MASTERS OF THE SHOALS

MASTERS OF THE SHOALS

Tales of the Cape Fear Pilots Who Ran the Union Blockade

Jim McNeil

Da Capo Press
A Member of the Perseus Books Group

First Da Capo Press edition 2003.

Cataloging-in-Publication data for this book is available from the Library of Congress.

ISBN 0–306–81280-0

Published by Da Capo Press
A Member of the Perseus Books Group
http://www.dacapopress.com

Da Capo Press books are available at special discounts for bulk purchases in the U.S. by
corporations, institutions, and other organizations. For more information, please contact
the Special Markets Department at the Perseus Books Group, 11 Cambridge Center,
Cambridge, MA 02142, or call (800) 255-1514 or (617) 252-5298, or e-mail
j.mccrary@perseusbooks.com.

1 2 3 4 5 6 7 8 9 10 — 07 06 05 04 03

In memory of my parents,

James Augustine McNeil Sr. and Gertrude Gause McNeil,

and for my sisters, Sally and Trudy,

my grandchildren, Kristin and Stephen,

and the other descendants of the

Cape Fear pilots who ran the blockade.

Contents

Acknowledgments   viii

Prologue   xiii

1. The Art and Mystery of the Pilotage   1
2. The Blockade at Cape Fear   13
3. The Trade   29
4. The Pilots of the *Mary Celestia*   53
5. Thomas Brinkman and the *Condor*   59
6. The Burriss Boys of Federal Point   63
7. The Misfortunes of Thomas Dyer   71
8. The Pilot Who Became a Preacher   77
9. The Tale of Julius Potter   89
10. Christopher Columbus Morse   101
11. Through the Eyes of a Girl   109
12. Thomas Mann Thompson   123
13. The Legacy of the Cape Fear Blockade Runners   129

    Epilogue: The Cape Fear Pilots after the Civil War   133

    Appendix: The Cape Fear Pilots, 1861–1865   149

    Notes   157

    Bibliography   177

    Index   183

Acknowledgments

I SHALL ALWAYS BE GRATEFUL to the people who helped make this book possible. None deserve my thanks more than my sister Sally McNeil.

Sally got me started on the project. She asked me in the spring of 1997 to write a short piece for the Southport Historical Society's newsletter on the Cape Fear pilots who ran the blockade. She had done some research and had gathered information on pilots who ran the blockade at Cape Fear, including the family blockade runners. I took this information and starting reading it. Then I began looking for more. And more. Soon the project had taken on a life of its own. My brief article for the newsletter became, eventually, this book.

Along the way Sally, who knows much more about history than I ever will, lent encouragement and helped in many other ways. My other sister, Trudy Hufham, helped as well, talking to people in Southport on my behalf and tracking down hard to find information. I have all my life been blessed with two wonderful big sisters.

Many others graciously shared information and gave their time and energy to the project. Captain Roy Daniel and his wife Cheryl are two who unquestionably deserve special mention. I grew up next door to Roy and knew Cheryl in high school. But I didn't realize until I got involved with this project that both of them are history buffs, and exceptionally knowledgeable of the Civil War.

Over the years Roy amassed a substantial collection of books, maps, and other materials about blockade running. Years ago he had gone to the Special Collection Library at Duke University and gotten a copy of the logbook used to record the licensing of Cape Fear pilots during the Civil War, a key document that was a great help to me as I got started on the project. Roy's a Cape Fear pilot so he understands as well as anyone how it must have been to bring a blockade runner across the bar in pitch darkness. His help was a godsend.

Cheryl, I found, had long been a mainstay in the Southport Historical Society. Both she and Roy offered me encouragement and support from the beginning of the project to the end. Cheryl organized a blockade-running cruise of Cape Fear that took place in the fall of 1998. She brought together as our tour guides two exceptional people, Dr. Charles V. Peery and Dr. Chris Fonvielle, who showed us the location of the wrecks of blockade runners and told us about the Civil War forts at Cape Fear.

Dr. Peery, who lives about ten miles from me in Charleston, South Carolina, is a medical doctor. But if anyone on earth could be called a doctor of blockade running it is Charlie Peery. Over more than thirty years he has assembled an astonishing collections of "things" related to blockade running during the American Civil War. Surely the finest private collection of its sort ever assembled, most of it now resides near Charlie's home at the South Carolina Historical Society. Today it's known as the Peery Southern Maritime Collection.

When I first ventured to Charlie's home on Church Street, I was overwhelmed by his treasures. And I brought away with me a treasure of my own: a print of a painting Charlie has of the blockade runner *Helen*, the steamer piloted by my great-grandfather Ephraim Gause. This picture was one of many Charlie provided for this book.

Charlie traveled all over to obtain his "things." In some cases he brought them up from the sea bottom himself, diving to wrecks at Cape Fear such at that of the blockade runner *Ella*. I was truly blessed by having Charlie's help on this project. No one today understands what the business of blockade running was like better than this gentleman from Charleston.

Dr. Chris Fonvielle is not a medical doctor like Charlie Peery, but a superb historian. He is *the* expert on Civil War Wilmington and the forts in the region. His book on the Union effort to take Wilmington, *The Wilmington Campaign: Last Rays of Departing Hope,* was the product of exhaustive research and rare insight into the people and forces involved in the Union campaign to take the last seaport of the Confederacy. Chris graciously read my manuscript, and made the suggestion that I include endnotes, which I hope will add value to the book for many readers.

Another person to whom I shall always be indebted is Captain Robert Potter of Saint Marys, Georgia. I think that Robert's beautiful illustrations add immensely to the book. I had seen and admired Robert's work in illustrating a delightful little book published in Charleston, *Tales of the Anna Karrue*, by Captain Buddy Ward. Robert, who comes from a Southport family with a long maritime tradition, is a pilot himself, but rather than bringing ocean-going ships across the bar he spent much of his career docking nuclear submarines at Charleston and at Kings Bay, Georgia.

From the beginning of the project I was fortunate to have the help of the good folks at the North Carolina Maritime Museum at Southport, Mary and Wayne Strickland. The museum served as a focal point for pictures and information I sought from the Southport area. Mary and Wayne also graciously shared with me historical materials in the museum.

Leslie Bright of Carolina Beach read the manuscript, including an early version of the chapter about Julius Potter, and helped make the book much better with his suggestions. For many years Leslie dived the shipwrecks of the blockade runners at Cape Fear as a member of the Underwater Archaeology Unit of the North Carolina Division of Archives and History at Fort Fisher, and wrote a book, *The Blockade Runner Modern Greece and Her Cargo*, on one of the most interesting wrecks. He is also exceptionally knowledgeable of the history of Federal Point. Richard Lawrence of the Underwater Archaeology Unit also graciously shared photographs and other historical materials in the files at Fort Fisher.

Captain Robert B. Thompson of Southport took the time to share with me some of his experiences during his thirty-two years as a Cape Fear pilot, including how my grandfather Charles Gause helped him get the job in 1932. His efforts helped me better understand what it must have been like to pilot a steamer at Cape Fear during the Civil War.

My niece Katherine Harper of Southport helped arrange for photographs for the book. And Jim Harper, the award-winning photographer of what must be one of America's best weekly newspapers, Southport's *The State Port Pilot*, provided a splendid photograph that he took of Cape Fear.

Betty Cappo of Wilmington shared the fruits of her research about the Burris pilots of Federal Point. Her family stories helped me bring alive the memories of some of these men, and of a little girl who shook her fists at the damned Yankees trooping ashore near her home. I appreciate the time she spent with me, including one rewarding day at the New Hanover County Public Library.

Three people whose books helped make my book possible were James Sprunt, Bill Reaves, and Stephen Wise. Mr. Sprunt ran the blockade himself as a youth of seventeen and became the chronicler of the Cape Fear blockade runners. His writings served as the foundation for many of my stories of the pilots. Mr. Reaves, a respected Wilmington historian, produced a multi-volume chronology of Smithville (Southport) that includes many references to pilots. His work served as the basis for much of my material in the first chapter. And Dr. Stephen Wise, of course, needs no introduction to Civil War history buffs. His *Lifeline of the Confederacy, Blockade Running During the Civil War* is the definitive book on blockade running. His appendices on port arrivals and departures of steam blockade runners and his capsule histories of the various ships proved to be godsends as I worked to trace the careers of the Cape Fear pilots.

I also benefitted from the work of Kevin Foster on the design of the blockade running steamers. His East Carolina University masters thesis provided the best information I could find on ship design and performance.

The following people also graciously shared with me information about the pilots who ran the blockade:

Lucy Murial Sellers Blocker of Bowie, Maryland
Ellen Price Butlers of Margate, Florida
Susie Carson of Southport, author of the delightful book about the history of the town, *Joshua's Dream*
Wilbur Dosher of Cincinnati, Ohio
Mike Edge of Snow Hill, North Carolina
Louise Hollard of Charlottesville, Virginia
Jean Horrell

Acknowledgments

Joseph Loughlin of Piqua, Ohio
Greg Marquis of Saint Mary's University in Halifax, Nova Scotia, author of *In Armageddon's Shadow: The Civil War and Canada's Maritime Provinces*
Helen Thomas Pearce
Patricia Ruark of Wilmington
The staffs of the following institutions helped immensely with my efforts to locate historical materials:
The Barnwell, South Carolina Public Library, especially Terri Mull
The Bermuda Archives, Hamilton, Bermuda
The Bermuda Historical Society, Hamilton, Bermuda
The Cape Fear Museum, Wilmington, North Carolina
The Charleston Library Society in Charleston, South Carolina
The Charleston County Library in Charleston, South Carolina
The Chicago Historical Society
The Confederate Museum of Charleston, South Carolina, especially Jane Wells
The Fort Fisher Museum, Kure Beach, North Carolina, especially Morris Bass
The Halifax Regional Library, Halifax, Nova Scotia
The Library of Congress
The Mariners' Museum of Newport News, Virginia, especially Claudia Jew
The Maritime Museum of the Atlantic in Halifax, Nova Scotia
The Mitchell Library, Glasgow, Scotland
The National Archives
The Naval Historical Center
The New Hanover County Public Library in Wilmington, especially Beverly Tetterton
The North Carolina State Archives, especially Steve Massengill
The Point Lookout POW Organization, Virginia Beach, Virginia
The Public Archives of Nova Scotia, Halifax
The Franklin D. Roosevelt Library
The South Caroliniana Library at the University of South Carolina, especially Robin Copp
The Special Collections Library at Duke University
The United Daughters of the Confederacy, Richmond, Virginia
The University of North Carolina at Wilmington
The United States Army Military History Institute
The University of North Carolina

I deeply appreciate the help of these people and institutions.

Jim McNeil

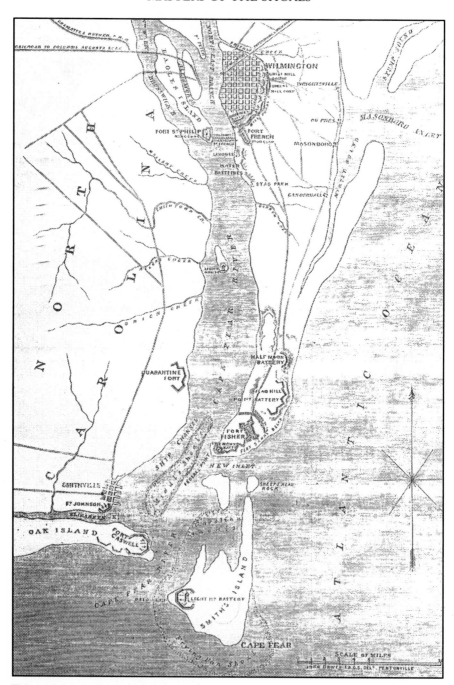

This map appeared in the *Illustrated London News* in February 1865. Although the artist captured the main elements of the coastline, he erred in many details, such as the layout of Fort Fisher and the names of the creeks. (Courtesy of North Carolina Maritime Museum at Southport)

Prologue

WHEN I WAS LITTLE I often accompanied my mother on her shopping trips to Wilmington. We usually took the Packard. I remember watching the silver flying lady lead us along the narrow, winding road which followed the river, listening to the huge straight eight murmuring beneath the long black hood, the tall whitewalls humming on the asphalt.

My mother hummed, too. Often it was the "Old Rugged Cross," the favorite hymn of her father, Charlie Gause. I sat beside her on the front seat and listened to her stories about the early days along the Lower Cape Fear.

My mother seemed ill-suited for the twentieth century. She should have been the mistress of an antebellum plantation, surrounded by a host of servants. She would have loved such a genteel life. Instead she lived in Southport, a quiet little town tucked in the southeastern corner of North Carolina, mistress of a drafty Victorian house that leaked whenever it rained hard, wife of the man who ran the Esso station. But her mundane existence never kept her from dreaming of a more glorious past.

My mother loved history. She read *American Heritage.* She was a member of the Brunswick County Historical Society. Genealogy was her passion; the history of the region where we lived she cherished. She loved nothing better than digging through old courthouse records, surrounded by mounds of musty deed books and ancient wills.

My mother tried her best to infuse in me her love of history. She gave me for Christmas when I was fifteen *I Rode With Stonewall,* a book that would sit unread, gathering dust in the bookcase which used to stand by our front door, for two generations. She told me about her grandfather Ephraim Gause, and her great-grandfathers, Archibald Gutherie and Charles Dosher, all Cape Fear pilots who ran the Union blockade during the Civil War. Attempting to stir my interest in history must have seemed like trying to stir sunbaked clay. She knew I did not listen: "Everything I say goes right in one ear and out the other."

In our home there certainly was ample evidence of our heritage. Portraits of family blockade runners stood on the table by the bay window in the parlor. Inscribed first editions of the books of James Sprunt, who ran the blockade himself and became a chronicler of blockade runners, rested on the bookshelves. I paid scant attention to these things.

But my mother never stopped trying. Then, twenty years after she was laid to rest in the Gause lot in the Old Smithville Burying Ground near her grandfather the blockade runner, I finally came to realize the significance of our heritage.

I never realized until then that a first edition of the 1877 book of Captain John Wilkerson, *Narrative of a Blockade Runner*, had been in our family for a long time. I picked it off the bookshelf in the home of my sister Sally. I wanted to think that it belonged to Mama Guffie. A portrait of her as a young girl hangs in Sally's living room, near the bookshelf that now holds Captain Wilkerson's book. Mama Guffie was Sarah Ann Crapon Gutherie, the wife of Archibald Menzies Gutherie, who was the second Cape Fear pilot of the *Robert E. Lee*, the famed blockade runner commanded by John Wilkerson. Archibald died in 1870, but Sarah lived for many years afterward, so the book could have belonged to her. But actually, I learned that my mother had bought it from a used book dealer as a gift for Sally. My mother again.

As I think about the stories she used to tell me I try to imagine what the town where we lived was like during the Civil War. It was named Smithville then, "a pretty considerable village, having a Court House, church and hotel. In spite of unlimited sand . . . a quite handsome settlement, abounding in a glorious growth of live oak and other shade trees," according to one visitor to the town. Live oaks remain even today one of the hallmarks of Southport. In places they reach over the streets to embrace, casting deep, cool shadows on the hot summer afternoons.[1]

According to the Federal census of 1860, 736 people, not counting black slaves, had lived in Smithville township before the war. Among the residents were seven teachers and three physicians, including Dr. Walter Curtis who would later serve as mayor of the town and write the most detailed surviving account of life in Smithville during the nineteenth century. Twenty-four pilots lived in Smithville in 1860. The pilotage was the third most popular occupation among the residents; the pilots were outnumbered only by the forty-one farmers and thirty laborers who lived in the town.[2]

Before the war, the village served as a summer resort for residents of Wilmington. Their favored means of transportation were steamers that stopped at Smithville on their regular runs between Wilmington and Charleston. The captain of the steamer *Spray*, which ran only during the summer months, was John B. Price, a Smithville pilot. Two steam tugs used to tow vessels needing assistance were in service on the river then. Both captains were also Smithville pilots, Captain John Davis on the *Mariner* and Jacob A. S. Price on the *Equator*.[3]

The favorite Smithville eating house, both for the summer visitors and local residents, stood on the waterfront. It was owned by Mrs. Mary Duffy. Mrs. Duffy would arise at three A.M. and prepare breakfast for passengers making the trip to Wilmington. Pilots stopped by her place for a cup of coffee and a morning meal before putting out to sea in search of vessels.[4]

In the years before the war, the people of Smithville enjoyed an active social life, especially during the summer months, which, in 1853, was enhanced by the presence of the men of the United States Coast Survey. Under the command of Lieutenant

This view of Smithville was drawn by an English artist in 1865. (Photo courtesy of North Carolina State Archives.)

John Newland Maffitt, they were charting the Cape Fear waters as part of a survey of east coast harbors. Young Maffitt, who brought his new bride to Smithville, formed a theatrical company which put on popular plays of the day. Maffitt himself, stage manager and "the most brilliant star," would later become, in the words of one popular writer, "the prince of blockade runners."[5]

But by 1862, the days of summer plays were long past. In Smithville lived mostly women and children and men too old to fight, along with Cape Fear pilots who managed to spend a few days at home from time to time in between their runs through the blockade.[6]

Across the river, to the northeast of Smithville, lay the vast earthworks at Fort Fisher, located on Federal Point, renamed Confederate Point with the onset of war, where many of the Cape Fear pilots lived. Federal Point had long been home to families whose men traditionally became pilots: Craig, Burriss, Newton, Adkins, and St. George. On the river side of Federal Point lay Craig's Landing.[7]

South of Fort Fisher then lay an open expanse of water between Zeke's Island and Battery Buchanan on the tip of Federal Point, because in those days New Inlet afforded a second entrance into the harbor and the port of Wilmington. And to seaward, you could have counted as many as thirty-five Federal warships divided into two blockading squadrons.[8]

As I reflect on these things, and think about the long history of the pilotage at Cape Fear, I realize how much the pilots meant to the struggling South during the Civil War. The guns of the Cape Fear forts prevented an enemy invasion by sea and provided a protective shield for Confederate blockade runners leaving or entering the harbor. In the South, the captains of those blockade-running ships were treated as heroes, for they carried cotton, the South's "white gold," to exchange for precious war supplies and sometimes luxuries for an impoverished land. But at Cape Fear they could never have done this without the aid of pilots who knew intimately the local waters and their shifting shoals, and possessed the skills, usually learned at the hands of their fathers, and the daring needed to guide blockade-running steamers safely past armed warships and hidden shoals on the darkest nights.[9]

Lt. John Newland Maffitt
(Sketch by Captain Robert Potter)

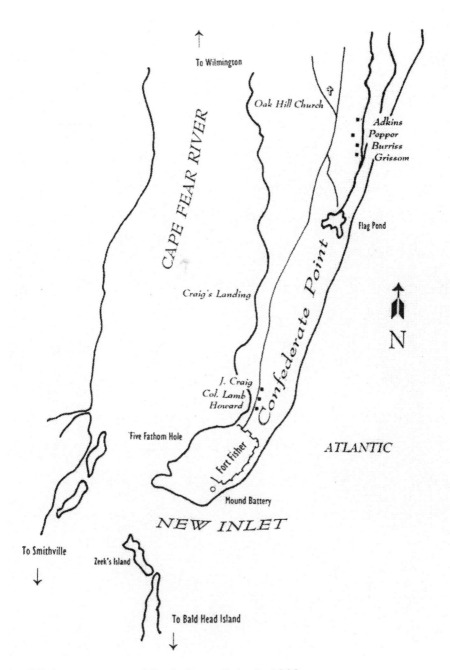

Federal Point was renamed Confederate Point in 1862.

A bird's eye view of Cape Fear. (Courtesy of Jim Harper)

CHAPTER 1

The Art and Mystery of the Pilotage

"... Destituted of all pilates ... they stranded their vessel on the Middle Ground of the harbours mouth, to the Westward of the Channel, where the Ebbe presently left her, and the wind with its own multeplyed forces and the auxiliaryes of the tide of flood beat her to peeces."

—*John Sandford's report of the 1665 loss at Cape Fear of the fly-boat of Sir John Yeamans for want of a local pilot.*[1]

Southport, the town where I grew up, lies on the northwest shore of the Cape Fear River. You can stand on the waterfront beside the pilot tower and look three miles across the harbor to Bald Head Island and North Carolina's oldest lighthouse. Take the ferry to the island and climb the 110 steps to the top of the lighthouse. Look around. The creek beside the lighthouse would bring to mind a silver serpent meandering through the marsh. In the springtime, blossoming dogwoods splash among the live oaks, like whitecaps upon an emerald sea. Ocean waves roll mutely against the windward shore. Seaward, Frying Pan Shoals—the scourge of mariners of centuries past—stretch endlessly out into the Atlantic.

Looking to the west, across the shipping channel at the harbor's entrance, you would see the remains of Fort Caswell. Across the waters of the harbor you could make out with binoculars the houses on the Southport waterfront, the water tank, and the pilot tower. To the northwest, the Cape Fear River runs broad and deep on its journey to Wilmington. To the east of the river, just beyond the horizon, lies Federal Point and the ruins of the old earthworks at Fort Fisher.

This is Cape Fear, a place of undeniable beauty. But these lovely waters where pirates roamed, where steamers ran the blockade, where pilot schooners raced on Independence Day, conceal countless shifting shoals. No captain worth his salt would risk his ship there, even today, without the help of a local pilot.

A view across the harbor from the Bald Head lighthouse. On the left lies the tip of Oak Island where Fort Caswell stood. In the distance appears the Southport waterfront. (Photo by the author.)

The pilotage was always the best job in town. Before Southport came into being—the town in 1887 changed its name from Smithville—Smithville had always been a town of pilots. Even before Smithville was founded in 1792, pilots lived in the region. And by that time several pilots also lived across the river at Federal Point.[2]

These men, with their intimate knowledge of the local waters, were necessary for safe passage of ships through the harbor and up and down the Cape Fear River. Avoiding the shallows was an art mastered only by men who knew the local waters from long experience.[3]

In the Early Years

One of the earliest descriptions of the harbor at Cape Fear was written by an Englishman in 1664:

> The river is barred at the entrance, but there is a channel close aboard the cape that will convey in safety a ship of three hundred tons; and as soon as the ship is over the bar, the river is five or six fathoms deep for a hundred miles from sea. The bar is a great security to the colony against a foreign invasion, the channel being hard to find by those that have not experience of it, and yet safe enough by those who know it.[4]

Safe enough by those who know it. The writer captured in those seven words the essence of the pilotage at Cape Fear: the critical importance of an intimate knowledge of the harbor, its currents and its shifting shoals to those who would venture there in ships.

The most difficult obstacle to safe navigation lay at the harbor's entrance. Here, as with the mouths of other rivers, sand and silt, stirred by the flow of the outgoing tides, tended to accumulate. Tidal movement over the millennia created "the bar," an enduring shoal that had to be surmounted to enter the deeper harbor. "Crossing the bar" became a common term used to describe the mariner's biggest challenge in navigating the American coastal waters before the entrances to major seaports were eventually deepened by jetties or dredging or by a combination of the two.[5]

From the earliest years, attempting to sail a ship through the harbor without the aid of a local pilot was to invite disaster. In 1665 the fly boat of Sir John Yeamans, "Governor of the County of Clarendon neare Cape Feare," was wrecked near the bar on a shoal known as the Middle Ground. In 1718 two ships under the command of William Rhett of Charleston captured the pirate Stede Bonnet in the harbor in what became known as the Battle of the Sandbars. Sailing without local pilots, the Charleston vessels and Bonnet's sloop the *Royal James* all ran aground and could not move until the tide rose and set them free.[6]

In the years which followed, ship traffic through the harbor increased with the growth of Brunswick Town in the 1730s and 1740s, the construction of Fort Johnston in 1749, and the development of the seaport of Wilmington up the river. So, too, did the need for local pilots.[7]

One of the few surviving records of the early Cape Fear pilots can be found in the diary of Janet Schaw, a Scotswoman from Edinburgh, who in 1773 visited Brunswick Town to see her brother who owned a plantation on the river.[8]

The village of Brunswick Town, which was located on the western bank of the Cape Fear River some twelve miles above Southport, was for a few years one of the most important ports in the British Empire. It became the largest exporter of naval stores—tar, pitch, rosin, and turpentine—in the colonies. Brunswick Town lay downstream of The Flats, shoals in the river at the mouth of Town Creek where at low tide there was only twelve feet of water. So larger vessels in the years before the Revolution stopped at Brunswick Town instead of proceeding up the river to the larger town of Wilmington. Brunswick Town served for years as the seat of royal government in North Carolina. The governor's house, Russelborough, stood on the northern outskirts of the town on a high bluff overlooking the river.[9]

Janet Schaw arrived on the brig *Rebecca* on a cold and dismal February afternoon. As the pilot guided the brig across the bar, she saw before her "a dreary Waste of white barren sand, and melancholy nodding pines." The only sign of human habitation she could see was Fort Johnston. She turned to the pilot standing beside her and asked, "Pray sir, does anybody live hereabouts?"[10]

The pilot found her aristocratic airs insulting. "Don't you see how thick it's settled?" he said. He then pointed to a spot on the bank near Walden Creek, which she could barely make out in the distance. "Ay. Ay. I told you so," he said, "That there is Snow's plantation and ye look there; don't ye see another? Why sure you are blind, it is not above five miles off."[11]

After this exchange, her first encounter with a North Carolina colonist, Miss Schaw hurriedly retired to her cabin as the pilot turned his attention back to the vessel.[12]

Miss Schaw's pilot was one of a dozen or so men in the area who made their living in those years guiding ships across the bar, through the harbor, and up and down the river. This task requires an intimate knowledge of the local waters, including the sandbars at the entrances to the harbor and of Frying Pan Shoals. These shoals, which reach seventeen miles into the Atlantic, claimed many lives in shipwrecks of the eighteenth and nineteenth centuries. And the pilots have to know the deep, land-locked tidal basin itself that stretches five miles from the harbor's entrance at the northern end of Oak Island past Southport and up the river toward Wilmington. They have to know each of the twenty-one turns a ship must make winding her way through the channel to Wilmington.[13]

Think of the captain of a large ship at Cape Fear as a blind man entering an immense strange house, cluttered with unfamiliar furniture and other hazards, with only one entrance and one exit. Using a cane to feel his way along would be like taking soundings, casting the lead in the early years, a tedious process which, by itself, would not prevent an accident. The blind man would be unable to safely make his way through the house. But if another man, who has lived in the house for many years and knows its every nuance, were to take the blind man's hand, he could easily guide him straight through the house and out the door.

A pilot's knowledge of his local waters must of course be combined with other skills. He must have a feeling for the sea. This, especially in the early years, usually came at the hands of his father. Sons of pilots at Cape Fear could get their first boat at the age of six. In addition to seamanship, a pilot must know the age-old conventions that govern ship passage around the world, the "rules of the road."[14]

Before the days of steam, the pilotage was an especially dangerous profession. In the eighteenth century, and in much of the nineteenth century, most pilot boats were small schooners, two-masted craft of shallow draft. The pilot and his mate would sail across the harbor. As they approached the ship outside the bar, the mate would carefully guide their schooner along the leeward side of the larger vessel. The pilot would then scramble up the Jacob's ladder and climb aboard the ship, leaving his mate to bring the pilot boat about and return to home. Often the early pilots of Cape Fear used rowboats—sturdy sea dories—instead of the little schooners.[15]

Young men became qualified pilots only after serving a long apprenticeship. Some began learning the trade as young as thirteen.[16]

State Regulations

The state found it necessary to regulate the pilotage. Actually, the first legislation to regulate the Cape Fear pilots was enacted in 1751. Colonial policy makers limited the maximum number of pilots to seven. Later in 1784, the state legislature drafted an Act for Regulating the Pilotage and Facilitating the Navigation of the Cape Fear River.[17]

The 1784 act provided detailed regulations. The maximum number of pilots to be licensed to operate below Wilmington was set at ten. A five-man commission known as the Board of Navigation and Pilotage was established. The board was given the authority to license new pilots and to collect a bond from each of those licensed. The act set rates, based on vessel length, for taking ships up and down the river. It also provided a measure of protection both for the pilots and the captains of the piloted ships. It decreed that no call for a pilot could go unanswered by the licensed pilots. It also specified that if the captain chose to navigate the channel on his own, he still had to pay the pilot. If a pilot boarded a ship outside the bar, and bad weather delayed entry into the harbor, the captain would have to pay a set fee for the pilot's time aboard.[18]

The 1784 act was amended two years later. The changes specified that each pilot would keep at least one apprentice (but not more than two) and "instruct him in the art and mystery of a pilot." The dividing line between river and harbor pilots was established as Fort Johnston. The pilot rate schedule provided for vessels with drafts up to nineteen feet, an optimistic figure certainly; such deep-draft vessels could be brought into the harbor only if they were considerably lightened to clear the bar.[19]

In 1800 a book was published titled *The Cape Fear Pilot, or Commerce and Navigation of Wilmington, N.C.* It contained regulations, rates of pilotage, and the names of pilots. Among the pilots listed at the turn of the century were: Charles Betts, James Clary, Benjamin Craig, Elias Craig, Henry Craig, Thomas Craig, Benjamin Cray, Caleb Davis, Isaac Davis, Wilson Davis, Cornelius Galloway, William Grissom, Henry Long, Samuel Long, John Nash, Edward Newton, James Newton, John Newton, Samuel Potter, William Todd, John Wade, and Thomas Wooten. From this list one can see that the maximum limit of ten pilots in the 1784 act was not being adhered to at that time.[20]

Captain Cornelius G. Smith, pilot of the blockade runner *Calypso*. (From a private collection.)

Like other seafaring men from time immemorial the Cape Fear pilots could be a rowdy bunch. In 1810 there was a riot between the pilots of Smithville and the sailors of some European ships, with many of the participants ending up in the blockhouse of Fort Johnston. In 1812, the Cape Fear pilots made ready to defend their harbor

Captain Charles William Craig, 1837-1890, Cape Fear pilot of the blockade runner *Margaret and Jessie*. He was taken prisoner when the steamer was captured trying to enter New Inlet on November 5, 1863. (See note on page 175; photo courtesy of Jean Horrell.)

from the British by organizing their own militia unit they called the "Sea Fencibles."[21]

The pilots acted swiftly to protect their interests and maintain the solidarity of their organization. In 1842 George Bowen defied his fellow pilots and was caught piloting a ship under new reduced rates set by the merchants of Wilmington that the majority of pilots opposed. Bowen paid for his transgression by being tarred and feathered. Thirteen pilots believed responsible were arrested, including: Christopher Burriss, John Burriss, Alfred Craig, Jessie Craig, James Newton Sr., Lewis Pepper, Elijah Price, John Price, and Raymond Sellers. All received fines and four spent ten days in jail.[22]

The War Years

At the beginning of the Civil War, the operation of the Cape Fear pilots was still governed by the state Board of Commissioners of Navigation and Pilotage for the Cape Fear River and Bar. Bonds were required as established in the 1784 act. And pilots received separate licenses for the river and the bar. At that time, a pilot's fee for taking a vessel from Wilmington to past the bar, or from the bar up the river to the port, was set at $200 each way. During the war, pilots of privately owned blockade runners could earn as much as $5,000 in gold per trip.[23]

During the war years some seventy-seven men served as pilots at Cape Fear. Most of them lived in Smithville or at Federal Point near Fort Fisher. A few lived on Masonboro Sound or on Bald Head Island. The main reason for such a large number of pilots during the war was attrition. Many were captured and spent the remainder of the war in Yankee prisons; because of their value to the Confederacy, they were seldom exchanged like other prisoners.[24]

Early in the war, before Wilmington became the dominant Southern blockade running port, a number of pilots served on Confederate gunboats in other capacities. For example, seven Cape Fear pilots served in the crew of the steamer CSS *Caswell*, most as seamen.[25]

Pilot assignments for ships leaving Cape Fear during the war were made in Wilmington by a Confederate naval officer. For a time this task fell to Lieutenant John Wilkerson, who later gained fame as captain of the *Robert E. Lee*, one of the most successful blockade runners. Records of the assignments he and others made no longer survive. But from other sources, it is clear that some captains favored certain pilots who stayed with their ships for long periods as they ran the blockade time and time again on voyages to Bermuda and Nassau.[26]

In September of 1864, General Whiting issued orders to the effect that all Cape Fear pilots of military age, eighteen to fifty, were in the service of the Confederate States. They were to be under the control of General Louis Hebert. The orders specified that pilot assignments would be made by the naval officer in

Captain Jacob Aker Smith Price piloted the blockade runner *Virginia*. Before the war he was captain of the steam tug *Equator*. Early in the war he served as pilot of the CSS *Caswell*. (See note on page 175; photo courtesy of Wilbur Dosher.)

This photograph was taken in Halifax, Nova Scotia, during the Civil War, in a studio near the Halifax Club, which was used to entertain prominent Confederates. Seated on the left is Captain Archibald Gutherie, Cape Fear pilot of the blockade runner *Robert E. Lee.* (See note on page 175; McNeil family photograph.)

A Federal Pilot

NOT EVERY CAPE FEAR PILOT served the Confederate cause. George F. Bowen of Federal Point was one who did not. "He was decoyed out by the *Gemsbok*, one of the first blockaders, thinking she was a trader," wrote Rear Admiral S. P. Lee. Bowen stayed on to pilot a number of Federal warships at Cape Fear, including the *Keystone State*. But he remained loyal to his fellow pilots and did not betray them when several were taken prisoner aboard the blockader.

Bowen had a wife and child at Federal Point. Owing to his circumstances, they remained separated from him for more than two years. During this time he heard that his wife had made several attempts to get to Beaufort to join him there but had been "stopped by the rebels and subjected to very harsh treatment."

In October 1863, Bowen was serving as pilot of the blockader *Nansemond* at Cape Fear. Her captain, Lieutenant Roswell Lamson, sympathized with the predicament of his pilot. The captain sent a party ashore at Federal Point under the cover of darkness and collected Mrs. Bowen and her child, along with Bowen's younger brother. Soon they were in Beaufort where Bowen would see them every two weeks as his ship returned there for coal.*

* *War of the Rebellion: The Official Records of the Union and Confederate Navies* (Washington, DC, 1896), hereinafter cited as *ORN*, ser. I, vol. X, p. 443; Clark, Walter, ed., *Histories of the Several Regiments and Battalions from North Carolina in the Great War 1861-65, Written by Members of the Respective Commands, Vol. V*, (State of North Carolina, 1901), p. 374, hereinafter cited as Clark, *Regimental History*; McPherson, James M. and Patricia McPherson, *Lamson of the Gettysburg* (New York, 1997), pp. 141-142.

charge of lights. They permitted pilots belonging to ships in port to live at home, subject to the orders of General Hebert.[27]

A logbook used for orders and daily happenings at Fort Fisher describes how pilot assignments were managed following these orders, when many Cape Fear pilots languished in Yankee prisons. Two Confederate officers were then in charge of the pilots, who were "subject to all rules & laws applied to soldiers they being in fact <u>enrolled soldiers</u>." Pilots in Smithville reported to Lieutenant Obediah H. Williamson; those at Federal Point to Lieutenant James A. Kelly. When a pilot came ashore after a run through the blockade, he was to report immediately to one of the officers. At nine o'clock each morning there was a role call, although senior pilots over fifty years of age were exempt from this daily mustering. Every Saturday each officer filed a weekly report to headquarters in Wilmington showing the status of each pilot and whether he was assigned to a ship.[28]

Early in the war the Union commanders recognized the vital importance of the Cape Fear pilots. In December of 1862, Lieutenant William B. Cushing devised a plan to capture some pilots using the prize schooner *Home*. After disguising her as an English vessel he was going to run into New Inlet chased by a blockader. When he was safely under the protection of Fort Fisher, he would wait for pilots or boats from the shore. He would grab the pilots and whoever else approached the schooner, and head back to sea.[29]

Lieutenant Cushing's plan was approved by Rear Admiral Lee and the acting secretary of the navy. The dauntless lieutenant sailed down the coast from Beaufort and made his way into New Inlet. But the wind failed to cooperate. "I failed to capture the Wilmington pilots because my schooner was three times becalmed, in shore, at the points where I desired to act," he wrote to Admiral Lee.[30]

But Mr. Cushing did not easily give up. He sailed further down the coast to Little River, having heard that there was a pilot station there. He failed again to find a pilot. But he did find a Confederate earthwork, which he and his men managed to capture without firing a shot.[31]

As the war continued, the importance of the Cape Fear pilots continued to mount. By late 1864, the shortage of pilots had become critical. On October 31 the steamer *Beatrice* inbound from Nassau ran into New Inlet with Sylvester Burriss Jr. as pilot. Sylvester was only eighteen. Since he does not appear on the pilot license rolls, he was probably an apprentice at the time. On November 29, Captain E. C. Reid had to bring the steamer *Emma Henry* into New Inlet without a pilot.[32]

In the decades following the war, many blockade runners recounted their adventures in eluding the Union warships which tried to close the Confederate ports. English captains of blockade runners told their tales, as did Confederate naval officers who commanded the swift, elusive steamers. A few chief engineers wrote about their ships—most, it seems, complaining about the poor quality of the coal they had to burn—and a number of passengers on blockade runners wrote about their voyages. But few of the Cape Fear pilots ever wrote about their experiences during the war.[33]

The Legacy of James Sprunt

Their legacy is preserved in the writings of one man: James Sprunt. Sprunt ran the blockade himself as a purser on the *Lilian*, an iron-hull sidewheel steamer built in Scotland which ran the blockade five times. Although Sprunt was just a teenager at the time, he knew the captains of the blockade runners and the Cape Fear pilots. He also later served for twenty-six years on the Board of Commissioners of Navigation and Pilotage. In his later years, he wrote numerous articles and several books about the exploits of the blockade runners at Cape Fear. Like many others, Sprunt was enamored with the grand adventures of those men. About the pilots, he wrote:

James Sprunt. (Photo courtesy of Charleston County Library)

> The story of their wonderful skill and bravery in the time of the Federal blockade has never been written, because the survivors were modest men, and because time obliterated from their memories many incidents in that extraordinary epoch in their history.
>
> Amidst almost impenetrable darkness, without lightship or beacon, the narrow and closely watched inlet was felt for with a deep-sea lead as a blind man feels his way along a familiar path, and even when the enemy's fire was raking the wheelhouse, the faithful pilot, with steady hand and iron nerve, safely steered the little fugitive of the sea to her desired haven. It might be said of him, as it was told of the Nantucket skipper, that he could get his bearings on the darkest night by a "taste" of the lead.[34]

James Sprunt went on to name some of the noted blockade runners and their pilots. His list, which is incorporated into the appendix, forms the most complete surviving record of the Cape Fear pilots who ran the blockade.[35]

These men, with their unique knowledge and skills, helped keep the hopes of the Confederacy alive during the last years of the Civil War. Before turning to their stories, let's first consider the blockade, the Union effort to seal the port of Wilmington, and then the business of blockade running as it was conducted during those times of appalling conflict between Americans from the North and the South.

The blockade runner _Lilian_ under chase. The iron-hull steamer was built in Scotland in 1864. (Courtesy of North Carolina State Archives.)

Drawing by Captain Robert Potter.

Some Blockade-Running Pilots and their Ships

James. N Adkins	*Ella and Annie*	Thomas B. Garrason	*Owl*
John W. Anderson	*Mary Celestia*	Ephraim D. Gause	*Helen*
James Bell	*Talisman*	Robert S. Grissom	*Little Hattie*
Joseph Bensel	*City of Petersburg*	Archibald Gutherie	*R. E. Lee*
Thomas Brinkman	*Condor*	John Hill	*Siren, others*
E. T. (Ned) Burriss	*Wando*	Henry Howard	*Orion*
George W. Burriss	*Hebe*	C. C. Morse	*Advance, others*
Joseph N. Burriss	*Hansa*	Thomas W. Newton	*Eugenia II*
Thomas E. Burriss	*Banshee*	William Julius Potter	*General Beauregard*
Thomas Gray Burriss	unknown	John R. Savage	*Ella II*
Charles W. Craig	*Margaret and Jessie*	Robert A. Sellers	*Venus*
J.W. (Jim Billy) Craig	*Lynx, others*	William R. Sellers	*Advance*
Thomas W. Craig	*Pet*	C. G. Smith	*Calypso*
E. T. Daniels	*Coquette*	Joseph Springs	*Alice*
Charles G. Dosher	unknown	William St. George	*Don*
Julius Dosher	*North Heath*	Joseph T. Thompson	*Index or Thistle II*
Richard Dosher	*Old Dominion*	Thomas M. Thompson	*Atalanta, others*
Thomas K. Dyer	*Giraffe, others*		

Note that in many cases, only one of several ships the men piloted appear in this abbreviated list.*

*Refer to the appendix for a complete list of sources. It stands to reason that there were African-American pilots at Cape Fear, but the record is mostly silent on this point. The naval records (*ORN*, ser. I, vol. VI, p. 85) mention that four black slaves, one who said that he had been river pilot of the steam tug *Uncle Ben*, escaped from Smithville on August 6, 1861 and rowed out to the *USS Penguin* and sought refuge with the crew of the blockader. The *Uncle Ben* was a Lake Erie tug chartered by the Union for an expedition to reinforce Fort Sumter. She never made it to Charleston. Violent winds forced her to put into Wilmington, where she was seized by the citizens and converted into a gunboat. During the summer of 1862, her engine was removed and installed into the ironclad *North Carolina*. (Navy Department, *Dictionary of American Naval Fighting Ships* (Washington, 1963-1981), vol. II, p. 577, hereinafter cited as Navy, *Ship Dictionary*.)

CHAPTER 2

The Blockade at Cape Fear

"I, Abraham Lincoln, President of the United States . . . have further deemed it necessary to set on foot a blockade . . ."

> —*From President Lincoln's declaration of a blockade of Southern ports.*[1]

*B*efore daybreak on the morning of April 12, 1861, residents of Charleston, South Carolina, awoke to the sound of cannon fire. The Civil War had begun. The first shots fired by Confederate shore batteries at Union-held Fort Sumter in Charleston harbor caused shock waves that rippled far beyond Cape Fear. They opened a deep fissure between the North and South, just as if a mighty earthquake had shook the earth and rent the nation. Even individual families would split apart as brothers would embrace opposite loyalties, and fathers and sons follow different flags. Over the next four years more than six hundred thousand American men and boys would die on battlefields and in makeshift prisons, from wounds inflicted by other American men and boys and from disease. Many more, maimed and crippled, would bear scars for the remainder of their lives. Even today, the scars of that long-past war still disfigure the nation's soul.[2]

In Charleston reminders of the war abound. Confederate cannons at White Point Gardens still guard the harbor. Arguments erupt from time to time over whether to remove from South Carolina's capitol grounds in Columbia the Confederate battle flag, but it still proudly flies. Everywhere in the South, men and boys drive pickup trucks bearing this flag as a symbol of rebellion. Despite civil rights gains in the past forty years, the division between black and white still can be seen and felt in many places throughout the South, indeed, throughout the country.

School children learn today that the Civil War was fought over slavery. It was, of course. But in the beginning President Abraham Lincoln and the Congress declared that the war's purpose was to preserve the union. And the seceding Southern states said they were fighting for their independence.[3]

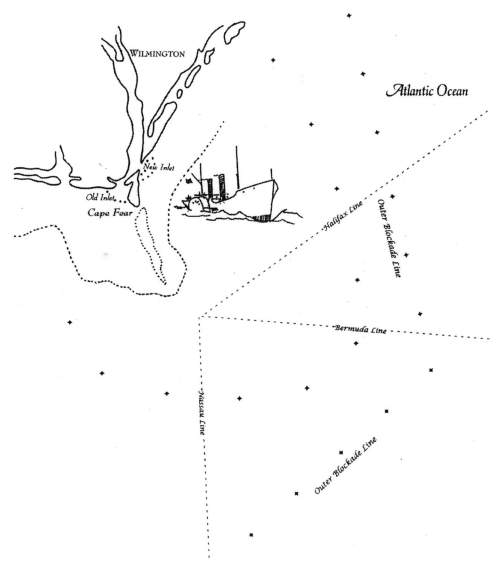

Typical positions of blockaders late in the Civil War.

Historians still argue about the political and social causes of the War Between the States. They point to deep cultural differences between the North and South, to states rights and slavery, the burning issues of the day. Of all who have written about the Civil War, few have done so with more insight and greater eloquence than historian Bruce Catton. He called the Civil War "probably the most significant single experience in our nation's existence." He observed that "It was certainly the biggest tragedy in American history and, at the same time, probably did more to shape our

General Winfield Scott, whose Anaconda Plan contained the seeds of Union victory. (Photo courtesy of U.S. Military Institute)

future than any other event." He spent most of his life seeking to understand the underlying causes of the war, including the "moving currents in the spirits of men."[4]

Such currents converged in Charleston harbor one spring day in 1861 and the war began. The blockade would shortly follow.

An insurrection against the Government of the United States has broken out . . . So began President Lincoln's proclamation that declared a blockade of the Southern coast. The blockade sent an unmistakable signal to the European powers that the United States no longer stood united. Blockades had long been recognized instruments of international maritime policy. But nations did not blockade their own ports.[5]

The American blockade was the eastern component of a strategy conceived by General Winfield Scott that became known as the "Anaconda Plan." Blockading the Confederate coast, coupled with seizing control of the Mississippi River, would slowly squeeze the life out of the Rebel states. While the old general would fall from favor and move on as Lincoln sought a more effective military leader, his plan would help mold the Union strategy throughout the war and, ultimately, help bring victory to the North.[6]

The blockade of Cape Fear began, on paper, on April 27, 1861, thirteen days after the fall of Sumter. President Lincoln proclaimed all Southern ports to be closed. It took many months to assemble the fleet necessary to make the Union blockade a reality, and then nearly two more years to make it effective. The United States Navy, with few ships, was not ready for war, much less for blockading more than 3,000 miles of coastline. Old vessels of various types were initially pressed into service as blockaders. Later, they were joined by many newer ships, including fast, well-armed steamers.[7]

The Purpose of the Blockade

The blockade was instituted to isolate the rebel states from world commerce, to prevent the Confederacy from exporting cotton, tobacco, and other Southern products and from importing war materials. The South had long depended on the more industrialized Northern states for many essential products. The Southern states

Captured blockade runners. (Courtesy of Mariners Museum of Newport News.)

lacked the industrial capacity to manufacture arms and ammunition in large quantities and to produce materials such as clothing and shoes for its armies. But the South did have cotton. And cotton, the Confederacy's "white gold," would be the perfect medium of exchange for the supplies that it would need to fight the war.[8]

Many Southern leaders saw cotton as the key to winning the war. They believed that England depended on Southern cotton so heavily for its textile mills that it would eventually come to the aid of the Confederacy. A Texas senator declared just before the war began:

> I say that cotton is King, and that he waves his scepter, not only over these thirty-three states, but over the island of Great Britain and over continental Europe; and there is no crowned head upon that island, or upon the continent, that does not bend the knee in fealty, and acknowledge allegiance to that monarch.[9]

During the war, letters from Southerners were often delivered in envelopes bearing patriotic messages. (Courtesy Duke University Special Collections Library.)

This was the "King Cotton" doctrine, in which the Southern states believed that the material, scarce in most other parts of the world, would become the salvation of the Confederacy. In the long run, of course, this theory proved to be a failure. But until the Union finally took Fort Fisher, cotton brought arms and badly needed supplies that sustained the Confederate armies for longer than many thought possible.[10]

The South's primary trading partner would be England. Great Britain immediately declared neutrality in the conflict. A royal proclamation issued on May 13, 1861, prohibited all British subjects from taking part in the hostilities between the states and expressed "the Royal determination to maintain a strict and impartial neutrality during the contest." But that position never prevented the United Kingdom from maintaining a mutually profitable trade with the Confederacy, however illicit such trade was viewed by the Federal government.[11]

The USS *James Adger*. When the war began, this large, fast steamship was seized and converted into a warship mounting eight 32-pounder guns. She saw blockader service at both Charleston and Cape Fear, where she helped capture several blockade runners. (See note on page 175; photo courtesy of Naval Historical Center.)

The Rules of the Blockade

The rules of the blockade were laid down at the beginning. Union blockaders could stop and search all vessels attempting to enter Confederate ports. Ships found to be carrying contraband would be seized. They would eventually be sold in a prize court in the North, with the crew members of the blockaders participating in the capture sharing one-half of the proceeds. This practice gave the crewmen on the blockaders a powerful incentive to capture blockade runners that went beyond their desire to win the war.[12]

Because the Union blockade followed international maritime practices of long-standing, other countries such as England and France were willing to acknowledge the legitimacy of the blockade while still maintaining relations with the Confederacy.[13]

On July 13, 1861, the small converted merchant vessel *Daylight* established the blockade at Cape Fear. In the beginning she attempted to guard the harbor alone, which proved to be impossible. On September 30, 1861, the steamer *Kate* made the first of many regular runs bringing arms and supplies into Wilmington, scarcely hampered by the few blockaders. But eventually more than thirty Union ships were assigned to enforce the blockade of the harbor. With additional ships, the effectiveness of the blockade improved.[14]

The steamer USS *Daylight* became the first blockader at Cape Fear. Alone, she could not stop blockade runners effectively. But before the war was over, she became involved in the capture or destruction of twelve runners. (See note on page 175; photo courtesy of Naval Historical Center.)

Ships and Crews

To run down the swift blockade runners, the Union needed fast steam-powered ships of its own. Such ships were obtained, some by converting merchantmen, others by construction for the U. S. Navy. The smaller, slower vessels such as steam tugs served as bar tenders, at night moving close to shore to guard the inlets. The fastest steamers cruised well off shore where they could give chase to blockade runners who escaped the harbor and those making inbound runs to the coast. They were divided into three rings of ships, one near the shore, another further out, and the third, with the fastest steamers, cruising the Gulf Stream well out to sea. The number of blockading ships at Cape Fear gradually increased as the war continued and, as other Southern ports were bottled up, the importance of Wilmington mounted.[15]

The blockaders of New Inlet stood well off the coast after Fort Fisher acquired its Whitworth cannons. These twelve-pounder rifled guns, deadly accurate at long range, had been salvaged from the wreck of the British merchantman *Modern Greece.* Colonel William Lamb, the fort's commander, said, "With these guns, we made the U. S. blockading fleet remove their anchorage from two and a half miles to five miles from the fort."[16]

One of Colonel Lamb's Whitworth guns. These long-range cannons were hauled by mules down to the beach where they could fire with deadly accuracy at blockaders five miles at sea. (Photo courtesy of Fort Fisher Museum)

The numbers of blockaders varied from time to time as ships left station for repairs and maintenance and to replenish their coal bunkers at regular intervals, which, because of rough seas off Cape Fear, could not be done on station. So most of the blockaders would frequently run up the coast to Beaufort, North Carolina, where the navy maintained a coal depot and a small repair facility. The largest ships, which could not cross the bar at Beaufort harbor, had to go to Hampton Roads for coal and needed repairs. Thus, with the need for coaling and repairs, a quarter of the blockaders or even more could be off station at any time.[17]

Among the blockaders at Cape Fear were heavily armed warships, such as the USS *James Adger*, a large, fast side-wheel steamer, along with smaller vessels. Converted tugs such as the lightly armed *Astor* were also utilized. Captured blockade runners were also armed and placed into Union service in the blockading fleets, a fate which befell the famous *Robert E. Lee*, after she had made five round trips through the Cape Fear blockade.[18]

Blockading duty could be exciting during the nighttime chases, but boring during the daylight hours. Robert Browning, in his book on the North Atlantic Blockading Squadron, quotes a sailor on the blockader *Florida* at Cape Fear who likened his "adventures" on blockade duty to going to the roof of a hotel on a hot summer day and then descending to the attic to drink tepid water full of iron rust, repeating this process throughout the day until it was time to go to bed.[19]

A Union naval officer wrote to the Boston *Traveler* newspaper in August of 1863 complaining about the ineffectiveness of the blockade at Wilmington:

> The blockade seems to be a farce to me, and I am ashamed and disgusted with the whole thing. The Niphon, the fastest vessel of the fleet, is stationed near Smith's Island, where there is nothing to catch. She was on the North Station a few days, and while there drove the Hebe ashore and destroyed her, but for some reason was sent back to Smith's Island.[20]

There was always that chance of prize money from captured blockade runners to keep the crewmen interested. But as the war continued and the size of the blockading fleet increased, the navy had mounting difficulties keeping the ships adequately manned. Late in the war, Confederate prisoners from Point Lookout in Maryland were brought in to serve in limited numbers as crew members.[21]

The USS *Niphon*. Built in 1863, she joined the Cape Fear blockading squadron that year. She captured the *Banshee*, the *Ella*, and the *Annie*, and collaborated with the *James Adger* in the capture of the *Cornubia*. (See note on page 175; photo courtesy of Naval Historical Center.)

Pilots of Union Blockaders

NEGOTIATING THE SHOALS WATERS of Cape Fear posed problems to the ships of the blockading fleet just as it did for the blockade runners. At least two Cape Fear pilots, George Bowen and John Savage, were pressed into Federal service to lend their knowledge of the coast to the Union cause.[22]

In August of 1861, four black slaves escaped from Smithville and made their way aboard the USS *Penguin.* One of these men was said to be a good pilot.[23]

The Port of Wilmington

The blockade at Cape Fear was established to close the port of Wilmington. At the beginning of the war, Wilmington was a good-sized town of some 9,500 souls. It was the largest settlement in North Carolina and, from a commercial standpoint, the most important. While the port of Wilmington was busy for a town its size, it ranked far behind New Orleans, Mobile, and Charleston in commercial importance.[24]

Wilmington during the Civil War. (Photo courtesy of North Carolina State Archives)

Wilmington before the war had been noted for its exports of lumber and naval stores—tar, pitch, rosin, and turpentine. The town was blessed with good railroad service; tracks led north to Virginia, to Columbia, South Carolina, and into the North Carolina interior. And it lay within reasonable distances from the British colonies of Bermuda and Nassau, which served as transshipment ports for most of the cargos moving between the Southern states and Great Britain. The harbor at St. George's in Bermuda is 674 miles from Wilmington, a three-day run for a typical blockade-running steamer. Nassau in the Bahamas, 570 miles distant, is even closer.[25]

Wilmington would eventually become the sole port in the Confederacy from which cotton could be shipped abroad. And it also became a rough sailor's town. According to Lieutenant John Wilkerson, captain of the *Robert E. Lee*, "The staid old town of Wilmington was turned topsy-turvy during the war." Speculators came from across the South to buy goods sold at auction. Fights occurred frequently between sailors on the steamers and soldiers in the town. Rogues wandered the streets, which were unsafe even during the daytime.[26]

But at least the streets were clean:

> "Two things about the city impressed me strongly: one was the great number of buzzards and their tameness. The other was the unusual cleanliness of the streets, especially the marketplace which was due to the presence of the buzzards."
> Johnny Tabb, captain's clerk of the *Robert E. Lee* [27]

To some, the heat of summer made the streets of Wilmington almost unbearable. "It is the hottest and most disagreeable place in the world and the very atmosphere seems laden with disease," wrote Rose Greenhow to President Davis in August of 1863, during a short visit to the city before departing for Europe. Chapter Six tells the story of the return to Wilmington of this lady, the famed Confederate spy known as the Rebel Rose.[28]

Despite complaints about the buzzards and the heat, Wilmington boasted handsome churches and fine homes. Actors at Thailian Hall managed to continue theater productions throughout the war. But many of the blockade runners preferred cock fights, wagering twenty dollar gold pieces on their favorite bird.[29]

In Wilmington cotton would typically sell for six to eight cents a pound; in Europe it brought nearly ten times as much. Thus its sale abroad was immensely profitable. Because of this, outward-bound blockade runners were literally stuffed with cotton. The bales were compressed and stacked so close together that one captain said, "a mouse could hardly find room to hide among them." He said that his blockade runner leaving Wilmington looked like "a huge bail of cotton with a stick [the foremast] placed at one end of it . . ."[30]

A Harbor With Two Inlets

The presence of two navigable entrances to the harbor made Wilmington the most difficult Southern port to blockade. And due to the presence of the Frying Pan Shoals, the blockaders were effectively divided into two separate squadrons. To avoid the perilous shallows, a vessel had to put to sea for a voyage of some forty miles to go from one inlet to the other, although the distance across to Bald Head Island was scarcely seven miles.[31]

For 118 years a fact of life for the pilots at Cape Fear was the existence of the two widely separated entrances to the harbor. During this period the traditional entrance was at the Western Bar, between Bald Head Island and the northern tip of Oak Island, an area known as Old Inlet. The other mouth of the Cape Fear River, New Inlet, lay seven miles north, past the east end of Bald Head Island just below Federal Point. At one point just below the tip of Federal Point, currents associated with the two inlets converged, creating an area of turbulence and shifting shoals known as "the Rip."[32]

New Inlet played a crucial role in the Civil War. One could argue that but for an act of nature—the hurricane which cut the inlet in 1761—the Confederacy would have fallen long before it did.[33]

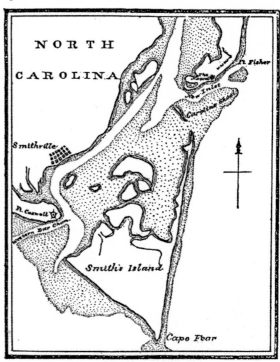

Entrances to Cape Fear River.

This chart appeared in J. Russell Soley's *The Blockade and the Cruisers* published in 1887.
(Drawing courtesy of Charleston Library Society.)

The two inlets made the approach to Wilmington unique. Some other Confederate ports had several ship channels—Charleston at one time had seven—but none had more than one entrance like Cape Fear. Inbound blockade runners could choose either entrance. Blockade runners leaving port could see the Union fleet, study its disposition and select the inlet with the better chance of success. More often than not, they chose New Inlet which was protected by the long guns of Fort Fisher. Until Fisher fell to Union forces in early 1865, war supplies continued to be delivered to Wilmington by the blockade runners, helping keep Confederate hopes alive. Without New Inlet, the Federal fleet could have much more easily bottled up the port.[34]

These engravings appeared in an 1864 edition of *Harper's Weekly*. The upper one shows the blockading squadron at Old Inlet, the lower view shows portions of the squadron standing off Fort Fisher. Note lying off the beach the wrecks of the blockade runners *Nighthawk* and *Lynx*. The Mound Battery on Federal Point—the best landmark for pilots on the low-lying coast—can be seen to the left of the wrecks.
(Courtesy of Charleston County Library)

Orders from the Admiral

By the third year of the blockade, the techniques of the blockade runners were becoming evident and the routine of the blockaders had become well established. On December 16, 1863, the commander of the North Atlantic Blockading Squadron, Acting Rear Admiral S. P. Lee, issued general instructions to his ships at Cape Fear. Among these instructions:

The primary day stations are:

New Inlet side: 1. Off the inlet (senior officer), 2. Off Masonboro, 3. Off the lower end of Smith's Island.

Old Inlet side: 1. Off the bar, 2. Off Folly Inlet, 3. Off the end of Smith's Island.

In clear weather by day these stations are occupied by the steamers at anchor, when an officer's watch and regular lookouts are kept, and the captain and first lieutenant especially, and the rest of the officers and crew, may sleep with the hammocks down.

At half an hour before sunset the blockader will have his anchor up, and as the shade of evening comes he will draw inshore, keeping the beach or other object in sight, yet regulating safely his approach to and occupation of his night station by the state of light.

In the dusk of evening and early dark the blockade is run by steamers (perhaps not showing black smoke) who thus get a safe and long run off the coast. At morning twilight and at night, guided by shore signals, the runners get in under the batteries.

Rear Admiral Samuel Phillips Lee, USN. Lee commanded the North Atlantic Blockading Squadron for two years beginning in the fall of 1862. With his share of the prize money from captured blockade runners he became one of the best-paid Federal officers of the war. (See note on page 175; photo courtesy of Naval Historical Center)

When a runner is seen coming out, it is desirable not to make the signal until his retreat can be cut off by getting between him and the bar or coast. It is best to capture or destroy runners when discovered, but not to throw away the chance of doing one or the other by prematurely alarming them and causing their retreat over the bar, or under the batteries, to escape under more favorable circumstances.

It is known that the runners run down the coast from just south of Masonboro and close to the surf, as the coast is clear, and in like manner they run up the coast and near the surf from Folly Inlet.

Heretofore it is believed that they have mostly run in and out by the coast and have also run out by Smith's Island and the shoals. Low and slow steamers are supposed to sneak out and large and swift ones to run boldly off. Some steamers of superior speed will, with special instructions from me, blockade off Cape Fear and Cape Lookout lights, to intercept blockade runners who may have run the inner line of blockade or who are hovering outside preparatory to running in.

The commanding officer of a steamer going to Beaufort for coal, or returning, will not depart from his direct route or delay on it to cruise; but it will be his duty to chase, if he has a fair prospect of success, any blockade runner he may discover on the way.

The senior officer present may, if he wishes it, station a steamer to show a light from a position known to all the others. On which they can take bearings; this steamer should be ready to move at a minute's warning, and in the event of doing so must lower the light.

Each commanding officer should make sure that no lights, other than signals, should be seen from his vessel, and that the lights on board are so covered, placed and used that they can not be seen through windows or portholes, in opening doors, mustering watch, etc.[35]

Admiral Lee's orders reflected the experience gained during the first year and a half of the blockade. At this point, the blockaders were becoming more and more effective in stopping the runs at Cape Fear. They were presenting a new challenge for the Cape Fear pilots. No longer could a pilot take a vessel into or out of the harbor in broad daylight as in peacetime. Navigating in darkness across the bars and through the elusive channel taxed the skills of even the best pilots. Armed warships posed new dangers beyond the usual concern over running aground. Underwater obstructions placed by the Confederates themselves to deter Yankee invasion by sea added to the danger, and at least one blockade runner sank after running into an obstruction in the harbor.[36]

Lightship drawing by Captain Robert Potter.

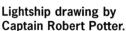

Burning of the lightship. Early in the war, the Confederates moved the Frying Pan lightship inside the Western Bar. She was burned in December of 1861 by boat crews from the blockader USS *Mount Vernon*. On the right in this picture one can see the Bald Head lighthouse. On the left stands Fort Caswell. (See note on page 175; photo courtesy of Southport Maritime Museum)

The success of blockade running at Wilmington and at other Confederate ports depended on the abilities of local pilots. They were as essential to the business as the captains of the steamers. In the next chapter we will focus on the business of blockade running—often referred to by the participants as "the trade"—to help complete our framework for the stories of the pilots who ran the blockade at Cape Fear.

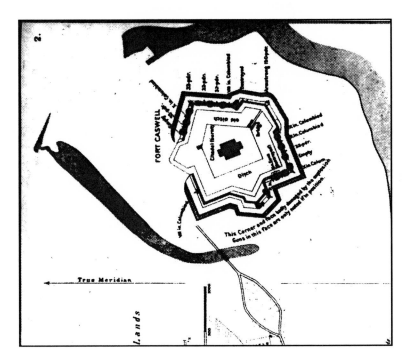

This map shows Fort Caswell as it appeared during the latter part of the Civil War. Fort Caswell guarded Old Inlet. (Map courtesy of North Carolina State Archives)

The Mound Battery at Fort Fisher. The 60-foot mound of sand mounted two long-range guns. Pilots referred to it—the most prominent landmark on the night-time coast—as "the Big Hill." (Photo courtesy of North Carolina State Archives)

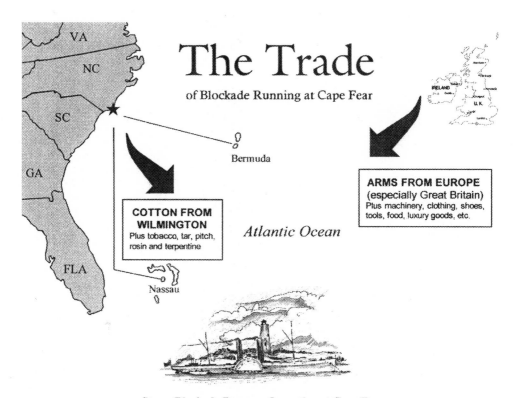

The Trade

of Blockade Running at Cape Fear

COTTON FROM WILMINGTON
Plus tobacco, tar, pitch, rosin and terpentine

Atlantic Ocean

ARMS FROM EUROPE
(especially Great Britain)
Plus machinery, clothing, shoes, tools, food, luxury goods, etc.

Bermuda

Nassau

VA

NC

SC

GA

FLA

IRELAND

U.K.

Steam Blockade Runners Operating at Cape Fear

Advance	*Blenheim*	*Emma II*	*Lilian*	*Rothesay Castle*
Agnes E. Fry	*Calypso*	*Eugenia II*	*Little Hattie*	*Robert E. Lee*
Annie	*Chicora*	*Flora II*	*Lynx*	*Susan Bierne*
Annie Childs	*City of Petersburg*	*General Beauregard*	*Margaret and Jessie*	*Talisman*
Antonica	*Coquette*	*Georgiana McCaw*	*Mary Celestia*	*Theodora*
Arabian	*Condor*	*Gibraltar*	*Modern Greece*	*Thistle II*
Armstrong	*Cornubia*	*Hansa*	*Night Hawk*	*Thomas L. Wragg*
Atlalanta	*Don*	*Hebe*	*North Heath*	*Venus*
Banshee I	*Elizabeth*	*Helen*	*Old Dominion*	*Virginia*
Banshee II	*Ella I*	*Hope*	*Orion*	*Vulture*
Bat	*Ella II*	*Index*	*Owl*	*Wando*
Beatrice	*Ella and Annie*	*Kate I*	*Pet*	*Wild Rover*

This list includes most of the vessels; there were others as well. The primary source was Stephen Wise's *Lifeline of the Confederacy*. Many vessels were renamed; only the best-known name is given.

CHAPTER 3

The Trade

"Our ships came together the next moment with a fearful crash, carrying away his starboard boat rail and part of his stem and cut-water."
—*Captain Frank Bonneau of the blockade runner* Ella and Annie *describing how he tried to run down a Union blockader.*[1]

Running the blockade. Even today these words ring of high adventure. And adventures there were, as the swift unarmed steamers attempted to slip through the Union blockading fleet under the cover of night.

After the war, as time passed and memories faded, the business aspects of the trade tended to diminish in the minds of those who ran the blockade, as they reminisced about shielding their eyes from the rockets' glare, about booming cannons and flying splinters, about the thrill of the chase. The glory associated with the blockade runners would outlast their lifetimes; their children and grandchildren would retell their tales of running the blockade to save the Confederacy.[2]

But blockade running was foremost a business. It also was the most important element in the South's military supply system. It became, in the words of Dr. Stephen Wise, the lifeline of the Confederacy. Before we turn to the pilots who ran the blockade and their stories, let's look at how this business got started, the men who ran it and those who delivered the goods, and the ships that carried them along with the ports on the Southern coast.[3]

The Confederate Seaports

To establish the foreign trade essential to support the war effort, the Confederacy needed seaports with suitable harbors, wharfs, and warehouses, along with rail or riverboat connections to the interior. Few met these requirements.[4]

The war began at the premier seaport on the south Atlantic coast: Charleston. The South Carolina city then ranked third among the Southern ports in total imports and exports, trailing only the gulf cities of New Orleans and Mobile. Four channels led into Charleston's broad harbor formed by the confluence of the Ashley and Cooper Rivers. The main ship channel, which varied in depth from seventeen to twenty-two feet, allowed the largest ships of the day to enter the port, including transatlantic sailing vessels which traded with England. Exports such as cotton, rice, and naval stores arrived in Charleston by rail and steamboat for shipment to Northern ports and to Europe.[5]

The South's other major commercial seaport on the Atlantic seaboard was Savannah. Located on the Savannah River which divides Georgia and South Carolina, Savannah's main export was rice, although the port surpassed Charleston in exports of cotton.[6]

Norfolk was the third busiest port on the south Atlantic coast, although the Virginia city ranked well behind Charleston and Savannah. Norfolk lies just south of the Chesapeake Bay and Hampton Roads, the deep anchorage at the mouths of the James, Nansemond, and Elizabeth Rivers.[7]

Some 150 miles south of Norfolk, just below Cape Lookout, lies Topsail Inlet, which opens into Beaufort Harbor. Two ports were situated on the harbor: the old colonial settlement of Beaufort and the new town of Morehead City. At high tide, vessels drawing eighteen feet of water could cross the bar at Beaufort Harbor. And thirty miles inland from Morehead City, up the Neuse River, stood the old town of New Bern.[8]

About ninety miles below Cape Lookout lies Cape Fear, with its twin inlets into the river which led to the port of Wilmington. Wilmington then as now was the most important commercial port in North Carolina. New Inlet allowed passage at high tide of vessels drawing twelve feet of water; Old Inlet was slightly deeper. Crossing the bar at either entrance with a medium-draft vessel could be tricky under the best of conditions, and the Cape Fear pilots had always earned their keep.[9]

South of Charleston, the Port Royal-Beaufort area offered deep-water access to the ocean, but lacked wharf facilities and railroad connections. In Florida, Fernandina, Jacksonville, and other deep-water harbors had not been developed to the extent that they could play significant roles in the war.[10]

Early in the war, the Union would occupy strategic points along the Confederate coast and establish support bases for blockaders at Beaufort in North Carolina and at Port Royal and Hilton Head in South Carolina. Tybee Island would fall into Union hands, hampering blockade running at Savannah. Norfolk would prove effectively useless for blockade running because of the presence of so many Union naval vessels in the area and because the Union Navy controlled the entrance to the Chesapeake. For the Confederacy, the most important seaports would be Charleston at the beginning of the war and Wilmington at the end.[11]

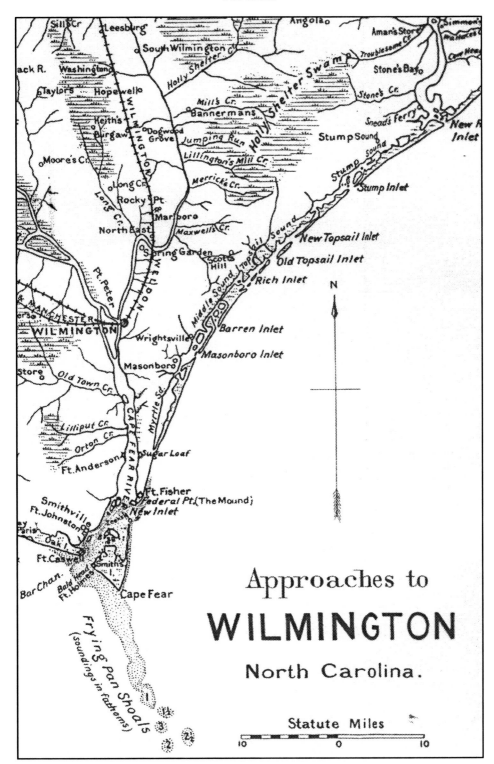

Approaches to

WILMINGTON

North Carolina.

Statute Miles

The Beginning

At the beginning of the war, the South clung to the notion that the economies of England and other European nations were so dependent on cotton that they would come to the aid of the Confederacy. Southern planters and merchants, with the open support of local politicians and newspapermen and the tacit support of the Confederate government, deliberately withheld its cotton from foreign commerce with a self-imposed embargo. The South waited. No aid came. The 1861 cotton harvest, one of the largest ever, stayed home. Finally, the South could wait no more and efforts to export cotton to exchange for arms began in earnest.[12]

Sailing ships were the first vessels to run the blockade. Virtually every type of vessel was employed in the first year of the war. Schooners were fast but lacked sufficient cargo capacity. And larger sailing vessels proved too slow and lacked the maneuverability to elude the blockaders.[13]

In October of 1861, the *Bermuda*, a new iron-hulled merchantman owned by the Charleston trading firm of Fraser, Trenholm and Company, became the first steamer to challenge the blockade. In Scotland, she took aboard a huge cargo for the Confederate Army: 18 rifled cannon, 4 larger guns, 6,500 Enfield rifles, powder, shot, 200,000 cartridges, 180 barrels of gunpowder, 60,000 pairs of shoes, 20,000 blankets, and an assortment of medical supplies. On September 18, 1861, she arrived in Savannah. The next month she left Savannah bound for Liverpool with 2,000 bails of cotton. The cotton was sold in England for a huge profit. The voyages of the *Bermuda* established in the minds of Southern businessmen and the Confederate military two key facts: cotton, which was scarce in Europe, would indeed be the perfect medium of exchange to buy war supplies, and fast steamers could successfully penetrate the Union blockade.[14]

The Transshipment System

The voyages of the *Bermuda* would prove to be flukes. It would not turn out to be practicable for large ocean-going cargo ships to sail directly from England to the Southern ports. Most of the accessible Confederate harbors were too shallow to readily accommodate the larger ships, which also lacked the speed and maneuverability to elude the blockading cruisers.[15]

Several early attempts with larger vessels were doomed to failure. In June 1862 the *Modern Greece*, a large deep-draft steamer, attempted to run arms into Wilmington and ran aground off Fort Fisher.[16]

The English owners of the *Modern Greece* displayed an apparent lack of knowledge of the coastal waters where they sent their ship; her draft was too deep to have ever crossed the bars at Cape Fear with a load of cargo. She was a large freighter inappropriately pressed into service as a blockade runner. Most of her cargo would remain aboard the hulk for more than a century, until it was recovered by divers of the U. S. Navy and the North Carolina Department of Cultural Resources.[17]

Contemporary reports said she also carried 1,000 tons of gunpowder and rifled cannon, four of which were salvaged by the soldiers of Fort Fisher.[18]

Wrenches used then for working on steam engines look just like those in use today, as did the hammers, knives, and scissors. The arms, of course, would be the most important cargo of the runners. But the surgeons' bone saws would also be an essential import, as many Confederate veterans could later attest.[19]

For the Confederate blockade runners operating out of Wilmington, two British ports would serve as intermediate ports: St. George's in Bermuda and Nassau on New Providence Island in the Bahamas.[20]

Bermuda lies 674 miles east of Wilmington. In those days it was a favorite stopover point for vessels crossing the Atlantic. The best harbor in the island group was at St. George's, which was close to open water. St. George's and the Bermudian capital, Hamilton, both had extensive warehouses and wharfs, and the business infrastructure for commercial shipping. Warehouses were necessary because English law did not allow goods to be moved directly from one ship to another in commerce with a blockaded nation. The blockade runners had to obtain clearances from local custom houses. But the ship's papers always listed a neutral port as the destination, a ruse, however transparent, intended to mislead potential captors. As sailors' towns the island ports also had places where the men went to let off steam, such as the dives of Shinbone Alley in St. George.[21]

THE CARGO recovered from the *Modern Greece* shows better than most cargo manifests the goods needed by the South, at least early in the war. It included:

Enfield rifle
Enfield carbines
pistols
bullet molds
knives
percussion caps
Whitworth cannon bolts (projectiles) and shot
Lead ingots
Tin ingots
Tin-plated sheet steel
axes
chisels
ratchet drills
Surgical instruments (including bone saws)
pipe dies
files
hammers
saws
hatchets
hoes
screwdrivers
flatirons
wrenches
bayonets
scissors
nails
frying pans

Many Bermudians first learned of the Civil War on June 4, 1861, when the steamer *Merlin* arrived from Halifax bearing mail from England, including the royal proclamation of British neutrality in the conflict. Most Bermudians, with close ties

Some writers have identified the steamer depicted in this painting by D. J. Kennedy as the *Modern Greece*. A contemporary report said that the *Modern Greece* ran aground three-quarters of a mile from shore. She became a total loss, although part of her cargo was salvaged by soldiers from Fort Fisher, including four Whitworth 12-pounder rifled cannons. (See note on page 175; photo courtesy of Naval Historical Center and Franklin Delano Roosevelt Library)

to the South, sympathized with the Confederacy. Bermudian merchants such as John T. Bourne seized the opportunity for making profits from receiving and shipping goods. By the summer of 1863, Confederate blockade runners had begun arriving with loads of cotton to exchange for European arms and other supplies imported from England.[22]

Nassau, the chief port of the Bahamas, stands on the northeast coast of New Providence Island. It lies some 570 miles below Wilmington and 515 miles from Charleston. Like Bermuda, it was ideally suited to serve as an intermediate port for shipping materials to and from the Confederacy. The first blockade runner to arrive in Nassau was the *Theodora* in October 1861.[23]

One drawback of the tropical port was the prevalence in the summer months of yellow fever. This infectious disease could bring high fever, hemorrhage, and the so-

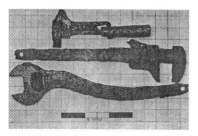

Wrenches rocovered from the *Modern Greece* by divers from the Fort Fisher Underwater Archaeology Unit at Kure Beach, North Carolina. (Photo courtesy of Underwater Archeology Unit, Fort Fisher.)

Sleek blockade runners mingle with transatlantic freighters in St. George's harbor in Bermuda during the Civil War. (Photo courtesy of Chicago Historical Society)

called black vomit (of blood), and kill within a week. During the 1860s, people were not aware that it was transmitted by mosquito bites. Outbreaks of yellow fever in Nassau—and sometimes Bermuda—eventually lead to quarantine of blockade runners arriving in Southern ports, but not before Wilmington had been devastated by an epidemic of yellow fever brought by the *Kate* in the fall of 1862.[24]

Another intermediate port for blockade runners was Havana, Cuba, which served the gulf ports of New Orleans and Mobile, and the limited blockade running from the Florida coast. But the Spanish colony was too far from Cape Fear to make it a suitable intermediate destination for blockade runners from Wilmington.[25]

Loading cotton in Nassau. (From Frank Leslie's *Illustrated News*.)

Halifax harbor in the 1860s. (Drawing courtesy of Halifax Memorial Library.)

One other foreign port visited by blockade runners was Halifax in Nova Scotia. Halifax served as a coaling and repair station for English ships crossing the north Atlantic. Throughout the war, trading ships sailed regularly back and forth between Halifax, the mother country, and the British colonies in Bermuda and the Bahamas. But Halifax never developed into an intermediate port for blockade running because of its distance from the Southern ports and the toll on lightly built ships of the heavy seas of the north Atlantic.[26]

There were, however, exceptions to this rule. In August of 1864, for example, the *Old Dominion* and the *City of Petersburg* arrived in Halifax with 2,000 bales of cotton after a five-day run up the coast from Wilmington. The *Helen* also made two runs to Halifax in the fall of 1864.[27]

The Owners and Operators

The men behind the business of blockade running ranged from Confederate Army officers doing their best to arm and outfit the armies in the field, to speculators looking to run in luxury goods for quick profits. Most ships were owned by private firms, a handful by the Confederate government, and one fast steamer by the state of North Carolina.[28]

Early in the war, the Confederate Ordinance Bureau moved to establish a program to import arms and supplies from Europe. Colonel Josiah Gorgas, the Bureau's chief, sent Captain Caleb Huse to England to make arrangements for the purchases.

The captain left with high hopes but little money. He stopped by Trenholm Brothers in New York to obtain some funds to get started. There he received $500 in gold along with a warning that if the Yankees discovered his business he "would be hanged from the nearest lightpost." Soon Huse was joined by Major Edward Anderson.[29]

To provide a source of funds, the Confederacy enlisted the support of a Charleston firm which would become its greatest ally: John Fraser and Company. Together with its Liverpool branch of Fraser, Trenholm and Company, it would become known as the banker of the Confederacy. George Alfred Trenholm, who directed both branches, would eventually become the secretary of treasury of the Confederate government.[30]

George Alfred Trenholm, the Charleston businessman who became the patriarch of blockade running. (Photo courtesy of Confederate Museum of Charleston)

Trenholm at the beginning of the war was one of America's wealthiest businessmen. He owned hotels, plantations, cotton presses, wharves, and steamships. Trenholm's companies also operated five sailing ships which made round trips between Charleston and Liverpool. They would operate more blockade runners than any other firm or organization.[31]

Many other private firms entered the business, some established just to run the blockade. Alexander Collie & Company, a British firm, was among the most successful. Collie owned the *Annie*, the *Condor*, the *Hansa*, the *Index,* and the *Don*. Crenshaw & Company, another British firm, owned the *Agnes E. Fry*, the *Armstrong*, and the *Mary Celestia*, and jointly owned, with Collie, the *Hebe* and the *Venus*. Southern businesses such as the Chicora Importing and Exporting Company also owned and operated blockade runners.[32]

To help raise money to purchase arms, the Confederate government issued cotton bonds. Secured by cotton purchased early in the war, these bonds earned interest and could be redeemed for Confederate cotton at a sizable profit to their owners. The popular bonds paid off handsomely both to their owners and to the government.[33]

After private firms demanded higher rates for shipping Confederate cargos, Major Edward Anderson bought for the government the *Fingal*, an iron-hull propeller steamer. With Anderson aboard, she made a successful run into Savannah in November of 1861, with enough supplies and equipment to outfit ten regiments. But

After a single run through the blockade, the *Fingal* was converted into an ironclad warship and renamed CSS *Atlanta*. (Courtesy Mariners' Museum of Newport News, Virginia.)

neither Anderson nor the ship ran the blockade again. Anderson stayed to help with Savannah defenses, the *Fingal* was turned into an ironclad warship.[34]

The Confederate government bought several other ships early in the war and purchased part interest in several more. But it did little to regulate blockade running until late in the war. Instead it relied mainly on privately owned runners to carry its cargoes, despite the high costs, as the fortunes of its armies grew ever more dependent on foreign arms and supplies. Some historians have attributed this policy to the Confederate government's emphasis on states' rights, that is, the desire to avoid strong centralized control of the enterprise.[35]

One state that refused to leave the fortunes of its soldiers in the field in the hands of businessmen or the Confederate government was North Carolina. Governor Zebulon Vance, who put the interests of his state before those of the Confederacy, bought his own blockade runner, the *Advance*. (In Chapters 10 and 11 stories appear about this fast and famous ship, about Kit Morse, the *Advance's* Cape Fear pilot, and about a young girl who planned to run the blockade with her family aboard the governor's steamer.)[36]

The owners, both government and private, needed middlemen to make the system work. For a handling fee, these people made arrangements for warehousing, wharfs, and stevedores, and took care of other details associated with handling of the cargoes. John T. Bourne served this purpose in Bermuda. A local businessman, he managed wharf and warehouse arrangements for a number of companies including

North Carolina Governor Zebulon Vance
(Photo courtesy of North Carolina State Archives.)

the Trenholm firms. Bourne also handled cargo for the Confederate government and the state of North Carolina. Copies of his business letters from that period, recorded in three tissue-leaved books, tell of the comings and goings of the ships and the cargos they carried to the Confederate coast. They serve as one of the best surviving records of the trade.[37]

Confederate army officers also served as middlemen. At Bermuda, Major Norman Walker and Major Smith Stansburg served as Confederate agents, representing the government's interests. Stansburg's letter book also survives. An entry in a letter dated September 14, 1863, concerned problems with one of the captains, Frank Bonneau of the blockade runner *Ella and Annie:*

> My faithful and efficient clerk Mr. Gibson and myself toiled to get the "Ella and Annie" off with her precious cargo. If Captain Bonneau had taken the same interest, I am satisfied that his steamer could have left a week earlier than she did . . . In the meantime Captain B. beguiled his time in Hamilton 12 miles distant. He says that he was sick, but if common report is to be credited, a woman who came over with him was the magnet, which detracted him from his duty.[38]

The Captains

Among the captains of the blockade runners were English naval officers, on leave from the Royal Navy, who ran the blockade for profit and for adventure. Some captains were furloughed Confederate naval officers who had served in the U. S. Navy before the war. And some had been captains of merchant ships before the war, men such as Captain Bonneau.[39]

"A splendid, handsome, courtly gentleman," according to one contemporary, Captain Bonneau's amorous nature was matched by his audacity. He was the only blockade runner captain who tried to run down a Union blockader. This happened early on the morning of November 9, 1863, as the *Ella and Annie* was steaming off the beach heading for New Inlet. As Captain Bonneau told the story:

> Just as the day was dawning we touched the beach slightly, but did not stop, and while hauling away from it, saw a gunboat standing directly across our bow (she

must evidently have heard our wheels), and was steering so as to cut us off from the beach. We being in three fathoms of water, I was much surprised to find a boat running so boldly for us. To pass outside of him would be to lose my ship, for he would then cut me off from the support I expected from our own batteries in a few miles more. To run my ship ashore at this point would have been madness, for the beach here is an outer one, the sound extending inside of it for miles, and consequently I could expect no protection, and my whole ship company would either be destroyed on this bold beach or taken by the enemy prisoners. To turn back to the sea was to give the ship to the enemy without an effort to save her.[40]

The blockader was the *Niphon*. Not liking his other choices, Captain Bonneau aimed the *Ella and Annie* directly for the smaller but heavily armed steamer:

> . . . As we approached each other rapidly, I could hear the noise of his men preparing for action, &c., and when about one hundred and fifty yards from him I hailed him, telling him that he would be afoul of us, hoping to induce the thought that I was one of their own ships, but was soon made aware of my mistaken opinion by a broadside of grape and canister, accompanied by a volley of musketry. I then

The *Ella and Annie*, one of the few American-built steam blockade runners. The iron-hull paddlewheeler was constructed in Wilmington, Delaware, in 1860 as the *William G. Hewes*. Renamed *Ella and Annie* she ran the blockade for the Importing and Exporting Company of South Carolina. On the day of her capture she was loaded with arms, lead, and saltpeter, along with beef, pork, salt, and brandy. The Wilmington *Daily Journal* reported that she was carrying "the heaviest cargo ever tried by a blockade runner—394 tons of dead weight, all Government property."
(See note on page 175; drawing courtesy of Naval Historical Center.)

ordered my ship pointed for her, and hoped to strike her just forward of her waist boat. Unfortunately, he perceived this move of mine, and shifting his helm, causing his vessel to swing away from me, and making it impossible to strike fair.

Our ships came together the next moment with a fearful crash, carrying away his starboard boat rail and part of his stem and cutwater. My engine kept working to its full capacity, as I had but one chance of getting clear of him, and that was to force my ship past him before he could board, as I distinctly heard him call away his boarders. In this last attempt I failed, as the ships were going ahead, and now he swung broadside into us while in this condition, and almost at the same time boarding us on the port quarter and wheelhouse guard. Then ensued a scene which none but an eyewitness would believe. Officers and men rushing along our deck, shooting and cutting at everything that came in sight . . . They went below and broke up everything that came in sight, state-rooms, trucks, boxes, &C., officers and men quarreling over trunks for the contents . . .[41]

Frank Bonneau went on to describe how the flagship *Shenandoah* arrived and how her officers put an end to the plunder by the *Niphon*'s crew. The *Ella and Annie* was sent to Beaufort as a prize and then on to Boston where she was sold to the U.S. Navy and renamed *Malvern*. Captain Bonneau accompanied her to Boston where he was released on parole. Her Cape Fear pilot, James N. Adkins, ended up in prison at Fort Lafayette on New York harbor.[42]

Confederate Naval Officers

As the United States moved toward civil war, naval officers loyal to the Southern cause resigned their commissions and offered their services to the Confederacy. Since the South had few warships it faced a surfeit of captains. Some went on to command Confederate raiders; others took charge of blockade runners. Some did both. Two such men who stood out among their colleagues were John Newland Maffitt and John Wilkerson.[43]

"Since I was born a son of Old Neptune, I was duty bound to offer my allegiance to the sea," Maffitt once remarked. Son of an Irish minister, he was born in 1819 aboard a British sailing ship in the north Atlantic.[44]

At age thirteen he joined the U. S. Navy as a midshipman. He spent most of the next few years aboard the USS *St. Louis* in the West Indies. And, as mentioned previously, Maffitt spent time in the Smithville area before the war surveying the coastal waters of Cape Fear. [45]

After his work on the coast survey, Maffitt commanded the U.S. brig *Dolphin* and, later, the U.S. steamer *Crusader*. In the weeks following the fall of Sumter, Maffitt resigned his commission in the U.S. Navy, received a commission as a lieutenant in the Confederate Navy and was placed in command of the steamer *Savannah*, a coastal packet.[47]

Tinker Runs the Blockade

CAPTAIN MICHAEL P. USINA of Savannah said he was known to fellow blockade runners as "the man that owned the dog." Tinker, his terrier, had been left to him by a shipmate who died at sea, and as he was dying, kept calling out to his little dog. Tinker, according to his new master, was "an excellent ratter, and fond of the sea."

"He seemed to know when we were approaching the enemy, and to be on alert, and when under fire would follow me step for step," said Captain Usina. Tinker developed such a reputation for bringing good luck that an English captain once offered $500 in gold to borrow the dog for a single trip through the blockade. His master refused.

After the capture of Fort Fisher, Captain Usina headed for England, saddened by the loss of the last gateway to the Confederacy, knowing that the dream of Southern independence was coming to an end. Saddened, too, was Tinker. "When blockade

The man who owned the dog
(From a private collection.)

Tinker (From a private collection.)

running ceased, his spirits drooped, and he soon sickened and died," said Usina about his devoted mascot. "I buried my faithful Tinker among the icebergs of the north Atlantic and every man on board stood uncovered when he was consigned to his watery grave."

Early in the war, Lieutenant Maffitt served as a naval aide to General Robert E. Lee. As one of the foremost experts on the Southern coast, he assisted with construction of shore batteries and river obstructions. Impressed with his knowledge and ability, George Trenholm offered Maffitt command of the *Cecile*. Although Maffitt did not take command of this sidewheeler, which Trenholm sold, he gained fame as captain of the Confederate commerce raider *Florida*. Later he commanded the blockade runner *Lilian* and, near the end of the war, the *Owl*. Master of the Confederate coast, experienced in command, brave under fire, and respected by his crew, he was

John Newland Maffitt stands on the inboard side of the paddlebox and peers at a Union cruiser chasing the *Lilian*, in this drawing by Frank Vizetelly, artist-correspondent of the *Illustrated London News*. The artist himself appears in the picture, to the left of the smoke stack. Vizetelly, who saw the Civil War from both sides, was a dinner guest of Colonel Lamb and his wife Daisy at the Cottage at Fort Fisher. James Sprunt was purser of the *Lilian*. Her Cape Fear pilot was Thomas Grissom. (See note on page 175; drawing courtesy of North Carolina State Archives.)

The Lockwood brothers of Charleston, Robert (left) and Thomas, were typical of the Southern steamship captains who commanded blockade runners. Both worked for John Fraser & Co. (See note on page 175; photos courtesy of Robert Lockwood of Huger, South Carolina, and the Confederate Museum of Charleston.)

Lt. John Wilkerson of the Confederate States Navy. Born in Norfolk, Virginia, he enlisted as a midshipman in the U.S. Navy in 1837 at age 16. (Courtesy Charleston County Library.)

a consummate professional, certainly among the best of the blockade-running captains.[48]

John Wilkerson shared many of these same qualities. After the war began he resigned his commission in the U. S. Navy and joined the Confederate Navy. Commissioned as a lieutenant, he went to England in the summer of 1862 and helped buy for the Confederate Ordnance Bureau the *Giraffe*, the sleek but rugged sidewheel steamer that was renamed *Robert E. Lee* upon her arrival in Wilmington. Wilkerson ran the blockade twenty-one times on this ship. He said she "carried abroad between six thousand and seven thousand bales of cotton, worth at that time about two million dollars in gold, and had carried into the Confederacy equally valuable cargoes."[49]

The Brits

Many British captains ran the blockade, some mainly for the adventure. Two of the best known were post captains on leave from the Royal Navy, Charles Augustus Hobart-Hampden and William N. W. Hewett.[50]

Son of the Earl of Buckinghamshire, Hobart-Hampden before the war had commanded the H.M.S. *Driver* and, for a time, Queen Victoria's yacht. In the American Civil War he saw an opportunity for adventure. He also saw an opportunity for enormous profits, which he seized with a firm grip. Shortly after the war he wrote as "Captain Roberts," his blockade-running alias, a thinly disguised account of his experiences called *Never Caught*.[51]

"For if ever a cool head, strong nerve, and determination of character were required, it was while running, or endeavoring to run, through the American blockade of the coast of the Southern States," he wrote. Hobart-Hampden's career shows that he possessed these qualities. His ship was the *Don*, a new twin-screw steamer built in London. Operated by Collie & Company, she made ten successful runs through the blockade.[52]

Hobart-Hampden was one of those captains who ran his own goods through the blockade to make extra money. (His salary amounted to one thousand pounds in gold per voyage.) On his first trip into Wilmington, he brought along Cockle pills, a popular patent medicine in England, and toothbrushes. Neither found a ready market: "Regarding the former, I am sorry to say that my endeavors to induce my Southern friends to try their efficacious powers were of no avail . . . my tooth brushes [were] not in the slightest degree appreciated in Wilmington . . ." He ended up trading the pills for matches in Nassau and sent the toothbrushes to Richmond where they were better appreciated and "sold for seven times their cost."[53]

During the layovers on his runs into Wilmington, Hobart-Hampden enjoyed the hospitality of Colonel Lamb and his wife Daisy at the Cottage at Fort Fisher, as did another Royal Navy captain, William Hewett.[54]

Captain Hewett, like Hobart-Hampden, used an alias for his blockade running, Samuel S. Ridge. But unlike his fellow officer, his venture met with failure, and a spectacular one at that. Hewett commanded the *Condor*, which attempted on her maiden voyage to run into New Inlet carrying arms and the Confederate spy, Rose Greenhow. The story of the *Condor* appears in Chapter Six.[55]

Captain Charles Augustus Hobart-Hampden served in the Turkish navy after the Civil War. (Photo from a private collection.)

Along with naval officers, a number of British merchant captains also ran the blockade. A British captain—the sailing captain—would bring a British blockade runner across the Atlantic on her first voyage to the Southern coast. Many sailing captains such as Johanes Wylie of the *Advance* remained on the ship in another capacity such as first officer after an American captain took charge. Others such as Jonathon Steele of the *Banshee* continued in command.[56]

Crews of the British-built blockade runners were mostly British. Hobart-Hampden said that his entire crew was English. Seamen from other countries were common as well, along with Southerners. The crew list of the *Advance* in February of 1864 included men from the following states: North Carolina (12), Virginia (4), Maryland (2), Pennsylvania (1), New York (1), and Rhode Island (1). Crewmen from other countries included Ireland (14), England (10), Scotland (4), France (3), Sweden (2), Portugal (2), and Canada (1). But when a

The cottage at Fort Fisher. (Photo courtesy of New Hanover County Public Library.)

Colonel William Lamb (Courtesy of North Carolina State Archive)

blockade runner was caught, most Southerners claimed British citizenship because citizens of neutral countries were released.[57]

The Blockade Running Steamers

As Kevin Foster has pointed out in his study of the evolution of the blockade-running steamships, the Civil War brought remarkable innovations in ship design.[58]

At the time of the Civil War, a revolution in marine propulsion was taking place. Although the changes would take the better part of a century, sails were being supplanted by steam. The days of the clipper ships—fast, long, slender, sharp-bowed, majestic vessels—were numbered. White clouds of sail rising from the beautiful clippers were being supplanted by black clouds of smoke billowing from the steamers' stacks. The high-water mark of wind propulsion had been reached and, so far as commercial shipping was concerned, the tide was going out.[59]

In 1807, Robert Fulton had built the first successful paddlewheel steamer. Before long, steamboats fueled by coal began to appear in the rivers and inland waters of the United States and Great Britain. In 1819 the converted coastal packet *Savannah* became the first steamship to cross the Atlantic. By 1840 the steamships of the Cunard Line were crossing the Atlantic on a regular schedule. By this time, some steamers used screw propellers instead of paddlewheels to drive the ships. The seagoing steamers still carried sails to use if an engine failed or the fuel supply ran out.[60]

In contrast to ships powered by the wind, the fuel supply was a significant operating limitation for the steamers. A typical blockade-running steamer would burn fifty to sixty tons of coal per day. Two hundred tons of coal—enough for a run from Wilmington to Bermuda—would weigh as much as seven hundred bales of cotton and take up considerable space. The best coal then available was Pennsylvania anthracite, hard coal that burned without smoke. Engineers considered Welsh coal second best. Among the worst was from North Carolina, soft bituminous coal which burned with less heat and produced telltale black smoke.[61]

Coal wasn't the only fuel used by the blockade runners. In times of peril, speed counted most. In a steamer, this meant hotter boilers. Captains were known to burn cotton soaked in turpentine to gain a few extra knots to elude a fast blockader. Lieutenant Wilkerson of the *Robert E. Lee* used this technique on one occasion to increase his steamer's speed by forty percent.[62]

Another change taking place in ship design involved the material of the hulls. Wood, fortunately for the few remaining forests of Great Britain, was beginning to

After purchase by the Confederacy, the *Giraffe* was taken into drydock in Glasgow for conversion into a blockade runner. She carried two oscillating engines, six horizontal boilers, and two furnaces. Each boiler contained 158 three-inch diameter tubes. Corrosion of boiler tubes was always a concern of engineers. She was renamed *Robert E. Lee* on arrival in the Confederacy in December of 1862. At 268 feet with a 28-foot beam and a 12-foot depth of hold she was one of the longer blockade runners. Ruggedly built, her top speed of 13¼ knots was obtained while burning cotton soaked with turpentine, according to her captain, Lt. John Wilkerson. (See note on page 175; photo courtesy of Museum of Transport, Glasgow Museums, Glasgow, Scotland.)

give way to iron. First, wooden planks covered iron frames. Then iron replaced the wooded planks. Then steel, with its higher strength, would replace iron in the outer skin. The metal plates were shaped to the curvature of the hull and fastened in place with rivets.[63]

Early in the Civil War, as the few Southern shipyards were taxed to capacity building warships, the blockade runners turned to England and Scotland. The coastal paddle steamers that carried passengers, mail, and freight around the British Isles proved to be ideal blockade runners. They were fast, seaworthy, and of light-draft. Many had been built on the Clyde River near Glasgow, making the term Clyde-built steamer virtually synonymous with blockade runner.[64]

After purchase as blockade runners, these vessels underwent conversion.

The USS *Fort Donnelson*, formerly the *Giraffe* and the blockade runner *Robert E. Lee*, in Norfolk in 1864. The *Lee* was captured in November 1863. Many blockade runners ended up as blockaders before the war was over. (See note on page 175; photo courtesy of Library of Congress)

Luxurious accommodations for passengers were ripped out to make room for cargo holds and bigger coal bunkers. Rigging was reduced to a bare minimum. Bows were reinforced to withstand the Atlantic crossing. Hulls and superstructures were painted to make the ships hard to see at night. Some eighty of these British river steamers would run the blockade.[65]

As the war proceeded, most of these ships fell prey to Federal cruisers or the shoal waters of the Confederate coast. And British shipyards turned to building steamers specially designed to run the blockade.[66]

Experience showed that success on the coastal runs required fast ships of shallow draft and great maneuverability that could pass blockaders quietly in the night without being seen. Meeting these requirements would challenge the British builders to produce advances in ship design that would endure well into the twentieth century.[67]

Increased speed came from longer ships with narrowed beams and lighter hulls made of steel. Streamlined "turtleback" forward decks allowed the runners to knife through the waves, requiring raised bridges with enclosed helms—forerunners of the modern steamship bridge structure. Steam pressures doubled in the finely tuned engines. Twin propellers replaced single screws, increasing maneuverability as well as speed, although the fastest paddle steamers still maintained a slight edge in speed. (One reason for this was the shallow draft size, which limited the size of the propellers.)[68]

The quest for stealth started with the camouflage paint scheme, the first such use for ships. Blockade runners were painted various shades of light grey to blend in with the background of the nighttime coast. Low freeboard and minimal deckhouses produced low silhouettes, making the vessels even harder to spot. Masts and rigging were reduced, leaving a place for the lookout on the forward mast and just enough sail area to aid ship stability. Some runners were built with telescoping funnels to further reduce the vessel's profile.[75]

Builders also worked to reduce noise. Piping was routed so that steam was vented underwater. Some runners carried canvas curtains to place over the paddleboxes as a further quieting measure.[76]

Several British dockyards stood out among the builders of blockade runners. One prolific builder was Caird & Company of Greenock, Scotland. The company built its first ship in 1840. Among the blockade runners it constructed were the *City of Petersburg*, the *Old Dominion*, the *Agnes E. Fry*, and the *Fox*, along with arguably the two fastest of the sleek ships: the *Advance* and the *Margaret and Jessie*. Jones & Quiggin of Liverpool built the first steel-hull blockade runner, the *Banshee*. It also constructed the *Lucy*, the *Wild Darrell*, the *Badger*, the *Lynx*, the *Owl*, the *Bat*, and the *Colonel Lamb*.[77]

They Even Burned the Bacon

GREAT SPEED gave some blockade runners an edge over the fastest of the Union blockaders, warships such as USS *Fort Jackson* and USS *Santiago de Cuba*. Of the captured blockade runners taken into Federal service, the USS *Gettysburg*, the *ex-Margaret and Jessie*, was probably the fastest. But even she could not catch fast runners such as the *City of Petersburg*.[69]

Engineers such as George Morrison of the *Advance* loved to brag about the speed of their ships. The debates continued long after the war was over. In 1894 Morrison was still trading letters with James Sprunt in the Wilmington *Morning Star* over whether the *Advance* could make nineteen knots. Sprunt wrote that the fastest blockade runners seldom exceeded fourteen knots. But Morrison appeared sure of himself: "I am positive that the speed (19 knots) as stated by me is correct. With a strong flood tide, such as was had at the time that run was made, I would be willing to stake everything I have that it could be done again."[70]

George Morrison was referring to a run on the Cape Fear River made by the *Advance* after the war, when she was known as the USS *Frolic*. The navy engineers said they could only get eight or nine knots out of the ship. Morrison showed them how they had a steam damper set improperly; changing the setting boosted the speed well beyond what the navy engineers thought possible.[71]

Another well-known blockade-running engineer, George McDougal, said that the *Margaret and Jessie* was considered to be a faster boat than the *Advance*. Yet her log when she was in Federal service as the *Gettysburg* showed her top speed to be fifteen and one-half knots. Her captain then, Roswell Lamson, said she once made sixteen knots.[72]

In practice, the speed of the Civil War steamers depended upon a number of factors. A heavy sea would slow the ships. The condition of the hull was another important factor, as marine growth (the sailors called it grass) could cut speed by a couple of knots. Speed also obviously depended on the load being carried; runners under chase would often throw part of their cargo overboard to lighten their ship.[73]

But fuel was the biggest factor. Bad coal cut speed. Fuel which would burn hotter than coal increased speed. Just about anything that would burn made its way into the furnaces as the ships raced each other off the Confederate coast. Cotton soaked with terpentine was favored by some engineers. Wood was used on occasion. Under dire straights, firemen would even throw in barrels of pork or sides of bacon.[74]

Strategy at Cape Fear

To make their way through the blockade at Cape Fear, the inbound blockade runners developed a strategy of closely hugging the coastline, running in shallow waters where the deeper-draft Union vessels did not venture. Another advantage of this route was that the roar of surf breaking upon the beach prevented the noise of the paddles from being heard by the blockaders.[78]

Many pilots and captains favored the northern approach, steaming toward Masonboro Inlet, some twenty-five miles from the cape, then sprinting down the coast until they reached the protected area within range of the guns of Fort Fisher, where Federal cruisers dared not venture, and finally making their way into the harbor through New Inlet. Other blockade runners would use the southern approach, steaming up the coast until they crossed the Western Bar at Old Inlet and came under the protective shield of Fort Caswell.[79]

One reason for choosing the northern approach was the Mound Battery at Fort Fisher, which on clear nights was visible against the skyline, making an excellent landmark. The Mound, constructed of sand by the builders of Fort Fisher, stood sixty feet high, mounted two guns, and served effectively as a lookout tower for the Confederate defenders.[80]

On rare occasions, a blockade runner would steam right through the blockade. But a wise captain would always choose a dark night and a high tide to make his run, regardless of his approach.

During their nighttime approaches, the pilots of blockade runners were guided by lights ashore. There was a range light on a brick tower located some five miles north of Smithville (the Price's Creek lighthouse); it still stands today just above the ferry landing. During some periods, a light burned atop the Mound Battery at Fort Fisher. Lieutenant Wilkerson also noted that there were "numerous salt works on the coast, where evaporation was produced by fire, and which were at work night and day, that were visible before the low coast could be seen."[81]

But crossing the bar at night was a dicey proposition. Leadsmen stood at the bow of the vessel, casting their weights to measure the depth and quietly calling out their soundings. Lieutenant Wilkerson recalled one voyage where "The bar was a sheet of foam and surf, breaking shear across the channel; but the great length of *Lee* enabled her to ride over three or four of the short chopping seas at once, and she never touched the bottom."[82]

The Obnoxious Ensign

When blockade runners cleared a foreign port, they listed as their destination a port in a neutral country, and then made for Charleston, Wilmington, or another Southern port. As merchant ships, they sailed unarmed. At sea the captains would

The *Colonel Lamb*. **Named for the commander of Fort Fisher, the guardian angel of the blockade runners at Cape Fear, the broad-beam, shallow-draft, steel-hull side-wheeler averaged nearly seventeen knots during her builder's trials. She ran the blockade at Wilmington twice late in the war. One expert called her the finest of the blockade-running steamships.** (See note on page 175; photo courtesy of Naval Historical Center)

sometimes show American colors to a passing ship. But most blockade runners flew Confederate flags and made little pretense of their intent as they attempted to slip through the blockade.[83]

They also flew Confederate flags in neutral ports, sometimes to the residents' chagrin, as reported in the Bermuda *Advocate* in May of 1864:

> Whilst the steamers "Let Her Be" and "Badger" were coaling at St. Thomas's, they continued to fly the Confederate flag at their respective staffs. The authorities sent them orders to haul down the obnoxious ensigns—compliance was refused. The authorities sent off again, giving three hours and threatening that if the flags were not hauled down they—the authorities—would have them hauled down themselves. The three hours elapsed and the flags were still flying—The authorities sent off a force to haul them down, when it was found out in each case, the flag was nailed to the staff, the halyards removed, and the pole greased![84]

The *Mary Celestia* made eight runs through the blockade in 1864. The iron-hull steamer was built in Liverpool. (Photo courtesy of Museum of the Confederacy, Richmond, Virginia.)

CHAPTER 4

The Pilots of the Mary Celestia

"He directed the ship's course among the enemy's ships, through
the shoals and safely in over the bar . . ."

—*Captain M. P. Usina describing how Smithville pilot John
Anderson brought the* Mary Celestia *into the harbor at Cape
Fear.*[1]

T he *Mary Celestia* (sometimes referred to as the *Mary Celeste*) was an iron-hull sidewheeler built in Liverpool by William C. Miller and Sons in early 1864. Originally named the *Bijou,* she was purchased by the Crenshaw brothers of Richmond to run the blockade. From May of 1864 until the following September, she made eight runs through the blockade at Cape Fear, hauling cotton to Bermuda and bringing back war supplies and other goods to Wilmington. Records show that the *Mary Celestia* had three pilots during her brief career as a blockade runner. Each one was named John.[2]

Her first Wilmington pilot was John William Anderson, one of the true heroes among the Cape Fear pilots who ran the blockade. Anderson in 1861 was living at Federal Point. During the latter half of that year and in part of 1862, Anderson served as quartermaster on the CSS *Caswell.* During the summer of 1864, he took the *Mary Celestia* across the bar at Cape Fear on a run to Bermuda.[3]

When Anderson boarded the steamer at Smithville, Captain Mike Usina of Savannah, the man that owned the dog, was in command. Captain Usina remembered his pilot well. On Independence Day in 1893 he recalled in a talk to the Confederate Veterans Association of Savannah: "In the summer of 1864 I took with me to Bermuda a young Wilmington pilot, John W. Anderson was his name. There was at that time an epidemic of yellow fever at Bermuda, the worst I have ever heard of—a veritable epidemic."[4]

At St. George's in Bermuda, the steamer took on a cargo of two bales of clothing, one case of glass pipes, 27 bales of blankets, a barrel of hams, and 392 barrels of pork. And the *Mary Celestia* also took aboard yellow fever. Several of the crew died of the disease in the few days she lay in St. George's harbor. Others took ill as well, among them John Anderson. As the blockade runner returned to Wilmington, Anderson grew sicker and sicker. Captain Usina grew apprehensive about how they would make it through the blockade, for Anderson was the only one onboard who knew the local waters.[5]

James Sprunt described the inbound passage through the blockade in his book *Chronicles of the Cape Fear River* in the flowery words of a Wilmington writer:

> At last the critical hour arrived, when, in the uncertain light of the dawn, they found that they had run near a blockader and had been seen by her. The blockader opened fire on the Mary Celeste and pursued her. Like a seared greyhound she made straight for New Inlet Bar, then visible several miles away, and after her steamed the blockader, from whose bow gun every few minutes would leap a flame followed by a shell which would pass over her or through her rigging and burst into the air, or, striking the sea, would flash a great column of spray towards the sky. By this time poor Anderson was dying in his berth, and the officers of the ship began to realize the terrible situation in which they found themselves, with the enemy in pursuit and before them a bar over which it was almost certain destruction for any one aboard except Anderson to steer the Mary Celeste. Anderson heard the firing and knew what it meant before they told him. He knew, too, that he was dying and had no further interest in this world's affairs; but the sense of duty asserted itself even in the presence of death.
>
> He was too weak to go up, but he demanded to be taken on deck and carried to the man at the wheel. Two strong sailors lifted him up to the wheelhouse. They stood him on his feet and supported him on either side. His face was as yellow as gold, and his eyes shown like stars. He fixed his unearthly gaze upon the dim line of pines that stood higher than the surrounding forest, then at the compass for a moment, and said calmly, "Hard starboard." Quickly revolved the wheel under the hands of the helmsman; slowly veered the stem of the rushing steamer, and a shell hurtled over the pilothouse and went singing towards the beach.
>
> Anderson kept his gaze fixed on the breakers, and in the same calm tone said "Steady." On ploughed the steamer straight for her goal, while the group of men in the pilot house stood in profound silence but fairly quivering with suppressed excitement. The blockader, finally seeing that it was impossible to overtake her and not desiring to come within range of the big guns of Fort Fisher, abandoned the chase with a farewell shot, and the Mary Celeste, now nearly on the bar, slackened her pace a little, and nothing but the swash of the sea and the trembling thud of the ship under the force of the engine could be heard. The dying pilot, though failing fast, continued in the same calm tone to give his directions. They were now crossing the bar, but had passed the most dangerous point, when he bent his head as if to cough, and the horrified men saw the last symptom which immediately proceeds dissolution - black vomit - and they knew the end was very near . . . At last the bar was safely crossed, smooth water was reached the engine slowed down, the Mary Celeste glided silently into the harbor, stopped her headway gradually, loosed her anchor

chains, dropped her anchor, and as the last loud rattle of her cable ceased, the soul of John William Anderson took its "flight to the undiscovered country."[6]

Captain Usina remembered that Lou Hutchins, the chief officer, held Anderson in his arms as the dying pilot "directed the ship's course among the enemy's ships, through the shoals and safely in over the bar . . ." Usina said that after they anchored in the bay across from Smithville, he sent for Anderson's wife. A half-hour later she came aboard the steamer, but by then Anderson had died.[7]

As the body of John Anderson was being laid to rest in the Old Smithville Burying Ground, the *Mary Celestia* was being held in quarantine in the Cape Fear River near Fort Anderson. Finally, she steamed up the river to Wilmington to unload her cargo and take aboard another load of cotton. She also took on a new captain, Arthur Sinclair, and a new pilot, John Wesley Galloway Sr.[8]

John W. Galloway was born in Georgia around 1812. His grandfather, also named John Galloway, was a Cape Fear pilot who in 1768 lived beside Fort Johnston. He became a member of the Sons of Liberty and helped lead the local resistance to the Stamp Act prior to the American Revolution.[9]

In 1838 John W. Galloway worked for Captain Alexander Swift of the United States Engineer Corps in the construction of Fort Caswell. The two became good friends and Galloway named his first son Alexander Swift Galloway in honor of Captain Swift. By 1850 Galloway was a licensed Cape Fear pilot living in Smithville. In 1858 he was serving as keeper of the Frying Pan Shoals lightship.[10]

Early in the war Galloway organized a company for local defense in the lower Cape Fear area. Known as Captain Galloway's Coast Guard Company, it was mustered into service in Smithville at Fort Johnston on August 14, 1861. Comprised of pilots, fishermen, and seamen, the unit's services would include working with the

---

LICENSED CAPE FEAR pilots serving in Captain Galloway's Coast Guard
Company included:

John Davis	James Gutherie
John Wesley Galloway Sr.	John R. Savage
Thomas B. Garrason	Cornelius G. Smith [12]

Signal Service and the Engineer Corps, serving the Confederate States Navy, and furnishing pilots for blockade runners. During most of the war Captain Galloway's company was stationed at the beach below Fort Caswell.[11]

On or about August 24, 1864, Captain Galloway took the *Mary Celestia* out of the harbor on a run to Bermuda. She arrived safely a few days later. But the British colony remained in the grasp of the yellow fever epidemic. John Galloway became

The *Mary Celestia* sinks near Bermuda.
(Drawing courtesy of Mariners' Museum, Newport News, Virginia.)

the second Cape Fear pilot of the *Mary Celestia* to fall victim to the disease. He died in Hamilton, Bermuda, on September 27, 1864. General Whiting wrote, "Capt. Galloway, being a very experienced pilot, detached in an emergency to take out the ship *Mary Celestia*, unfortunately contracted yellow fever and died. His death was a great loss to the command."[13]

On the same day that Captain Galloway died, the *Mary Celestia* departed from St. Georges harbor and headed back toward the coast. Just off the Bermuda coast she struck a reef and sank. All hands made it safely to shore, save the first cook, who drowned. Many blamed the Bermuda pilot, John Virgin, for failing to heed a warning from the first officer who saw breakers in the path of the ship.[14]

In his book *The Blockade-Runners*, Dave Horner quotes a song about the demise of the *Mary Celestia*. Composed by a Bermudian, Blind Isaac Harvey of Somerset, it goes:

> The Mary Celeste was run ashore
> She will never run the Block any more
> So Johnny fill up the glass
> Johnny fill up the glass
> And we'll all drink stone blind.

How did the Mary Celeste get ashore?
Oh, Pilot Virgin runned her ashore—
She'll never run the Block any more
So Johnny fill up the glass
And we'll all drink stone blind.

Us boys may just as well go ashore
We won't be wanted on board any more —
Now boys we need not mind
So Johnny fill up the glass
And we'll all drink stone blind.[15]

The last resting place of the blockade runner *Mary Celestia*.
(Photo courtesy of Underwater Archaeology Unit, Fort Fisher.)

Thomas Brinkman stands on the left in this group of six Cape Fear pilots who ran the blockade. To his left stands Joseph Bensel. Joseph Newton stands on the far right. Seated on the left is Julius Dosher. The other two men are unidentified. (Photo courtesy of Joe Loughlin and Lois Jane Brussels Herring.)

CHAPTER 5

Thomas Brinkman and the Condor

"Both vessels crowded on steam, and an exciting chase began. It did not take my uncle long to see that his charge was in great danger, and the solid shot tore up the water . . ."

—*James Price describing how the* Condor, *the steamer piloted by his uncle Thomas Brinkman, was chased by a Union blockader.*[1]

T he name of Thomas Washington Brinkman will be forever linked to the story of the Rebel Rose, and how in the fall of 1864 she returned to her beloved Confederacy on the steamer *Condor.*

Thomas Brinkman, the son of John Jacob and Susan Brinkman of Oak Island, was born in 1838. In April of 1861, he married Mary Ann Piver of Smithville, who the year before had been living with the family of Joseph T. Thompson, a Cape Fear pilot. Thomas and Mary, who lived in Smithville, had nine children. A number of their descendants still live in Southport.[2]

Brinkman was one of the youngest Cape Fear pilots; when the *Condor* ran the blockade, he was only twenty-six. One of the few bar pilots to carry a restricted license, being limited to vessels of no more than nine-foot draft, Brinkman probably boarded the *Condor* at Halifax to pilot her into the harbor at Cape Fear.[3]

The *Condor* was a magnificent steamer specially built to run the blockade by Randolph, Elder and Company of Govan, Scotland. Built for Alexander Collie and Company, Collie himself considered the *Condor* and her three sisterships—the *Falcon,* the *Flamingo,* and the *Ptarmigan*—to have no superior among blockade-running steamers. She was long and low, with a turtleback forward deck, three raked stacks, and painted white.[4]

Her maiden voyage from Greenock, Scotland, in the fall of 1864 began with promise. Her captain was the famous British naval officer William Nathan Wrighte Hewett. On leave from the Royal Navy to run the blockade, Hewett was using the alias Samuel P. Ridge. Also aboard as a passenger was the well-known Confederate spy Rose Greenhow.[5]

The Rebel Rose

The widow Greenhow was a woman with connections. Friend of presidents and cabinet members, she could be seen in the years before the war walking down the streets of Washington on the arm of President Buchanan. In fact, she was attending a wedding with the president when he received the news of the secession of South Carolina.[6]

With the help of a Confederate army officer, Greenhow had organized a Confederate spy ring that gathered intelligence on Union plans for the war. She sent to General Beauregard secret information which led to the Confederate victory at Bull Run. A tall, statuesque brunette, she traveled widely in the North, charming secrets out of high-ranking military officers and members of Lincoln's cabinet, and through the South, working to build the morale of her people. As an official repre-

sentative of the Confederate government, she had traveled to Europe. During her time abroad she sought from every quarter support for the Southern cause. She also enjoyed the social life of Paris and the flattering attention of the literary set for her book, *My Imprisonment and the First Year of Abolition Rule in Washington.*[7]

On the voyage home, Rose Greenhow was carrying $2,000 in gold received as royalty from her book. She also carried, tradition says, vital dispatches for President

Rose Greenhow and her daughter in the Old Capitol Prison. Allan Pinkerton, who established Lincoln's Secret Service, arrested Mrs. Greenhow at her home in August 1862. He said she had "almost irresistible seductive powers."
(Photo courtesy of Library of Congress)

Davis. The gold she carried in a small leather bag which hung from her neck.[8]

After an uneventful voyage across the Atlantic, the *Condor,* loaded with war supplies, steamed into Halifax, Nova Scotia, on September 6, 1864. After taking on coal, she ploughed southward down the coast. Captain Hewett took the northern approach to Cape Fear, moving with strong northeast wind at his back, which made for rough seas. Running down the beach, the *Condor* eluded the blockader USS *Niphon* and moved swiftly towards New Inlet and the protective guns of Fort Fisher. Brinkman could make out in the darkness another vessel looming directly in his path. He brought the *Condor* hard to starboard to avoid running into the other ship. Moments later, all aboard the blockade runner felt her shudder and come to an abrupt stop. She had run aground, trying to avoid the wreck of the *Nighthawk,* which was stranded just off the beach, which Brinkman took to be a Federal cruiser.[9]

Aground

The hours that followed must have been ghastly. The wind howled. The waves pounded the stricken vessel. Flares soared into the sky. The *Niphon's* cannons boomed as she fired on the helpless *Condor.* Barrages from the guns of Fort Fisher finally drove away the Union cruiser.[10]

As daybreak approached, the *Condor* lay hard aground. Captain Hewett believed that the vessel, with its precious cargo, could be saved. But Rose Greenhow persuaded the captain to have her put ashore. Two seamen took her and another passenger in a lifeboat and set out into the breakers for the beach. But the boat was swamped. All survived except Mrs. Greenhow, who drowned in the surf, weighted down by the leather bag filled with gold sovereigns she always carried with her.[11]

A young soldier from Fort Fisher first saw her body lying on the beach and took the gold she had been carrying. After learning whom she was, he was said to have returned it to Colonel Lamb, the commander of Fort Fisher.[12]

It was Tom Taylor, supercargo of the foundered *Nighthawk,* who first recognized the body of Rose Greenhow. "It was I who found her body on the beach at daylight and carried her to Wilmington," he wrote in his memoirs. Her body was laid out in the chapel of General Hospital Number 4 for mourners to pay their respects, and she was buried with full military honors befitting her role in defense of her beloved land. Her tombstone can be seen in Wilmington today in Oakdale Cemetery.[13]

The *Condor* did not survive the grounding. Her hulk was eventually used for target practice by the 150-pounder Armstrong rifles of Fort Fisher.[14]

The Aftermath of the Accident

The pilot did make it to shore but found little but grief himself, according to his nephew James Eastus Price. Price was just seven years old at the time of the *Condor's* accident. Later he wrote of his uncle's ordeal, presenting a different view of the grounding of the *Condor* and the events which followed. In his words is, presumably, Thomas Brinkman's version of the incident:

> Although it was night, the low gray hull of this ship [*Condor*], which was diffi-
> cult to see, even by moonlight, was detected, heading for the bar, by the blockader.
> Both vessels crowded on steam, and an exciting chase began. It did not take my
> uncle long to see that his charge was in great danger, and the solid shot tore up the
> water all around. Heading straight for the nearest land, which was near Fort Fisher,
> the *Condor* was driven at full speed and struck bottom, unfortunately quite a dis-
> tance from shore. The enemy was pressing hard and, being unable to use the boats,
> the *Condor's* crew were compelled to swim for life. Uncle had with him a
> Newfoundland puppy, which, though a few months old, swam ashore through the
> breakers with master.[15]

James Price went on to describe how his uncle was falsely accused of uselessly running the steamer ashore. According to Price, as a result of this accusation, Thomas Brinkman was imprisoned first at Fort Johnston and then at Wilmington, and later in Salisbury, where at the end of the war, he still awaited trial.[16]

Brinkman's imprisonment apparently came months after the foundering of the *Condor*. Colonel Lamb wrote in his official diary that on November 5, 1864, the steamer *Blenheim* arrived from Nassau with Brinkman as pilot. The *Blenheim* was a paddle steamer built in Glasgow in 1848 that ran the Cape Fear blockade four times in late 1864.[17]

In any case, after the war Brinkman returned to the pilotage. In December of 1872, he drowned, along with four other Cape Fear pilots, when their boat was lost in a storm. Brinkman's remains were found near Battery Island. A ring he was wear-ing that day is still in the possession of his great-great-grandson Thomas Harrelson.[18]

CHAPTER 6

The Burriss Boys of Federal Point

"Sixteen fathoms—sandy bottom with black specs. We are not as far in as I thought, captain . . ."

— *Pilot Thomas E. Burriss of Federal Point reporting to the captain of the* Banshee *on a run to the coast.*[1]

For the better part of two centuries, men and boys of the Burriss family piloted ships at Cape Fear. Records show that at least five ran the blockade, although others likely did also.[2]

I remember the last in the line, the man who brought the battleship *North Carolina* up the river when others said it couldn't be done, Captain Bertram "Piggy" Burriss. The first was James Henry Burriss. Throughout the nineteenth century, menfolk of the Burriss family made their homes at Federal Point and made their living taking ships across the bar.[3]

The first members of the family to live at Federal Point were Captain John Burriss and his wife, who arrived shortly after the American Revolution. Their son James Henry was born there on July 5, 1784, in a house located between the present Fort Fisher museum and the river.[4]

In 1803, James Henry Burriss married Elizabeth Newton of Federal Point. Among their seven children who lived to maturity were four sons who became Cape Fear pilots like their father: Christopher William, John Henry, James Thomas, and Joseph Newton Burriss. Each of

Captain E. T. (Ned) Burriss
(Photo from a private collection)

these men was a licensed pilot during the Civil War. Joseph Newton Burriss was the Cape Fear pilot of the *Hansa*, a Glasgow-built paddle steamer operated by Alexander Collie and Company which ran the blockade twenty times.[5]

At least four grandsons of James Henry Burriss ran the blockade. Edward Thomas "Ned" Burriss, Christopher's son, piloted the *Chicora*. Originally named the *Let Her Be*, this steel-hull sidewheeler was built in Liverpool to run the blockade. She made fourteen successful runs through the blockade in 1864 and 1865.[6]

The Pirate Who Kept His Whiskey in His Coffin

George Washington Burriss piloted the *Hebe*. George, according to family tradition, kept his coffin under his bunk and in his coffin he kept his whiskey. George is also remembered in family stories as a pirate. Betty Cappo, a descendent of Burriss pilots, believes that this idea came from his service aboard the Confederate commerce raider *Tallahassee*, which the Yankees often referred to as a pirate ship.[7]

In any case George's service on the *Hebe* lasted only two months in the summer of 1863. Built in London that spring, the twin-screw steamer made one successful run into Wilmington and carried out a load of cotton. On her return voyage she carried a cargo of clothing, coffee, medicines, and bales of silk, arriving early on the morning of August 18, to find Cape Fear in the grip of a northeaster. The *Hebe* steamed down the beach plowing through heavy seas, heading for New Inlet, and met the USS *Niphon*. To avoid capture, George and the captain ran their steamer ashore.[8]

George and the other crewmen took to the ship's boats and made it safely to the beach. In the hours that followed a fierce fire fight ensued. Boarders from the *Niphon* set fire to the blockade runner. They came back on deck only to discover that their own boat had sunk, so they hurriedly returned below deck to put out the fire. In the meantime, two more boats set out from the *Niphon* to rescue the men aboard the stranded steamer. Lieutenant William Cushing, commander of the blockader USS *Shokokon*, sent another boat to the rescue. On the beach Confederate riflemen fired at the Union boats. Two Whitworth guns positioned behind a sand dune sent shot after shot at the *Niphon*. One of the Union boats capsized, another was driven ashore in the heavy surf. As the day ended, the guns of the *Shokokon* were pounding the stranded *Hebe* and the Confederate Whitworth battery was maintaining a deadly fire at the Union ships. The engagement cost the *Niphon* the lives of fifteen men.[9]

But the battle was far from over. Soldiers from Fort Fisher salvaged cargo from the *Hebe*. In an attempt to thwart their efforts, Rear Admiral Lee ordered his flagship the USS *Minnesota*, the USS *James Adger,* and four other gunboats to destroy the blockade runner. They not only did this but sent men ashore and captured one of Colonel Lamb's precious Whitworth guns, a loss lamented by General Whiting who said, "I have met with a serious and heavy loss in that Whitworth, a gun in the hands of the indefatigable Lamb has saved dozens of vessels and millions of money to the Confederate States." The Wilmington *Daily Journal* reported on another result of the skirmish: "The houses, and fences and woods in the neighborhood were riddled with shot and shell. Four shots passed through Mr. James Burriss' house. The hills around the wreck are furrowed like a ploughed field . . ."[10]

The next summer would find George Burriss in Halifax. He likely arrived on the *Tallahassee*. The newly armed cruiser steamed out of Old Inlet on the night of August 6, 1864, under the command of Captain John Taylor Wood, eluding the blockaders and heading around the Frying Pan Shoals and up the coast. Three days later the *Tallahassee* had claimed her first victim, a schooner from Boston which she sent to the bottom. Other victims quickly followed. A week after the raider left Cape Fear, the headline of the *New York Times* read "HIGHLY IMPORTANT: A Rebel Pirate Off The Coast."[11]

If George Burriss was aboard the *Tallahassee*, he would have appreciated the irony of an incident which occurred near New York harbor. With the *Tallahassee* twenty miles from the city, flying the Stars and Stripes, the pilot boat *James Funk* approached the Confederate raider. The pilot climbed aboard to take her in the harbor. Instead, he found himself aboard the "Rebel pirate ship."[12]

Twelve days after the *Tallahassee* passed the Bald Head light, she arrived in Halifax. On the way she had burned fifteen vessels and scuttled ten more. Townspeople crowded the docks to glimpse the now infamous raider. After replenishing her nearly empty coal bunkers, the cruiser headed back down the coast, and slipped back into the harbor at Cape Fear on August 25.[13]

George Burriss died in Halifax of yellow fever on August 22, 1864, and was buried in the cemetery there. He was twenty-eight years old. Whether or not he spent his last days aboard the famed Confederate raider we will never know for sure. Nor will we know whether the coffin that held his whiskey accompanied him on his final voyage so it could serve its more conventional purpose.[14]

The Confederate raider *Tallahassee* at Halifax, Nova Scotia, in August 1864. The twin-screw steamer was the former *Atalanta*, which was piloted by Thomas Mann Thompson of Smithville. George Burriss likely served aboard the cruiser during her raids on Yankee shipping. (Photo courtesy of Maritime Museum of the Atlantic, Halifax, Nova Scotia)

Tom Burriss and the *Banshee*

Another Burriss pilot who ran the blockade was Thomas Edward Burriss. Ned's older brother, Tom was the pilot of the *Banshee*. He also piloted two other blockade runners, the *Nighthawk* and the *North Heath*.[15]

His adventures in running the blockade were immortalized by Tom Taylor, the young, resourceful supercargo who managed the blockade running of the *Banshee*.[16]

The *Banshee* became the first steel-hulled steamer to cross the Atlantic. Built in Liverpool to run the blockade, the sleek, twin-funnel paddlesteamer, with her turtle-back forward deck, certainly looked the part. But she had problems, too—a leaky hull and poorly designed boilers which reduced her speed shy of the eleven knots she was designed for.[17]

But the *Banshee* was blessed with the presence of Taylor, who at twenty-one proved to be astute beyond his years, and her commander, the British merchant captain, Jonathon Steele. She was also blessed with a Cape Fear pilot who knew his business.[18]

After the war, Tom Taylor wrote down his experiences in a delightful little book. He never forgot the excitement: "Hunting, pig-sticking, steeplechasing, big-game shooting, polo—I have done a little of each—all have their thrilling moments, but none can approach *running a blockade*." In his book, Taylor left an indelible impression of his first run into Wilmington in May of 1863. The *Banshee* was loaded with supplies from Nassau, and was moving quietly under the guidance of her pilot, whose named he spelled *Burroughs*.[19]

> With everything thus in readiness we steamed on in silence except for the stroke of the engines and the beat of the paddle-floats, which in the calm of the night seemed distressingly loud; all hands were on deck, crouching behind the bulwarks; and we on the bridge, the captain, the pilot, and I, were straining our eyes into the darkness. Presently Burroughs made an uneasy movement—"Better get a cast of the lead, Captain," I heard him whisper. A muttered order down the engine-room tube was Steele's reply, and the Banshee slowed down and then stopped. It was an anxious moment, while a dim figure stole into the fore-chains; for there is always a danger of steam blowing off when the engines are unexpectedly stopped, and that would have been enough to betray our presence for miles around. In a minute or two came back the report. "Sixteen fathoms—sandy bottom with black specs." "We are not as far in as I thought, captain," said Burroughs, "and we are too far to the southward. Port two point and go a little faster." As he explained, we must be well to the northward of the speckled bottom before it was safe to head for shore, and away we went again. In about an hour Burroughs quietly asked for another sounding. Again she was gently stopped, and this time he was satisfied. "Starboard and go ahead easy," was the order now, and as we crept in not a sound was heard but that of the regular beat of the paddle-floats still dangerously loud in spite of our snail's pace. Suddenly

The *Banshee* was built in Liverpool, England, in 1863 by Jones, Quiggin and Company. She was the first vessel constructed specifically to run the blockade, and the first steel-hull steamer to cross the Atlantic. (Drawing courtesy of Mariners' Museum in Newport News, Virginia)

Burroughs gripped my arm,—"There's one of them, Mr. Taylor," he whispered, "on the starboard bow."

In vain I strained my eyes to where he pointed, not a thing could I see; but presently I heard Steele say beneath his breath, "All right, Burroughs, I see her. Starboard a little, steady!" was the order passed aft.

A moment afterwards I could make out a long low black object on our starboard side, lying perfectly still. Would she see us? That was the question; but no, though we passed within a hundred yards of her we were not discovered, and I breathed again. Not very long after we had dropped her Burroughs whispered, — "Steamer on the port bow."

And another cruiser was made out close to us.

"Hard-a-port," said Steele, and round she swung, bringing our friend upon our beam. Still unobserved we crept quietly on, when all at once a third cruiser shaped herself out of the gloom right ahead and steamed slowly across our bows.

"Stop her," said Steele in a moment, and as we lay like dead our enemy went on and disappeared in the darkness. It was clear there was a false reckoning somewhere, and that instead of rounding the head of the blockading line we were passing through the very center of it. However, Burroughs was now of the opinion that we must be inside the squadron and advocated making the land. So "ahead slow" we went again, until the low-lying coast and surf line became dimly visible. Still we could not tell where we were, and, as time was getting on alarmingly near dawn, the only thing to do was to creep down along the surf as close in and as fast as we dared. It was a great relief when we suddenly heard Burroughs say, "It's all right, I see the 'Big Hill'!"

The "Big Hill" was a hillock about as high as a full-grown oak tree, but it was the most prominent feature for miles on that dreary coast, and served to tell us exactly how far we were from Fort Fisher. And fortunate it was for us we were so near. Daylight was already breaking, and before we were opposite the fort we could make out six or seven gunboats, which steamed rapidly toward us and angrily opened fire. Their shots were soon dropping close around us: an unpleasant sensation when you know you have several tons of gunpowder under your feet. To make matters worse, the North Breaker shoal now compelled us to haul off shore and steam further out. It began to look ugly for us, when all at once there was a flash from the shore followed by a sound that came like music to our ears—that of a shell whirring over our heads. It was Fort Fisher, wide awake and warning the gunboats to keep their distance. With a parting broadside, they steamed sulkily out of range, and in a half hour we were safely over the bar . . . For my part, I was mighty proud of my first attempt and my baptism of fire.[20]

Thomas Edward Burriss died in 1869, a few years after his adventures on the *Banshee*. His widow Sarah lived until 1914. Their grandson James Henry Burriss III, who died a few years ago, was intensely proud of his family history, and assembled a genealogy of the Burriss, Newton, and allied families of Federal Point and even had a museum of sorts in his home where he kept family memorabilia. Among his treasured keepsakes was a black silk shawl brought from England during the Civil War on the blockade runner *Fanny and Jenny* by Thomas Edward Burriss as a present for his daughter Drucillia.[21]

Thomas Gray Burriss and his wife Nancy stand in front of their home on the Southport waterfront. (Photo courtesy of Betty Cappo)

Mr. Gray

Thomas Gray Burriss, the son of James Thomas Burriss and Maniza Craig Burriss, was born at Federal Point on October 4, 1843. Mr. Gray, as he was always called in his later years, became a Cape Fear pilot at an early age and served in the pilotage for most of his life. My great-aunt Esther Dosher Eriksen remembered that Mr. Gray ran the blockade. I could find no record of this. The pilot licensing records of the period are maddeningly ambiguous. They show a T. C. Burriss on the May 1863 list of bar pilots. Since there was no T. C. among the families who lived in the area, this was probably Thomas Gray. (I first thought that Thomas Gray was the Tom Burriss of the *Banshee*. But James Sprunt said that Tom Burriss was the brother of Ned, which means he was Thomas Edward Burriss.)[22]

Perhaps one day information will turn up that will accord Mr. Gray a less ambiguous place on the honor roll of Cape Fear pilots who ran the blockade. In any case, Mr. Gray was a hero to my family. He owned the home in Southport where Ephraim Gause, my great-grandfather who piloted the *Helen* through the blockade, lived for a time with his family. Mr. Gray taught my grandfather Charles Gause to read. And one winter after Ephraim died, when young Charles Gause had no coat, Mr. Gray gave him one of his which Charles's mother Rebecca cut down to fit him.[23]

Over the years few families made a bigger contribution to the pilotage at Cape Fear than the Burriss clan, especially during the Civil War.

The home of Mrs. Gray still stands. (Photo by the author)

A good example of a Clyde-built steamer was the *Giraffe*, shown here in this 1860 lithograph by William Clark. This iron-hull paddle steamer was built in Govan, Scotland, by James and George Thompson in 1859. For the next several years, she carried mail and passengers between the Clyde River ports and Belfast, Ireland.
(See note on page 175; photo courtesy of Mariners' Museum, Newport News, Virginia.)

CHAPTER 7

The Misfortunes of Thomas Dyer

"God almighty, man, there isn't a rock as big as my hat in the whole damned state of North Carolina."

> — *Cape Fear pilot Thomas Dyer responding to a report of the lookout of the steamer* Giraffe, *who thought he spotted a rock in the path of the ship as she approached the bar at Cape Fear.*[1]

O f all the Cape Fear pilots who ran the blockade, perhaps the least fortunate was Thomas Dyer. Dyer was born in Massachusetts. In 1860 when he was twenty-six, he lived in Smithville with his wife Sarah and their young son David. By then he was a licensed Cape Fear bar pilot.[2]

Dyer was a dark-haired man of middling height with a dark complexion and hazel eyes. In June 1861 he enlisted in the First North Carolina Regiment of Artillery as a private. A few months later he transferred to the Confederate Navy. He served as a seaman on the Confederate gunboats CSS *Beaufort* and CSS *Caswell*. The *Caswell* served as a tender in the Wilmington area. The *Beaufort*, an armed steam tug, saw action in the battles of Roanoke Island and Elizabeth City in February 1862, and distinguished herself as tender to the famous CSS *Virginia* (ex-*Merrimack*) off Hampton Roads the following month. But by the fall of 1862 Dyer's brief naval career came to an end and he returned to his calling as a Cape Fear pilot.[3]

Dyer may have been a fine pilot. Certainly, he was entrusted with at least three different blockade runners during the war. His blockade-running career began with promise, when he brought Lieutenant John Wilkerson's *Giraffe* across the bar on her first voyage into Wilmington. But his other wartime efforts would meet with a singular lack of success.[4]

Aboard the *Giraffe*

In the fall of 1862, the Confederate government purchased the steamer *Giraffe*. After fitting out at Glasgow, the sidewheeler took aboard a cargo of Enfield rifles, ammunition, cloth, and medical supplies.[5]

The *Giraffe* moved down the Clyde River on November 15, 1862, to begin her transatlantic voyage. According to a local newspaper, she sailed under the command of "Captain Duguid and a crew of fifty, plus thirty passengers who are described as more useful than ornamental." The passengers included twenty-six Scottish lithographers coming to the South to print Confederate paper money.[6]

Lieutenant Wilkerson had chosen the northern approach to Cape Fear. In the dark the *Giraffe* steamed down the beach toward New Inlet. At her helm stood the quartermaster, an old-timer named McLean. Wilkerson and Dyer talked in whispers as Dyer passed the helm orders to McLean. At about ten o'clock, as they were moving swiftly past the blockaders, the *Giraffe* ran hard aground. She had struck "The Lump," a small, sandy shoal about three miles off the bar.[7]

Wilkerson acted swiftly. He ordered a passenger, Major Price, to take a brace of pistols below to the engineering room and kill the engineers if they refused to obey orders. He ordered his clerk, Johnny Tabb, to fetch two demijohns of nitric acid (he called it aqua fortis) to be used to blow up the ship to prevent it from falling into enemy hands, if they were unsuccessful in getting off the shoal. He then sent out a boat with a kedge anchor. He lowered another boat and sent the Scotsmen to Fort Fisher. With steam hissing as the stern windless pulled against the kedge anchor, and aided by a rising tide, the blockade runner broke free.[8]

Wilkerson remembered that as they approached the bar that night the lookout called out, "There's a rock straight ahead, Mr. D." The reply of Thomas Dyer: "God almighty, man, there isn't a rock as big as my hat in the whole damned state of North Carolina."[9]

Thomas Dyer was a man who had difficulty holding his tongue, even when circumstances called for discretion. Lieutenant Wilkerson said that he had to discharge Dyer as pilot of his steamer because of Dyer's continual arguments with the vessel's sailing captain. Wilkerson described an encounter between Dyer and Captain Duguid in Wilmington:

> An hour or more after my return to the ship, while sitting in the cabin, I heard loud and angry altercation overhead; and going up on deck, I saw Dyer pacing up and down the wharf, along side which the Lee was lying; while the sailing captain was bidding him defiance from the steamer's deck; Dyer with a drawn knife in his hand, and the captain with a handspike. They had exhausted their vocabulary of abuse, but neither was disposed to invade the enemy's territory. At last Dyer cried out "Come ashore you d—d English hog, and I'll make mince meat of you!" I shall never forget the expression on the captain's face at this cruel taunt. He was literally struck speechless for a moment; then turning to me and drawing himself up with a thumb in his armhole, he exclaimed, "Now sir, isn't that too bad. Do I look like a Henglish og?" To this pathetic appeal, I could but answer "no," but the fact was they bore a ludicrous resemblance to two boars about to engage in mortal combat; the captain, with his jolly, rosy face and portly figure, not at all unlike a sleek, well fed

"White Chester" and Dyer quite as much resembling a lean, lank, wiry "razor-back" native to his own pine woods.[10]

After Dyer left the *Lee*, Archibald Gutherie of Smithville replaced him as her Cape Fear pilot.[11]

Claimed by the Reaper Shoal

During the last few months of 1863, Dyer brought the *Antonica* through the Cape Fear blockade five times. The *Antonica* was an iron-hull sidewheel steamer of 450 tons burden, which was built in England as the *Herald*. She was purchased for blockade running by Fraser, Trenholm and Company who operated her for a year until November of 1862, when she was sold to the Chicora Importing and Exporting Company of Charleston. Renamed *Antonica*, she proved so successful in running the blockade at Charleston that her profits enabled the Chicora Company to buy another British steamer, the *Havelock*. (The *Havelock*, renamed the *General Beauregard*, would make four voyages from Wilmington to Nassau and back with Julius Potter as her Cape Fear pilot.)[12]

The *Antonica* was known as the slowest of the Fraser, Trenholm and Company blockade runners, but was said to handle well. Most of her career she sailed under the command of Captain Louis Coxetter, a middle-aged, mild-manner Hollander. Despite his mild demeanor, Captain Coxetter developed such a reputation in running the blockade that he was declared by the Union to be a pirate. The captain took this situation seriously. On one occasion as the *Antonica* was leaving Charleston he seated himself on the ladder leading to the engine room and pointed a Colt revolver at his chief engineer and politely informed him that if the engine stopped before he was clear of the fleet, then he, the engineer, would be a dead man.[13]

The *Antonica* left Wilmington on her last run to Nassau on or about December 7, 1863. She returned to Cape Fear on December 19. Dyer and her master, then Captain W. F. Adair, had chosen to come in through Old Inlet. Between eight and nine o'clock that evening, the *Antonica* approached Little River Inlet, about forty miles south of Cape Fear. Upon sighting two blockaders, she stood off the coast and steamed northward toward Lockwood's Folly Inlet, fifteen miles from the Western Bar.[14]

As they drew closer to the cape, Dyer and Captain Adair could see standing near the bar two blockaders, the *State of Georgia* and the *Emma*. At eleven P.M., as Dyer was taking the *Antonica* past the two ships, lookouts on the blockaders spotted her. Rockets flared. The USS *General Buckingham*, a new screw steamer mounting six guns, slipped her anchor and steamed toward the *Antonica*. The blockader's captain, Acting Volunteer Lieutenant W. G. Saltonstall, could see the runner in the moonlight on the other side of the breakers on the bar, close to Bald Head Island. Dyer guided

Captain W. F. Adair.
(Photo courtesy of Confederate Museum of Charleston)

the *Antonica* offshore where he and Captain Adair waited for the moon to set, and lookouts on the *General Buckingham* lost sight of her.[15]

Then at 2:30 the next morning, the moon slipped below the horizon. In the darkness, Dyer guided his steamer toward the narrow channel near Bald Head. At three A.M., she ran hard aground on Frying Pan Shoals.[16]

Captain Adair ordered the crew to man the boats to try to make it to the island before daylight. At five o'clock, the *General Buckingham* got underway. Captain Saltonstall reported:

> While cruising slowly toward the shoal at dim dawn, made a steamer ashore on shoal to eastward, evidently a blockade runner. At once called away launch and second cutter to board her. While lowering our boats, two small boats were discovered, filled with men, pulling from grounded steamer to the nearest land (Smith's Island). Sent our boats to intercept them and opened fire upon them. They were soon captured and brought alongside, containing in all 26 men, comprising the commanding officer and crew of Confederate steamer Antonica, formerly the Herald, of Charleston, a notorious blockade runner.[17]

The blockaders moved swiftly to claim their prize. After sunrise, the USS *Aries* arrived from westward and sent boats to the grounded steamer. But "large quantities of liquor were on board and exposed and unfortunately much drunkenness prevailed for a time among the men." The boarders managed to get the engines running but could not get the *Antonica* to move off the shoal. At nine o'clock, a Confederate battery three miles away on Bald Head opened fire on the stranded steamer. The *General*

Buckingham moved in toward the shore and returned the fire with her 100-pounder. Little damage was done by either side.[18]

Throughout the day, the blockaders worked to free the *Antonica* from the shoal. Captain Saltonstall sent his officers to the wreck to destroy the liquor "to keep it from the men." Some of the cargo was loaded on a prize schooner. That afternoon at high tide, the steam tug USS *Violet* attempted to pull the *Antonica* free. But the hauser broke. That night a strong southwesterly wind drove the blockade runner farther ashore. In the morning, the Union sailors found the *Antonica* taking on water. She became a total loss, one more victim of the "Reaper Shoal."[19]

In the meantime, the crew members of the *Antonica* were taken prisoner. The captain of the *General Buckingham* allowed them to bring "a little personal luggage," which his crew carefully searched. From the wreck Union sailors recovered the chronometer, the octant, and the ship's papers. From the prisoners they took $1,005.28 in Confederate money.[20]

Shortly afterward, the prisoners were transferred to other blockaders and eventually were released. Dyer returned home to his family in Smithville to await another assignment to pilot a blockade runner.[21]

The Final Voyage of the *Georgiana McCaw*

Dyer's final assignment came in late May of 1864 in Nassau, where he boarded the *Georgiana McCaw* bound for Wilmington with sixty tons of provisions. The *McCaw* was a Liverpool steamer on her first run to the coast. Dyer and the captain chose the Old Inlet approach to Cape Fear.[22]

As she attempted to cross the Western Bar, she encountered the USS *Victoria*. The captain of the Federal cruiser later reported to his superior:

> I have the honor to report that at 3 a.m., of this date, and while drifting in three and one-half fathoms water, Bald Head light bearing east, saw white water near the beach to the south and westward, which I supposed to be a steamer. I immediately steamed ahead toward the beach in order to cut her off. On near approach I discovered her to be a side wheel steamer, steering for the bar.
>
> As he crossed my bow I rounded to in his wake and discharged at him my starboard 8-inch gun, loaded with one 5-second shell and stand of grape, and kept firing my 30-pound rifle as I continued the chase, until 3:30 a.m. She struck on the bar. I immediately ordered the first and second cutters to board and fire her . . . On arrival on board they found that two boats, with their crews, had escaped to the shore. They, however, succeeded in capturing twenty-nine of the crew, including the captain and most of the officers, together with three passengers. They fired her in several places, and she continued to burn until 10 a.m., when she was boarded from the shore.[23]

The people in Smithville heard the *Victoria's* cannon fire. Shortly afterward they learned by telegraph from the signal stations that the ill-fated steamer was the *Georgiana McCaw*. Fourteen men from the blockade runner had managed to escape to shore. Thomas Dyer was not among them. The boarders from Fort Caswell found his body still on the vessel; apparently he had been murdered by one of the crew, although this was never proven. One account says that Dyer had stayed aboard to guard a quantity of gold.[24] John Wilkerson recalled in his memoirs:

> The poor fellow's fate was a sad one. While acting as pilot of a blockade-runner inward bound, he committed the folly one day of saying that he would put a steamer under his charge ashore, before he would be captured. The remark was overheard and treasured up by some of the crew; and a night or two afterwards the steamer ran aground on the bar in an attempt to enter Cape Fear River, and was deserted. As she was under the shelter of the guns of Fort Caswell, a boat from shore was sent to her the next morning and poor Dyer was found in a dying condition on the deck with his skull fractured.[25]

For many years, the bones of the *Georgiana McCaw* lay buried in the sands off Caswell Beach. In 1881 some machinery on the ship was salvaged by the crew of the schooner *Wave*. There were also rumors that part of the wreck was salvaged in 1932. But if any gold was ever found, the news never reached Southport.[26]

CHAPTER 8

The Pilot Who Became a Preacher

"The marsh grass was full of sandfiddlers . . . I pretended to be surprised and asked the guard what these things were, saying they would be called lobsters in my country if they were much larger."

—*Federal Point pilot Jim Billy Craig in prison at Fort Macon, pretending to be a foreigner.*[1]

James William Craig, known as Jim Billy during his youth, was one of the youngest of the Cape Fear pilots to run the blockade and one of more than a dozen Craig men from Federal Point who during the nineteenth century served as pilots, at Charleston as well as at Cape Fear. He piloted six different blockade runners during the war.[2]

Among the first of the Craigs to become a pilot at Cape Fear was Benjamin Craig. Benjamin, who served in the Revolutionary War, obtained his pilot's license in about 1797. In 1850, among the sixteen pilots who lived at Federal Point were seven Craigs: Thomas Sr. (70), Thomas Jr. (39), Lewis (73), Joseph (37), James N. (32), Jessie Sr. (52), and Jessie Jr. (32).[3]

Lewis Craig was Jim Billy's grandfather. Jim Billy's father was James N. Craig, who was born in 1818 at Federal Point. His mother was Mary Elizabeth Grissom Craig. The Craigs lived on the river at Craig's Landing, where Jim Billy was born. Jim Billy's mother's family, the Grissoms, were another Federal Point family whose men traditionally became pilots.[4]

Thanks to James Sprunt, the blockade-running career of Jim Billy Craig was one of the best documented of those of the Cape Fear pilots. The two men were shipmates on the *Lilian* and became lifelong friends. Jim Billy Craig recounted his Civil War adventures to Sprunt who included them in his *Chronicles of the Cape Fear River* and in some of his other writings. The following account is based primarily on the *Chronicles.* Jim Billy Craig's story begins:[5]

I was born in May, 1840, and piloted my first vessel into the Cape Fear River when I was seventeen years of age . . . I acted under the protection of my father, who was a full branch pilot; in other words, he was permitted to carry in vessels of any depth suitable for the water then available. I was an apprentice to him.

When the war broke out I was twenty-one years of age and, in view of certain circumstances favorable to my reputation, I was given by the Board of Commissioners of Navigation and Pilotage a license for twelve feet, the laws having been changed a year or two before the war in respect to the method of issuing licenses.

My father, James N. Craig, lived a short distance from Fort Fisher on the river side at a place called Craig's Landing and his house and landing were both used later by the commander of Fort Fisher, Col. William Lamb, who was so intimately engaged with my father that he gave him general charge of the duty of setting lights for the benefit of blockade runners, under certain restrictions which had been provided. I was therefore engaged for nearly two years after the outbreak of the war in assisting my father, and became more familiar with the channel and the approaches of the channel than many other pilots who had not the opportunity of sounding, as we had frequently, under government instructions.[6]

This experience would serve Jim Billy Craig well during the war. His first opportunity to take a ship through the blockade came in the fall of 1863 on the *Gibraltar*.[7]

Craig's Landing at Federal Point during the Civil War. (Drawing courtesy of Southport Maritime Museum.)

Baffled Repeatedly

The *Gibraltar* was an iron-hull screw steamer built in England. Originally named the *Havana*, she was fitted out in New Orleans by Lieutenant Raphael Semmes as the cruiser *Sumter*. In 1861 Semmes, who would later gain fame as captain of the Confederate raider *Alabama*, took the *Sumter* into Northern waters where he captured eighteen Yankee merchantmen. Semmes then took her to Gibraltar for repairs and afterward she ended up in Liverpool under the ownership of Fraser, Trenholm and Company. Renamed *Gibraltar*, her guns were removed and she was converted back into a merchant ship.[8]

When the Confederacy was looking for a vessel to deliver two huge Blakely cannons to Wilmington, the *Gibraltar* was available. In July of 1863, she left England under the command of Captain E. C. Reid, the immense guns stowed vertically in her hold so that they appeared to be extra smokestacks. The *Gibraltar* arrived a few weeks later at New Inlet, boldly flying the United States flag as she passed through the blockade. Only after she entered the protective shield of Fort Fisher did the blockaders realize that the *Gibraltar* was not one of their own ships.[9]

After unloading the Blakely guns, which eventually were taken to Charleston, the *Gibraltar* took on a load of cotton. Captain Reid brought her down the river and anchored off Old Brunswick landing while he waited to find a pilot. He chose Jim Billy Craig and offered him $1000 in gold if he could take his ship out successfully and reach Bermuda.[10]

The *Gibraltar* drew eleven feet of water. Jim Billy Craig, intimately familiar with New Inlet, knew that this deep draft would pose problems for the steamer he called by her old name, the *Sumter*. It did. In his words:[11]

> I made several ineffectual attempts to get the *Sumter* outside, but, owing to the lack of water and the vigilance of the blockading fleet, we were baffled repeatedly. At last I took her out successfully over the bar at New Inlet, the fleet in the meantime having concentrated at the Western Bar, expecting to capture her there, and Captain Reid subsequently told me that he proceeded to Bermuda and to England without sighting a single hostile vessel during the whole voyage.[12]

The Second Run

Jim Billy Craig's second run through the blockade, which came a short time later, was entirely fortuitous. He and another Federal Point pilot, Thomas Newton, were at New Inlet setting lights to guide an outbound run of the *Cornubia*. As the steamer passed them, her pilot C. C. Morse called out: "Don't take your lights in too soon, because if we run afoul of a blockader outside, he may run us in again, and we want the benefit of the lights."[13]

Craig and Newton watched as the *Cornubia* faded into the night. A few minutes later another large steamer appeared. The two pilots took it to be a Federal blockader. In Craig's words:

> We were still more surprised, and really frightened, when they lowered a boat and pulled close to us in the semi-darkness and demanded to know who we were . . . They asked if we were pilots, which we admitted was the case. The voice, which proved to be that of chief officer of the blockade runner *Orion*, a very fine ship, then replied, "We have been trying to run into Charleston, and failed to do so. We are groping around for the New Inlet Bar. Will you take us in?" We at once agreed, and proceeded to the ship and brought her over the bar and anchored her in safety under the guns of Fort Fisher.[14]

Jim Billy Craig's next assignment came on the *Don*. Her regular Cape Fear pilot, William St. George, had taken sick. The *Don* was an iron-hull twin-screw steamer commanded by one of the English adventurers who ran the blockade, Charles Augustus Hobart-Hampden. Craig took his steamer out on a run to Nassau and back into the harbor on the return voyage. Afterward, William St. George, having recovered from his illness, resumed his role as the steamer's regular Cape Fear pilot.[15]

Under Contract

Shortly after his runs on the *Don*, Craig signed a three-month contract with Alexander Collie and Company to pilot their steamers at Cape Fear. His first ship was to be the *Annie*, like the *Don*, an iron-hull twin-screw steamer. He was ordered to Nassau where he boarded her for the voyage to the coast. He brought her into Cape Fear without incident.[16]

Craig took the *Annie* out on a second run to Nassau. Below is his description of the return voyage:

> We again loaded the *Annie* in Nassau and cleared for Wilmington, but fell in with a hurricane shortly afterwards, and were obliged to heave to for about forty hours, and so lost our reckoning. Failing to get observations for three days, we waited until the gale subsided, and then anchored the ship in smooth water, by a kedge, until the captain succeeded in getting an observation of the North Star, by which he worked out his position. We then shaped our course for the blockade off Fort Fisher.
>
> At that time, and subsequently, it was the custom for the flagship of the blockading squadron to carry a large light, and this, being the only one visible, often served the purpose of guiding the blockade runners until they could get the bearings of the Mound Light. On this particular night of May 6, 1864, we came very near running afoul of the Confederate iron-clad ram *Raleigh* outside the bar, but, supposing her to be one of the blockaders, got out of her way as quickly as possible.[17]

Soon after this voyage Jim Billy Craig's contract with Collie and Company expired. Then, once again, he was in the right place at the right time for another assignment:[18]

My term of three month's service having expired, I was proceeding in my skiff from Craig's landing to Wilmington when I was overtaken by a very swift blockade runner, with two rakish funnels, a perfect model of its kind, called the *Lynx*, and, having been given a towline, climbed aboard and found, to my great surprise and delight, that the ship was commanded by my old friend, Captain Reed, who immediately requested that I would arrange to go with him, as his engagement of a pilot was only for the voyage inward.

To this I consented on condition that General Whiting would approve it, and I received a few days afterwards a telegram to go on board the *Lynx* at Fort Fisher. I was in a hurricane on this ship in which she fared badly, the paddleboxes, sponsons, and bridgework being partly carried away; but we at last limped into Bermuda and, after repairing damages, proceeded again to Wilmington. [The *Lynx* cleared Bermuda on July 8, 1864, with a cargo of lead, steel, saltpeter, rifles, pistols, and sugar and arrived in Wilmington about ten days later.]

Chases

The longest chase of which I was a witness during the war occurred while I was on the Lynx, which was chased for fifteen hours by the very fast cruiser *Fort Jackson*. The Fort Jackson's log and official report subsequently showed that she was making sixteen knots an hour, which at that time was considered phenomenal speed (the

The *Lynx*, built in England in 1864, was a steel-hull, twin-screw steamer. She made nine successful runs through the blockade. She was chased ashore and destroyed near Fort Fisher on September 25, 1864. (Drawing courtesy of Naval Historical Center)

average blockade runner seldom exceeding fourteen knots an hour), and on this occasion I remember that the safety-valves of the *Lynx* were weighted down by the iron tops of the coal bunkers, which of course imperiled the life of everyone on board, but increased the speed of the *Lynx* to more than sixteen knots an hour and ultimately allowed her to escape. [This dangerous technique of disabling the pressure relief valves enabled the steam pressure to rise to increase the ship's speed; it could also have caused the boiler to explode.][19]

After completing two round trips on the *Lynx*, Craig was assigned to another steamer, the *Lilian*. His story continues:

Quite a number of the Wilmington pilots had been captured by the enemy, and the force available for ships belonging to the Confederate government waiting in Bermuda and Nassau was in consequence greatly reduced. The regular pilot of the *Lilian* was Thomas Grissom, and I was one of four extra pilots (the other three being Joseph Thompson, James Bell, and Charles Craig) who were ordered by General Whiting to proceed to Bermuda and take charge of certain ships to be designated by Maj. Norman S. Walker, the Confederate agent at that port.

Trouble began before we got outside. An armed barge from the fleet had come close inside the Western bar and lay in our track in the channel, and immediately upon our approach, sent up a rocket and fired a gun, which was instantly answered by the whole fleet outside, and I remember that we crossed the bar in a bright flash of Drummond lights and rockets which made the night as bright as day. Every one of the blockaders was firing at us or over us as we headed out to sea, and when the next morning, Sunday, dawned, we had just succeeded in dropping the last of the cruisers, which had chased us all night.

We were congratulating ourselves after breakfast that morning that we would have a clear sea toward Bermuda—and, by the way, the sea was as smooth as glass—when the lookout in the crow's nest reported a vessel of war ahead, shortly afterwards another on the starboard bow, and a little later a third on our port bow, and in a few minutes a fourth on our beam. We had unfortunately run into the second line of blockaders, called the Gulf Squadron, and it was not more than two hours before they were all in range and pelting us with bombshells.

The chase lasted until half-past one in the morning, when a shell from the cruiser on our starboard beam, called the *Gettysburg*, formerly the blockade runner *Margaret and Jessie*, struck us below the waterline, making a large hole through which the water rushed like a mill-stream.

All our efforts to stop the leak with blankets were unavailing. We had previously thrown over our deck-load of cotton, but it was impossible to reach the aperture from the inside, as the hold was jam full of cotton; and in a short time the vessel began to steer badly and gradually sank almost to the level of the deck. Finding further efforts to escape utterly fruitless, the captain stopped the ship and surrendered to the boats that immediately surrounded us.

I remember that when the ship was hove to and the Federal officers came on board, our sullen and dejected commander was standing on the starboard paddle-box, with his arms folded, and his back turned to the approaching Federals. One of them, with a drawn sword, approached and asked if he was in command of the ship. Captain Martin responded with an oath: "I was in command, but I suppose you are captain now."

Although every effort had been made to escape, those of us who knew Captain Maffitt, the former commander of the *Lilian*, regretted very much his absence on this occasion, as he would most likely have been more fortunate in getting away.[20]

As Jim Billy Craig indicates, things may have turned out differently had Captain John Newland Maffitt been in charge. Maffitt's intimate knowledge of the coast and his unquestioned bravery contrasted sharply with Captain D. S. Martin's incompetence. James M. Morgan, a Confederate naval officer who was aboard the *Lilian* during a run into Wilmington with Captain Martin, bitterly described the commander's cowardice under fire when another officer had to take over the ship because Martin retired to his berth with a bottle of brandy and lay dead drunk.[21]

Craig's narrative continues:

Knowing how eager the Federals were to identify the pilot of the ship, they being in blissful ignorance that there were no fewer than five Wilmington pilots on board, we all agreed to personate firemen or members of the crew, and succeeded in passing ourselves off as such. Subsequently all of us escaped except the ship's pilot, who was detained at Point Lookout until the end of the war.[22]

The *Lilian* was captured on August 24, 1864. Her captors found about five hundred bales of cotton aboard. Union sailors from the *Gettysburg* and the *Keystone State* fished from the sea another eighty bales, the *Lilian's* deck load which had been pitched overboard during the chase.[23]

The pilot imprisoned at Point Lookout was apparently Thomas Grissom. Point Lookout prison camp for Confederate soldiers and sailors lay on a low, marshy finger of land located where the Potomac empties into the Chesapeake Bay. In terms of number of prisoners—during the war over fifty thousand Southern men and boys were incarcerated there—it was the largest of the Northern prisons.[24]

With its sweeping vistas of the river, the Chesapeake, and the Maryland countryside, Point Lookout is a place of great natural beauty. Before the war it had been a popular resort with hotels and "cottages by the sea." But there was nothing beautiful about it to the miserable captives crowded into rotten tents. With the bay on one side and the river on the other, the point grows hot in the summer and bitterly cold in the winter. There was often no wood for fires on the coldest nights. Prisoners sometimes ate rats for want of food, or, as they would say, "to stand off the wolf." Diarrhea, dysentery, typhoid, and typhus remained their constant companions. As many as fifteen thousand prisoners at a time lived in the forty-acre hell. Four thousand were buried there. A number of Cape Fear pilots were imprisoned at Point Lookout; all somehow managed to survive the ordeal.[25]

Among the prisoners at Point Lookout was the poet Sidney Lanier. The young

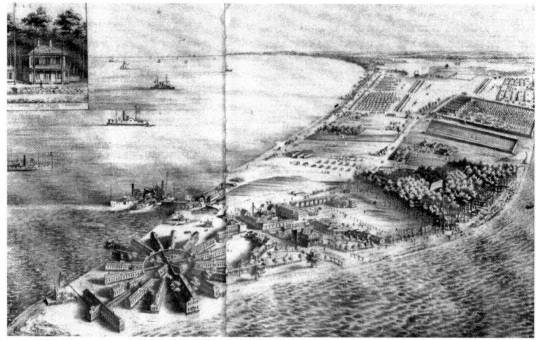

Point Lookout prison camp for Confederate soldiers and sailors lay on a spit of land located where the Potomac River empties into the Chesapeake Bay. (Drawing courtesy of National Archives)

signalman, captured on the blockade runner *Lucy*, brought along, smuggled in his sleeve, his beloved flute. It lent a touch of humanity to that dreary place. Some prisoners wept as they listened to the mournful notes. One wrote: "The night sky, clear as a dew drop above us, the waters of the Chesapeake far to the east, the long gray beach and the distant pines, seemed to have found an interpreter in him."[26]

Craig and the other three pilots who were aboard the *Lilian* were also imprisoned, along with the ship's purser, seventeen-year-old James Sprunt. He described their experiences while imprisoned at Fort Macon near New Bern, North Carolina:[27]

> The monotony of prison life affords so few incidents that my experience is hardly worth recalling, and yet I remember some diversions, which gave us much merriment at the time.
>
> While our friends from the *Lilian* were confined in for several weeks in a casemate of Fort Macon, that garrison consisted of what the Yankees called the First Regiment of North Carolina Volunteers. These men were known to us, however, as "Buffaloes," and they were a mean lot, as can be imagined from their having turned against their native State in time of great stress of war. Every day an officer and a guard took us outside our gloomy casemate and permitted us to stretch our legs along the beach, while we gazed our longing eyes across the intervening sound to Dixie Land. The marsh grass was full of sand fiddlers, which scuttled away at our

approach. I pretended to be surprised and asked the guard what these things were, saying that they would be called lobsters in my country if they were much larger. The old renegade looked at me with a most contemptuous expression and replied: "You know what they are; you've got millions of them in Smithville, whar you come from."

Another daily experience was the persistent, though unsuccessful, effort of the officer of the day to tease out of our young purser, James Sprunt, whom he thought an easy mark on account of his youth (17 years), betrayal of our pilot, little dreaming that we were five Wilmington pilots.[28]

Jim Billy Craig and his companions managed to escape from Fort Macon, as he explains:

> After our escape from prison, we made our way to Halifax, Nova Scotia, through the medium of some gold coins, which I fortunately kept close to my body in a waistband and which paid the passage of four of my companions, including Mr. Sprunt. I joined the steamer *Bat* at Halifax and proceeded as her pilot to Wilmington.[29]

The Voyage of the *Bat*

The *Bat* was a new steel-hull sidewheeler purchased by Fraser, Trenholm and Company to turn over to the Confederate government. She had been built in Liverpool and was making her first run to the southern coast. According to Craig, "When off the bar, and in the midst of the blockading fleet, which was firing heavily upon us, the captain lost his nerve and, despite my expostulations, persisted in stopping the *Bat*."[30]

Craig said that the captain lost his nerve upon hearing the screams of a terrified sailor. The man, whose name was Match Madick, was hiding forward under the turtleback and lost his leg when a shot struck the bow of the ship.[31]

Reports from the blockaders indicated that five Union warships converged on the *Bat* as she tried to run into Old Inlet early on the morning of October 9, 1864. The USS *Montgomery* fired the shell that struck the blockade runner and put an end to her maiden voyage through the blockade.[32]

The blockaders found the *Bat* to be an impressive steamer, "admirably adapted for blockade running." They observed that she had "double, powerful oscillating engines, 180 horsepower (nominal), 52-inch cylinders, of 4 feet stroke; draft when loaded, 6 feet 6 inches, and will carry coal for six days; has capacity for 850 bales of cotton; speed 13 knots; will do better when engines are in good working order."[33]

For Jim Billy Craig, it was back to a Yankee prison:

> For the second time I was made a prisoner of war and under the following circumstances, which I have mentioned but once before.

Before I became engaged in the blockade-running service, I was acting as mate on the Confederate steamer *Flora Macdonald*, a transport on the Cape Fear River, and when the Confederate privateer *Retribution* sent into Wilmington a prize schooner, which she has captured at sea, in charge of one of the *Retribution's* officers named Jordan, who had shipped with Capt. Joseph Price in Wilmington, I assisted in towing that vessel from the bar to Wilmington, and of course saw much of Jordan.

When I was captured by the *Montgomery*, I was taken to the Portsmouth Navy Yard, where we were boarded by a Federal officer in a captain's uniform, who proved to be none other than my quondam Confederate friend Jordan, who had gone over to the enemy, and who immediately recognized me and informed against me.

I was then put in irons and sent onboard the U. S. Man-of-war *Sabine*, where I was most kindly treated by its commander, Captain Loring, and while a prisoner on his ship, I was repeatedly approached by the Federal officers, who offered to pay any sum I would name if I would join their fleet off Fort Fisher and take part as a pilot in their attack against my home. I told them that the United States Government did not have enough money to induce me to accept such a proposition, and I accordingly remained a prisoner at Point Lookout until the war was over.[34]

All You North Carolinians, Stand up Quick!

During my . . . confinement on the *Sabine* as a prisoner of war, a large number of blockade runners who had been captured at sea were brought to that school-ship for confinement, and Capt. Loring tried in every way to surprise those suspected of being pilots into an admission of the fact. One fine day, while the prisoners were lying in the deck, he, looking like an old sea dog, bluff and hearty, paced up and down among them, and suddenly turning on his heel called out: "All you North Carolinians stand up quick!" I cast my eyes over a number of our pilots, fearing they would be taken by this surprise and betray themselves, but not a man stirred, and old Loring, who was really a good fellow and kind to us, went on his way.

I may add that while I was a prisoner on the *Sabine*, two of the Cape Fear pilots, C. C. Morse and John Savage, were brought on board as prisoners, under suspicion of being pilots, and, although they were intimate friends of mine, I took particular pains to treat them as total strangers and paid no attention to them, lest it might get them into further trouble. They were so much relieved when they discovered my purpose. Savage was subsequently released, but Morse, having been identified later by some other means, was made a prisoner with me until the end of the war. [Craig was imprisoned aboard the *Sabine* from October 31, 1864, until November 24, 1864.][35]

Jim Billy Craig, along with the other pilots at Point Lookout, made his way home after the end of the war. He continued his career as a Cape Fear pilot. He also became a Methodist minister at the little church near his home at Federal Point.[36]

The *Wilmington Star* observed that he performed a marriage ceremony for Mr.

D. B. Craig and Miss Winnie, daughter of Edward Rue, in December of 1870. Ten years later the same newspaper noted that Jim Billy Craig preached several sermons at the Smithville Methodist Church.[37]

During his sermons he drew on his experience as a Cape Fear pilot as he followed what he called "the lead of the Great Pilot." The following was one of his favorite homilies:

> The approach by sailing vessels in the olden time to the inlets of the Mediterranean Sea was often baffled by adverse winds, or calms; a little boat was then lowered, which carried into the harbor a kedge anchor that was dropped overboard. To this small anchor was attached a line by which the vessel was warped by the windless into the haven. The man who carried the anchor in was the forerunner, and, in the figure, he is Christ, the Captain of our Salvation; the line is the line of faith, and the man at the windless is a human soul who trusts in God."[38]

Drawing by Captain Robert Potter.

The Union's swift new sidewheeler USS *Fort Jackson* chased the blockade runner *General Beauregard*, piloted by Julius Potter, on several occasions.
(Photo courtesy of Naval Historical Center)

CHAPTER 9

The Tale of Julius Potter

"Steamer one point forward on the port beam!"

—*The lookout of the blockade runner* General Beauregard *reporting the sighting of the USS* Fort Jackson.[1]

For the tale of Julius Potter, I shall always be indebted to my friend Captain Roy Daniel. Roy was my next door neighbor when I was growing up in Southport. Today he's a Cape Fear pilot and blockade running enthusiast. But I remember him best as the boy who kept strange pets: a raccoon named Josephine for the lady across the street and a little alligator he walked on a leash.

Some years ago Roy dug through the Alexander Sprunt papers at Duke University and found a rambling manuscript referred to as the reminiscences of a Cape Fear pilot. The author turned out to be William Julius Potter of Smithville, the Cape Fear pilot of the blockade runner *General Beauregard.*[2]

William Julius Potter, the son of Nathaniel and Sarah Jane Hunter Potter, was born in Smithville on February 9, 1833. His mother died when he was eight months old. When Julius was seventeen—he was often called Julius, although he was also known as William—he worked in Smithville as a clerk. In 1856 he married Sarah A. "Sallie" Drew. Two years later their daughter Ida was born; her daughter, also named Ida, lived across the street from our home in Southport. My family always called that big two-story house of Mrs. Ida Potter Manson Watson, long since torn down to make way for a bank, Miss Ida Potter's house.[3]

By age thirty Julius Potter was a qualified Cape Fear pilot, both for the river and for the bar. After the war, he recounted his adventures aboard the *General Beauregard.* Laced with details of his voyages, the tale begins in Nassau where he signed on as pilot for a voyage into Wilmington for $3000 in Confederate money and $2000 in gold.[4]

The *General Beauregard* was built in Govan, Scotland, in 1858 as the *Havelock.* She served initially as a ferry between Glasgow and Dublin. An iron-hull sidewheel steamer, her 223-foot length and 26-foot beam were typical of the Civil War blockade runners. Loaded, she drew eleven and one-half feet of water, according to Potter, a deeper draft than most of her fellow steamers, which made it difficult for her to clear the bars at Charleston and at Cape Fear.[5]

She was operated by the Chicora Importing and Exporting Company of Charleston. Upon her arrival in Charleston in February of 1863, she was named for Pierre G. T. Beauregard, the Confederate commander at the city. She returned to Charleston twice more in the next two months bringing supplies from Bermuda and Nassau. On June 23, 1863, she departed Charleston for the last time, bound for Nassau. There she picked up her Cape Fear pilot and made way for Wilmington. For the rest of the year, she ran the Cape Fear blockade, carrying cotton to Nassau and returning to Wilmington with vital supplies for the Confederacy. Julius Potter joined the ship he and other crew members affectionately called the *Bora* in September of 1863.[6]

Potter's first trip to Nassau came on the blockade runner *Arabian*. She cleared Wilmington on or about July 17, 1863, under Captain Joe Moore. After dark that evening, Potter piloted the steamer over New Inlet bar, hauled up the beach to Masonboro, then turned her south-southeast before giving her back into the hands of the captain.[7]

After an uneventful voyage Captain Moore approached Nassau from the east to avoid the United States warship *Tioga*, which was cruising in the area. After leaving the *Arabian*, Potter apparently stayed in Nassau until mid-September. He found the busy Bahaman port much different from his native North Carolina. He seemed especially interested in the food in this place where pork was scarce but which had "splendid green turtle soup . . . which is the best soup in the world."[8]

The First Voyage to Wilmington

Potter's first voyage from Nassau on the *General Beauregard* began with a northeast wind and a smooth sea, and with Captain Thomas Lyon, commander of the *Bora*, keeping a watchful eye for the USS *Tioga*, which often gave chase to blockade runners leaving the island. Captain Lyon joined the lookout on the masthead, but they spotted only sailing vessels and black smoke coming from a blockade runner steaming toward Nassau.[9]

The captain was a cautious man who made sure that his crew was ready for any eventuality. Potter described a bulletin posted on the ship that gave directions for manning the ship's boats in the event of capture by a blockader. The four boats contained drinking water and bags of bread. The plan was to set the ship afire and take to the boats if necessary to avoid capture.[10]

The bulletin indicated that the captain was in charge of boat number one. Chief engineer Lockhart was to accompany him, along with ten other crew members and three passengers. Four kegs of gold, if there was any aboard, were also to be carried.[11]

As the Cape Fear pilot, Potter was in charge of boat number two. With him would be the second engineer, two oilers, two seamen, the leadsman, two coal passers, one quartermaster, two passengers, and two kegs of gold.[12]

In charge of boat number three was to be the chief officer, Harry Holgate. Aboard would be nine crewmen, the Bahamas pilot and two passengers, along with two kegs of gold. The second officer would be in charge of the fourth boat which would carry the remaining nine crewmen.[13]

On her second day out, the noon observation placed the *General Beauregard* 140 miles from Nassau. She was making eleven and one-half knots riding gentle swells in a mirror-smooth sea. The lookout kept a sharp eye for warships, and that evening spotted a man-of-war chasing a blockade runner well to the west.[14]

On the morning of the third day, the *General Beauregard* entered the Gulf Stream and by noon stood 150 miles off Cape Fear light. The captain called for an increase in speed to make the bar by eleven o'clock that night. He spent the afternoon aloft with the lookout, scanning the horizon with his glass, looking for blockaders. Potter stayed on the bridge with the chief mate, the chief engineer, and the quartermaster.[15]

At two o'clock that afternoon the lookout called out "steamer one point forward on the port beam." Heading straight for the blockade runner was the USS *Fort Jackson*, a swift new sidewheel steamer on her maiden voyage out of New York.[16]

The chase began. Captain Lyon swung the *Bora* around and headed north-north-east up the Gulf Stream. Captain Henry Walke of the *Fort Jackson* pushed his warship hard and began to close. The *Bora's* engineers threw "great Nassau bacon sides" into the furnace, along with lumps of rosin and cotton bales soaked with turpentine. The steam pressure gauge began to climb. The blockade runner, water flying across her bow, plowed ahead at fourteen knots. Gradually, the Union warship fell behind. By sundown, she had given up the chase.[17]

Once free of the Union cruiser, the *Bora* made her way toward the shore to the north of New Inlet. Potter took over. Under his guidance the *Bora* cut southward and steamed down the beach and, under the cover of darkness, crossed the bar. The next day she ran up the river to Wilmington where she was swiftly unloaded and piled high with cotton for her next run.[18]

Ready for sea, the *Bora* anchored at Five Fathom Hole, in the river behind Fort Fisher, where she could not be seen by the blockading fleet. After consulting with Colonel Lamb at the fort about the positions of the blockaders, Captain Lyon ordered his ship underway at nine o'clock in the evening. Potter got her safely across the bar at New Inlet, with her bottom dragging on the sand. He was guided by lights on the shore off the port bow which were set in alignment to mark the bar by "the faithful hands of uncle Jim Stokes and Jim Craig." [James N. Craig of Federal Point was in charge of setting lights to guide the blockade runners at New Inlet. Jim Stokes assisted him.] Potter guided the ship up the beach past the Mound Battery at Fort Fisher (which he called the Big Hill), then turned her southward and back into the charge of Captain Lyon for the voyage to Nassau.[19]

The *General Beauregard* encountered one blockader, which she easily outran. The rest of the voyage proved uneventful as the ship passed three other blockade runners on their way toward Wilmington.[20]

In Nassau, the cotton was unloaded. Divers cleaned the ship's bottom with brushes to remove marine growth and she was loaded with "dry goods, bacon, sugar, coffee, medicine, arms, ammunition, cotton cards, blankets, salt in sacks and other articles." Also taken aboard were lumps of rosin, turpentine, and a few bales of cotton to burn when the ship needed an extra burst of speed. After the captain paid the crew half of their wages in gold, the *General Beauregard* set out once again to Wilmington.[21]

The Second Voyage to Wilmington

On her second day from Nassau, 150 miles off Cape Fear, the *General Beauregard* was sighted by the *Fort Jackson*. Once again the swift blockader took up pursuit. Potter said the *Bora* "did burn the wind, the coal, the Nassau bacon and cotton bales wet with spirits of turpentine" as she tried to escape the Federal warship. Soon, with the aid of her newly cleaned hull, the *Bora* was "shaking herself to the tune of sixteen knots." Although the *Fort Jackson* pulled within range of her cannons, she eventually fell behind and, at five o'clock that afternoon, finally broke off the chase. Not long afterward, the Union warship limped into New York for repairs to a burned-out boiler.[22]

During her long, high-speed run, the coal reserves aboard the *Bora* fell dangerously low. All aboard grew apprehensive. Potter remembered going to his stateroom to decide which of his personal effects he would take with him if they were captured. At five o'clock the next afternoon, the lookout sighted the blockading squadron standing off New Inlet. Potter and the captain counted twelve vessels. The *Bora* headed north-northeast up the coast.[23]

After dark that evening, Potter guided the steamer toward the Mound Battery at Fort Fisher. He saw a light shining from the masthead of a blockader. She turned out to be the USS *Minnesota*, flagship of the North Atlantic Blockading Squadron. The *Bora*, dead slow, headed under the cover of darkness straight for the big steam frigate. Unobserved, she passed close under the blockader's stern, within a biscuit's throw of the larger ship, and Potter set her course for New Inlet bar. Working around the north shoal, he guided the *Bora* across the bar about three o'clock that morning.[24]

The next day the steamer proceeded just up the river to Fort Anderson where she was quarantined for a week because of the yellow fever epidemic in Nassau. When no one on board showed symptoms of the disease, the *Bora* steamed to Wilmington to be unloaded.[25]

After taking on a load of cotton, she proceeded downriver to Smithville, then across the harbor to Fort Caswell. Potter found the blockading squadron at Old Inlet "pretty well circled around the bar." About ten o'clock that night, on or about October 31, 1863, the *Bora* got underway, following the *Alice*, a blockade runner of lighter draft piloted by Joseph Springs of Federal Point.[26]

When Sages Let the Blue Pigeon Fly

Potter had difficulty getting the *Bora* across the bar that night. He tried once and failed and tried again unsuccessfully. At these times he relied heavily on his leadsman, Jimmie Sages. Sages, who was a Savannah pilot, had signed on as leadsman for the *Bora* after that port was closed by Federal blockaders.[27]

A skilled leadsman, according to Potter, was "the pilot's best friend." Standing precariously on the sponson (a small platform near the pilot house), the leadsman would hurl his lead weight into the water. As he retrieved it he would feel appendages on the line and quickly tell the depth. He would call out the soundings, such as "by the mark, four fathoms . . . by the mark, three and one half." There was a genuine art to casting the lead and taking soundings on a blockade runner moving through the dark at fourteen knots. Lead sounding weights such as the one used by Sages had a blue-gray cast. Pieces of leather attached to the line resembled feathers, hence the name "blue pigeon."[28]

The Lead. Hand lead—7 to 14 pounds—marked to 25 fathoms.
Deep-sea lead—30 to 100 pounds—marked 100 fathoms or upward.
Lines are generally marked as follows:

> 2 fathoms from the lead, with 2 strips of leather
> 3 fathoms from the lead, with 3 strips of leather
> 5 fathoms from the lead, with a white rag
> 7 fathoms from the lead, with a red rag
> 10 fathoms from the lead, with leather having a hole in it
> 13 fathoms from the lead, same as 3 fathoms
> 15 fathoms from the lead, same as 5 fathoms
> 17 fathoms from the lead, same as 7 fathoms
> 20 fathoms from the lead, a line with 2 knots
> 25 fathoms from the lead, a line with 1 knot
> 30 fathoms from the lead, a line with 3 knots
> 35 fathoms from the lead, a line with 1 knot
> 40 fathoms from the lead, a line with 4 knots

and so on.

A "blue pigeon." (Drawing by Captain Robert Potter.)

On the third attempt to cross the bar that night, the *Bora* was successful. She was moving slowly through the shoal waters when the quarter moon appeared from behind the clouds and the blockaders spotted the *Bora*. Rockets flared. Cannons boomed. Smoke drifted across the water. Shells fell all around the blockade runner. Chief Engineer Lockhart came to the bridge and asked Potter if they could turn back into the harbor. Potter told him no, because a warship stood between the *Bora* and the bar. The chief engineer declared that one of his main bearing journals was running hot and he was afraid that he would have to stop the engines.[29]

As the engineers hosed down the bearing journal, Potter turned the *Bora* on "the pitch of the cape," running south-southeast under a heavy fire. She moved close "down in the bite of the Frying Pan Shoal to the western knuckle," successfully avoiding the pursuing warships. Once the blockaders were out of sight, Julius turned the ship back over to Captain Lyon who set course south-southeast for Nassau.[30]

At two o'clock the next afternoon, the lookout on the masthead sung out "Black smoke, one point on the port bow." The ship turned out to be the *Antonica*, another blockade runner operated by the Chicora Company.[31]

The *Bora* proceeded on to Nassau without incident. While the ship was there, the crew used the time waiting on the dark side of the moon to prepare the blockade runner for her next voyage. They cleaned and painted the ship's bottom, while listing the vessel on one side and then the other. They painted the *Bora* all over a whitish gray. During this time the USS *Tioga* sent over a boat with sailors who, according to Potter, measured the Bora's draft "to see what places we could go in at the different keys in the Bahamas."[32]

Stuck on the Middle Ground

After loading her cargo, the *Bora* got underway in late afternoon during the second week in November. To avoid the ubiquitous *Tioga*, she took a route well eastward of her regular course. She made Abaco light by eleven P.M., and Captain Lyon set course north-northwest for Cape Fear. Steaming along at twelve knots in a smooth sea, the night passed quietly. But Potter recalled, "As daylight came on things began to become anxious, as we often fell in with cruisers in the locality, and when it became light many sailing vessels were seen and one steamer but it proved to be a blockade-runner on our starboard bow making plenty of black smoke to get away from us, for we were afraid of him and him of us, for we hauled away from each other, until we found each other out and knew that we were friends, then we both hauled back on our course."[33]

Captain Lyon's noon observation the next day placed the *Bora* 220 miles from Nassau. They plowed toward Cape Fear with the wind fresh from the northeast, and the sea "getting sharp, *Beauregard* making herself a Methodist by sprinkling herself all over . . ."[34]

That afternoon they narrowly escaped capture when a Union cruiser closed while the crew was cleaning out the *Bora's* fireboxes. But the engineers got the steam up in time to outrun the Union steamer, which hauled off south by east toward the Bahamas.[35]

As daylight came the next morning the *Bora* entered the Gulf Stream "with a good many vessels in sight." The lookout spotted black smoke again. According to Potter, the steamer proved to be the blockade runner *Lucy* bound to Nassau. He said those aboard the *Bora* were jubilant that she had gotten out of Cape Fear safely with a load of Confederate cotton.[36]

At eleven o'clock that night, the *Bora* passed by the Frying Pan lightship. Potter took charge of the steamer. He guided her "feeling our way by lead along the shoal." Two hours later they made Bald Head and "felt up around the Reaper Shoal to the eastern part of the Middle Ground . . ." But with the tide falling the *Bora* stuck fast on the Middle Ground.[37]

As the sun rose, the crew frantically worked to lighten the ship. They pushed overboard heavy machinery that had been stowed on deck. The blockaders pulled nearer and started firing. The guns of Fort Campbell and Fort Caswell returned their fire. People eating breakfast at Mary Duffy's place on the Smithville waterfront could see and hear the battle across the harbor. Finally, the rising tide freed the *Bora*. As she began to float, she would move forward "a length or two and stop and go again," her paddlewheels churning the water. As the engines strained, the crew continued unloading cargo until high tide came and then the *Bora* steamed "in right across the Middle Ground."[38]

After the usual quarantine, the blockade runner steamed up the river to Wilmington. After she was unloaded, the crew "painted and took another cargo of cotton." They also took on another captain. Captain Lyon resigned. Harry Holgate, the first officer, took command. Potter said that the beardless young man looked like a boy compared to the much older Lyon.[39]

When the moon was right, Captain Holgate took the *Bora* downriver and anchored in Five Fathom Hole. After dinner that evening, Potter, the captain, and several others went ashore to pay their respects to Colonel Lamb. Potter, like other blockade runners, held the colonel in high regard, referring to him as "one of the best men in the South, and one of the best helpers to the blockade runner . . ."[40]

Potter also paid his respects to three others important to the blockade runners at Cape Fear when he went "to see Uncle Elijah Piver and Uncle Joe Craig and Uncle James Stokes Newton to go with them to sound the bar and the rip and to decide where to set the lights . . ." Afterward, the three men came aboard the *Bora* to collect their fee for this service of $500 dollars each.[41]

Before departing, Potter and Captain Holgate talked to Colonel Lamb and some of his officers, and with Elija Piver, who Potter said was the pilot of the fort, about the disposition of the blockading fleet. The *Bora* weighed anchor at ten o'clock that evening, and slowly moved toward the bar. And immediately ran into trouble.[42]

A rocket flared, marking the blockade runner's path, from the deck of what

Potter referred to as "a miserable little tell tale tug," which had been lying at the inlet. But the *Bora* performed "like a new fiddle and she did play a tune for the Yanks that night." After dragging her bottom across the bar, she bolted swiftly up the beach and eluded the blockaders once again. Potter turned the ship back over to Captain Holgate who set course south by east for Nassau.[43]

The voyage to the island proved uneventful. The crew saw the usual sailing vessels going to and from the West Indies as the *Bora* passed through the Gulf Stream. At this point in his narrative, Potter mentions a ruse used by Union warships to confuse the blockade runners. He said that sometimes a warship would lay in the runners' route showing two lights on her masthead, mimicking the Frying Pan lightship. But Potter said that those aboard the *Bora* were not deceived by the decoy ship because they took soundings and "the blue pigeon never lies."[44]

Once again, the *General Beauregard* arrived safely at Nassau, unloaded her cargo of Southern cotton and took aboard cargo for the Confederacy. This included one thousand pounds of brown sugar, a thousand pounds of coffee, three boxes of candles, and fifteen hundred pounds of bacon. (One account, related by Dave Horner in his book *The Blockade-Runners*, also has gold aboard the *Bora*. But Potter did not mention any gold on this voyage, nor is there any record of any ever being found aboard the ship.)[45]

The Fourth Voyage to Wilmington

After waiting for the moon to wane, the *Bora* cleared for Halifax and then headed for Wilmington. Potter wanted to bring her in through Old Inlet across the western bar, for he knew that blockaders were more numerous at the other inlet and that they had "found the runners track down the beach from Masonboro Sound."[46]

Instead, the *Bora* came in on the north side of Cape Fear. On the voyage toward the North Carolina coast, Captain Holgate turned eastward on several occasions, after the lookout sighted steamers off the port bow. According to Potter, he would not allow hauling back on the original course and failed to take into account the currents of the Gulf Stream. Nor was his navigation as accurate as that of Captain Lyon, who could be depended on to make the place where the pilot wanted the ship to begin her run into the harbor. As a consequence, the ship ended up well north of Fort Fisher, anchoring that evening under the New River bar near Jacksonville until the following day, which was December 11, 1863.[47]

The *Bora* got underway that morning and moved down the coast. By twilight she had reached Masonboro Sound. She turned around and moved slowly up the beach, awaiting full darkness. Then she steamed southward just off the beach, and sent a signal to Colonel Lamb that the *Beauregard* was coming in. But the message came too late. There was not time for the defenders of Fort Fisher to haul the flying battery of Whitworth guns, which Potter referred to as " Colonel Lamb's little pocket pieces," down to the beach to protect the *Bora*.[48]

Potter recalled that the *Bora* was moving south at half speed when "we fell in with our first man-of-war, we only seeing the sparkling water breaking from his bow." The warship, about a half-mile distant, sent up rockets in the direction of the *Bora*'s path and began firing. Soon a second blockader joined in.[49]

By this time Potter's ship was moving down the beach at full speed. The *Bora* out-distanced the first blockader. She passed by the second so close that its shot passed overhead. Then a third blockader joined the chase, with even heavier fire. The *Bora* shot by that warship as well, then Potter saw yet a fourth blockader close to the breakers, directly in his path. He had no choice but to run his vessel ashore.[50]

The *Bora* ran aground some five miles from the bar at Fort Fisher. The captain ordered the engineers to keep the engine running and open the sea cocks to flood the ship and keep her on the beach. The captain also ordered the crew to man the boats because the blockader who blocked their path was still lying nearby.[51]

As the crew lowered boat number two, it filled with water. Potter ran up to the bow of the *Bora*, pulled off his long canvas overcoat, undercoat, boots, and hat and jumped overboard. As he was swimming for shore the crew finally launched the boat

Julius Potter jumps for his life.
(Drawing by Captain Robert Potter.)

and managed to pick him up. All four boats made it safely to shore. Wet and shivering from the cold, Potter walked to the nearest house, which belonged to Tom Newton, another Cape Fear pilot. He met Tom's family coming back from the river where they had taken refuge from the shelling.[52]

The blockader that ran the *General Beauregard* ashore was the USS *Howquah*, a compact sidewheel steamer. Captain Daniel Ridgely of the *Howquah* described his encounter with the *Bora* in his report to the commanding officer of the North Atlantic Blockading Squadron:

> On the evening of the 11th instant, between 7 and 8 o'clock, the *Howquah*, stationed at the northward, saw a blockade runner coming down the beach. She made the usual signals and gave chase, and by a good use of her guns compelled the runner to put his vessel on the beach. There was a heavy sea running at the time, and doubtless as soon as she struck she became a wreck.
>
> The next morning this ship and the *Tuscarora* went in to see if it would be necessary to use the guns on the wreck. I found the sea breaking over her, and the greater portion of her upper deck submerged. The two ships were opened upon by a battery to the northward and one to the southward of the wreck. The *Tuscarora* was struck in her quarter, and I am happy to say no one was injured.[53]

The *General Beauregard* went ashore "between Flag Pond Hill and Dick's Bay." The hulk of the blockade runner still lies just offshore of Carolina Beach, her paddle wheel hubs clearly visible at low tide.[54]

The wreck of the *General Beauregard* off Carolina Beach.
(Photo courtesy of Leslie Bright.)

After the war, Potter continued to serve as a Cape Fear pilot. He eventually became an agent of the American Tract Society, distributing religious literature as far away as the Bahamas and San Salvador. Captain Potter died in 1895 and was buried in the Old Smithville Burying Ground. A number of his descendants still live in Southport. [55]

A Union blockader bears down on a blockade running steamer.
(Drawing by Captain Robert Potter.)

Kit Morse made $3,000 for piloting the *Cornubia*.
(Courtesy of National Archives)

CHAPTER 10

Christopher Columbus Morse

"Every light on the vessel was out except one in the binnacle, and the strictest silence was observed except an occasional 'starboard' or 'port' from the pilot."

> —A passenger on the Cornubia describing Smithville pilot Kit Morse giving helm directions as the steamer headed for the bar on an outbound run to Bermuda.[1]

C. C.

"Kit" Morse served as pilot of three of the most successful blockade runners to operate out of Cape Fear: the *Kate,* the *Cornubia,* and the *Advance.* Together, they made fifty-five runs through the blockade.[2]

Kit Morse was born in Smithville on June 29, 1829. His father, Uriah, a boat builder, came from Oslow County, North Carolina. His mother, Mary Cratch Morse, died when Kit was just ten months old. When Kit was four, Uriah Morse married a widow who lived in Brunswick County, Margaret Ann Gause Gold. She bore him ten children.[3]

Among them was Edward Dudley Morse of Charleston, who became a captain of blockade runners, probably the schooners *Argyle* and *Anna Deans.* Two of Kit's younger half-brothers—John Morse and James Madison Morse—became pilots, John in Charleston and James in

Captain C.C. Morse
(Courtesy Charleston County Library)

Fernandina, Florida. James eventually became president of the pilot's association in the Florida port.[4]

In 1853, the year his father died, Kit married a young Brunswick County woman, Mary Virginia McKeithan. A few years later they lived in Florida where Kit was keeper of the lighthouse near Fernandina on Amelia Island. On the eve of the Civil War they lived in Smithville with their two young children. By then Kit was an experienced Cape Fear bar pilot, adept at taking vessels into and out of the harbor.[5]

On the *Kate*

The *Kate,* one of the steamers Kit Morse piloted across the bar at Cape Fear, ran the blockade twenty times. Her captain, Thomas Lockwood, and her owners favored Charleston but she also made several runs into Wilmington.[6]

The *Kate*, a wooden-hulled sidewheel steamer, was shorter (165 feet) and broader of beam (29 feet, 10 inches) than blockade runners built for the trade. She had been built in New York in 1852 under the direction of Captain Louis Coxetter as the *Carolina*. She was purchased around January 1862 by John Fraser & Company, and her name changed to *Kate* for the wife of William Trenholm.[7]

Shortly afterward, she left Charleston with 250 bales of cotton, arriving in Nassau flying the Confederate flag on January 18, where citizens greeted her singing "Dixie Land." Throughout most of 1862, she moved through the blockade unscathed, bringing in arms, gunpowder, and other munitions. The *Kate* grew famous for her repeated successes, becoming "one of the most renowned packet steamers of the war." The blockaders made her a special target. Once, while anchored behind Fort Caswell, blockaders fired at her, causing Captain Lockwood to move her across the harbor to the safety of Mrs. Stuart's wharf in Smithville. Mrs. Stuart's daughter Kate, who was eighteen at the time, presumably enjoyed having a namesake tied up at her mother's wharf in front of their home.[8]

But the *Kate* was remembered best for having brought yellow fever to Wilmington. On August 6, 1862, she arrived from Nassau heavily laden with supplies. Unknown to the townspeople, her crewmen were infected with yellow fever. The disease spread throughout the city. Many fled to the country, or down the river to Smithville, to escape the epidemic.[9]

Wilmington became a virtual ghost town. Normal activities ceased. Carpenters turned to making coffins. Aid came from as far away as Charleston, which sent doctors and nurses to the North Carolina city. Eventually, the disease claimed more than eight hundred lives.[10]

Finally, cold weather brought an end to the spread of new cases of the fever. On November 11, 1862, the Wilmington *Daily News* announced that "Our streets begin to look lively once more; people are coming back in and seem glad to get back." A week later the *Kate* passed the Western Bar on a successful run through the blockade. A soldier stationed at Fort Caswell wrote to his brother that day:[11]

This morning about 4 o'clock, the *Kate* ran in at this place. She ran against the obstructions in the river here, which caused her to leak very badly. She however succeeded in reaching Smithville, where they ran her as high up on the shore as they could. She soon went to the bottom. Her bow and upper deck in front are above water also her wheelhouse. The remainder is covered with water.[12]

Kit Morse and the other crew members made it safely to shore. That afternoon a detachment of soldiers from Fort Caswell helped unload the cargo. But the *Kate* was a total loss.[13]

It is unlikely that many in Smithville and Wilmington mourned the loss of the ship that had brought the deadly fever. Today the *Kate* still lies in her final resting place, just off Southport in twenty-five feet of water on the edge of the ship channel near the mouth of Bonnet's Creek.[14]

The *Cornubia*

In 1863 Kit Morse spent much of his time aboard the *Cornubia*, which ran like clockwork between Wilmington and Bermuda during that year. Built in England in 1858, the 190-foot iron-hull sidewheel steamer was one of the blockade runners owned by the Confederate Ordnance Bureau. Initially, she was manned by an English captain named Burroughs and an English crew. In the summer of 1863, Confederate Lieutenant Richard N. Gayle assumed command. The *Cornubia* was sometimes called the *Lady Davis*.[15]

As a government-owned ship, the *Cornubia's* crew pay scale was much lower than those of privately owned blockade runners. But Kit earned $3000 for piloting her at Cape Fear, according to a pay receipt dated in May 1863.[16]

Many of the *Cornubia's* runs were uneventful, such as one outbound run for Bermuda in September of 1863, which was described by Confederate Lieutenant William Conway Whittle Jr., who went along as a passenger:

Every light on our vessel was out except one in the binnacle, and the strictest silence was observed except an occasional "starboard" or "port" from the pilot. Just at 12 the moon rose increasing the danger of our being seen and chased. At 12:30 the lead colored, low sidewheel steamer *Cornubia* crossed the bar and stood boldly out with every eye on board cast ahead of the vessel, which was going at a rate of thirteen miles per hour, and straining every nerve to catch a glimpse of some Yankee blockader awaiting to catch rebels who attempt to run out. The moon was up now and as far as that was concerned the chances against us—another tell-tale which calculated to lead to our discovery was this—not withstanding all precautions to prevent some of the bad Wilmington bituminous soft coal got mixed with our good anthracite and just as we got into the dangerous neighborhood a black column of smoke came from our smokestack and I expected any moment to see ahead of us a signal rocket which always proceeds the boom of a Yankee gun—but I was agreeably disappointed. The black smoke had all passed out when an order was carefully passed to put the helm to starboard, that there was a Yankee right ahead. We discovered him not too soon and it was not long before we lost sight of his low black hull on our starboard quarter. The danger was now half over. We had passed through the inner line—about 10 mile further out we ran right close to another Yankee steamer underway—we were so near that we could distinguish that he was a walking beam side wheel steamer. He must have seen us and mistaken our vessel for one of theirs.[17]

Frederick Gregory, who was the signal operator at the Price's Creek Station north of Smithville, also accompanied the *Cornubia* on a voyage to Bermuda. He later recalled:

> We cleared the bar successfully, with Captain Burroughs in command, and C. C. Morse as pilot, and had a good voyage to St. George, Bermuda, where we unloaded out supply of cotton and returned with supplies for the Southern Army. On our returned trip we made the land fifty or sixty miles above Fort Fisher and coasted down to the inlet, our intention to get near the land inside the blockading fleet, which was obliged to keep off a certain distance on account of shoal water. As well as I can remember, when within fifteen to twenty miles of Fort Fisher, Captain Burroughs sent for me to come to the bridge, and asked if I had my light ready, and if I thought I could send a message ashore, Pilot Morse in the meantime telling me that he would let me know when we were opposite the signal station on the land, where a constant watch was kept all night for our signal. We had not gone far when Morse told me we were opposite the post. We were feeling our way very slowly in the dark. I was put down on the deck, with the gangways open, my lights facing the land and a screen behind, when I was ordered to call the station. The officers and sailors were highly interested in the movement and crowded around to watch the proceedings. I had called but a few times when I was answered from the shore with a torch. I turned to Captain Burroughs and told him that I had the attention of the land forces, and asked what message he wanted to send. He replied as follows: "Colonel Lamb, steamer *Cornubia*. Protect me. Burroughs."[18]

According to Gregory, the signal was passed to the fort, miles ahead of the *Cornubia*. When the blockade runner arrived ". . . we found Colonel Lamb down on the point with his Whitworth guns ready to protect us if necessary. The success of this attempt gave an impetus to the signal corps, and from that time every steamer that arrived applied to the Government for a signal officer before leaving port."[19]

The final voyage of the *Cornubia* as a blockade runner began in St. George's, Bermuda, on November 4, 1863. Her cargo manifest shows that she was carrying goods transported from England to Bermuda by five different ships:[20]

From W. L. Penno's warehouse, imported per *Harriet Pinckney*: 58 cases bacon, 3 casks bacon, 19 hogshead bacon, 3 cases cartridge paper, 1 case blankets.

From same warehouse, imported per *Rover's Bride*: 12 bales, 1 case.

From Hunter's warehouse, imported per *Glendower*, London: 15 cases caps, 36 pigs lead, 300 sacks saltpeter.

From A. J. Musson's warehouse, imported per *Miriam*, London: 64 cases rifles.

From Higgs and Hyland's warehouse, imported per *Harkaway*: 4 quarter casks brandy.[21]

Four days later, on November 8, the *Cornubia* was chased as she approached Wilmington by the USS *Niphon* and the USS *James Adger*. The *Cornubia* steamed down the coast, followed closely by the *James Adger*. The *Niphon* moved in from seaward to cut off the blockade runner. Captain Gayle had to beach his vessel eleven miles north of New Inlet. The passengers and the crew abandoned ship, except the captain, the carpenter, and one seaman. At 3 o'clock that morning, the *James Adger* towed the *Cornubia* free and she was sent to Boston as a prize, along with a bag of water-soaked mail she had been carrying, which one of the officers had thrown overboard.[22]

As it turned out, the documents had greater impact on the war than the loss of the *Cornubia*. The papers showed that the *Cornubia*, the *Robert E. Lee*, the *Ella and Annie*, and other steamers of that class were the property of the Confederate government, disclosing the operational system of the Confederate transport service. This disclosure marked the first time that the Federal government understood this arrangement and led to tighter sanctions on captured blockade runners. The *Cornubia's* captain lamented, "though the *Cornubia* is a small vessel, the Confederate government could have better afforded to lose almost any other . . ."[23]

The Governor's Long-Legged Steamer

Kit Morse's other blockade runner, the *Advance*, was a swift iron sidewheel steamer that began service as a ferry running between Glasgow and Dublin under the name *Lord Clyde*. According to her chief engineer, George Morrison, she could make nineteen knots, extraordinarily fast for her day.[24]

The governor of North Carolina, Zebulon Vance, had been looking for a fast vessel to bring in supplies to help equip North Carolina troops. So he sent his agent John White of Warrenton to Great Britain to arrange for the purchase. He bought the *Lord Clyde* for $171,000, including extra equipment, through the English firm of Alexander Collie & Company. Rechristened *Advance*, the steamer began her career as a blockade runner with a run into Wilmington, bringing much-needed supplies which were sent to Raleigh by railroad. Thus the *Advance* joined three other blockade-running steamers—the *Don*, the *Hansa*, and the *Annie*—jointly owned by the

The North Carolina steamer *Advance*. Along with cotton for England she often carried passengers; among them was Anna McNeill Whistler of Wilmington, subject of the famous painting by her son James. (Photo courtesy of Naval Historical Society and Charles Peery.)

state and the English company. As the war progressed, three more Collie steamers joined the trade—the *Constance*, the *Edith*, and the *Pet*.[25]

The design of the *Advance* was ideally suited for the trade with a single exception: she drew too much water to easily cross the bars at Cape Fear. Because of her twelve-foot loaded draft, James Sprunt said that she could not carry a full load of cargo into or out of Wilmington. But this limitation did not keep her from becoming enormously successful as a blockade runner for the state.[26]

On her third inbound voyage to Wilmington, the *Advance* made it into the harbor in broad daylight. A passenger recalled:

> Captain Crosson [Thomas M. Crossan] prepared to run up near enough to see what blockaders were within view and I supposed that he would then stand out to sea, lie off until night and then run in at his leisure. But to my astonishment, although it was about eight o'clock in the morning, the sun shining brilliantly and the sea as level as a floor and three blockaders guarding the entrance [New Inlet], he steamed straight on to Fort Fisher. The blockaders seemed confused for a few moments by the audacity of the movement, but presently they came about and all but three struck for the shore, intending to cut us off. They came on very speedily, but finding that we were running so swiftly they opened upon us with shrapnel, shell and solid shot. It was a scene of intense excitement. We could see the people on the shore watching the result . . . the shells were plowing up the water and tearing up the sand on the shore, bursting over and around us and yet not one struck us.[27]

Officers and Crew of the Steamer *Advance*

A LIST OF THE OFFICERS AND CREW MEMBERS for an inbound voyage in February 1864 showed a total ship's company of fifty-six. Included were men from England, France, Ireland, Portugal, Scotland and Sweden, as well as from five states. Among the officers and crew:

J. J. Gutherie, captain
Thomas J. Boykin, purser
Joannes Wylie, first officer
William C. Jones, second officer
B. Taylor, third officer
William H. Jones, boatswain
C. C. Morse, pilot
C. L. Neil, signal officer
George Morrison, chief engineer
William Maglenn, first assistant engineer
A. I. Barnes, second assistant engineer
George Curtis, third assistant engineer
four greasers
twelve firemen
one store keeper
three coal heavers
two watchmen
ten seamen
one seaman's mess boy
three cooks
five stewarts
one captain's clerk *

*From list in possession of Dr. Charles V. Peery of Charleston, S.C.

In August and September, the *Advance* made eight attempts to leave the harbor at Cape Fear, but could not because both bars were "swarming with boats." Actually, the Union blockaders were only one of many obstacles faced by the steamer during that frustrating period. An account of this time appears in the next chapter.[28]

Mary White spent much of August 1864 on the *Advance*.
(Photo courtesy of Naval Historical Center.)

CHAPTER 11

Through the Eyes of a Girl

"I tumbled over between the cotton but not before I had seen the bulwarks going away. All was in the greatest confusion and no one knew what was the damage . . ."

—Fifteen-year-old Mary White describing how another block-ade runner collided with the steamer Advance. [1]

*A*s one writes about blockade running during the Civil War, it is easy to get caught up in the spirit of adventure of the men who ran the Union gauntlet on nights of the black moon. *Bold, daring, dauntless, fearless*—adjectives roll like marbles on a hardwood floor as writers attempt to capture the essence of those running the blockade. The age-old romance of the sea reaches its crest when in the darkness just ahead lurk perils from enemy ships and hidden shoals.

But the experiences of a fifteen-year-old girl, set down in entries in her diary, complete with weeping captain and drunken pilot, cast blockade running in a different light. And they show some of the difficulties that could turn piloting a blockade runner at Cape Fear into a disheartening nightmare.

"I hope everything will be all right."

The girl's name was Mary J. White. In August of 1864, Mary, the daughter of North Carolina agent John White, embarked on a voyage on the state's premier blockade runner, the *Advance*. It promised to be a grand adventure.

White's family lived in Warrenton, North Carolina, a small town near the Virginia line. Her father was responsible for making arrangements to obtain arms, clothing, food, and other necessities of war for North Carolina troops. His duties often took him to England. During the summer of 1864, he decided to take along his family. Traveling with them as passengers on the *Advance* would be another family, the Boykins from Wilmington.[2]

John White was, of course, familiar with the ship they would take, having bought her for the state. She was a sturdily built steamer with a stout iron hull and twin paddlewheels, and had made seventeen successful trips through the blockade. Some thought her to be "the most trustworthy vessel at sea." John White certainly trusted her captain, the Scotsman Joannes Wylie. Captain Wylie, called by one contemporary "a warmhearted Scotchman . . . big, burly and red faced, full of enthusiasm, full of poetry, " had accompanied the *Advance* on her maiden voyage to America as her sailing captain and later served as her first officer. John White also trusted her Cape Fear pilot, Kit Morse. Otherwise, he would never have brought his family along.[3]

John White
(Courtesy Charleston Library Society)

Mary White's story begins on August 2, 1864, with the first entry in her diary:

> I left home for England with Father, Mother, Bro. Andrew, Hugh, Kate and Sue. Father had to go to buy supplies for the N. C. soldiers, and things were so awful here and Mother had suffered so much being separated and our baby sister Lizzie died while he was away, so he promised Mother he would never leave her again. The evening before we left, just after sunset, we all went together to say goodbye to the little graves at the back of the garden, where our precious little sisters, Sallie and Lizzie, are buried and our beautiful little Pattie, my first niece. It all seems very strange, but we are going with father and I hope everything will be all right.

Mary and her family traveled by train to Raleigh where the Confederate agent met with Governor Vance and other state officials. Then they went on to Wilmington to board the blockade runner. They arrived at ten o'clock on the evening of August 5 in the midst of a thunderstorm. Mary wrote:

> We left there Saturday morning for the S. S. AdVance, which was lying in the Cape Fear River, near Wilmington. We expected to run the blockade that night, but there was some mistake in the ship's papers and before they could be corrected, we were too late for the tide and had to cast anchor and lie there all night.

On Down to Smithville

The next day the *Advance* steamed down the river and anchored in the bay between Fort Caswell and Smithville. Near her lay the *Helen*, another iron-hull side-wheeler piloted by Ephraim Gause of Smithville. The following evening both vessels were ready to run the blockade.[4] Mary recorded:

> On the night of the 7th all was excitement on board, supper was over, the machinery all oiled, the steam gotten up and everything put in readiness for the run, finally the order was given for them to heave the anchor and when that was up the lights were all extinguished.
>
> Then we went below, stood on stools looking over the side of the ship and were watching the water sparkling, when the vessel got fast aground and all their efforts to get her off were unavailing for some time.

As the *Advance* crept through the harbor that night, Mary could see the *Helen* stuck fast on a shoal. The *Helen*, like the *Advance*, managed to work herself free that night and had to turn back into the harbor.[5]

As the *Advance* lay at anchor off Smithville, waiting for her next attempt at the blockade, Mary spent much of her time watching other blockade runners in the harbor. Her favorite vantage point was sitting perched on the cotton bales which were stowed on the main deck of the *Advance*. She could see the *Mary Celestia*, recently in from Bermuda, being held in quarantine. She heard that a man had died aboard the ship from yellow fever. (This was a shipmate of John Anderson, the heroic Cape Fear pilot who had brought the ship across the bar and died afterward.)[6]

Mary wrote that as the *Advance* waited to leave port, the captain made a wager with the captain of another blockade runner, the *Little Hattie*:

> The ship that gets to Bermuda in the shortest time is to have given to the Captain $10 and the same to be divided among the crew. Capt. Wylie seems to be confident that he will win the race, and I suppose the Captain of the *Little Hattie* is sure that he will get it.

As Captain Wylie and Kit Morse awaited a suitable high tide, other blockade runners of shallower draft crossed the bar. The *Little Hattie* safely cleared the harbor, piloted by Robert Grissom. Then the night of August 8 Ephraim Gause took the *Helen* out on a run to Bermuda. Mary wrote that the *Helen*, which "has been lying very near us all day, went out and as no guns were heard and no news from the ship it is supposed that she escaped uninjured."[7]

The following day, the *Annie* came in from Bermuda. Celebrations in Smithville for the safe return of another runner were tempered with the grim reality of the ship in the harbor under quarantine. Mary saw a boat carrying another coffin to the *Mary*

Celestia. She wrote, "How sad it is to look over there and see them signaling to the shore which is their only means of communication, and think that the poor fellows suffer and die and have no efficient nurse there to attend them."[8]

The Second Attempt

That evening, Captain Wylie and Kit Morse again attempted to get the *Advance* through the blockade:

> We . . . were over the rip, and it was thought that we would get out without much difficulty, but they did not steer properly and we missed the channel and fastened in the sand. The engines were worked and everything possible done, but there was no getting off and we had to lie there all night with eight large blockaders in sight.

According to Mary, the *Advance* finally got free of the shoal the next morning and steamed back up the river to Wilmington to wait "until the nights get dark again." The passengers went ashore. The next morning they took the small steamboat *Cape Fear* down to Smithville. They arrived at two o'clock in the afternoon:[9]

> We stopped at Mrs. Stewart's, a boarding house on the shore, stayed there an hour or so and then went to our quarters, just back of the boarding house. The house we are staying in belongs to a family named Cowan. It was their summer residence, but they haven't been here in some time. It is a very comfortable house with six rather small rooms and three piazzas. It is very amusing to see us sitting down to our meals. Dr. Boykin's family and ours have six teaplates, the same number of knives and forks and one teaspoon between us. We have one cracked dish and have been putting the salt, pepper and sugar on the table in papers until this morning, on an exploring trip, a cracked dish and an old broken teapot were found. These were very valuable and immediately washed and the teapot filled with sugar and the top with salt.
>
> Capt. Wylie came down with us today. The "City of Petersburg" came in today. [The *City of Petersburg*, one of the fastest blockade-running steamers, was piloted by Joseph Bensel of Smithville.]

The next day Mary wrote in her diary:

> Father and Capt. Wylie have just left for Wilmington. Father expects to go home to Warrenton before he returns. He expects to be back the last of next week. This evening, Tom, the boy who waits on us, went bathing in the river with the boys and they thought it great fun, but the people down here say there are many sharks in the water, so I don't think mother and Mrs. Boykin will let them go anymore.

Mary Stuart's boarding house on the Smithville waterfront, where Mary White stayed, was a favorite of visitors to the town well into the twentieth century. It was built in 1842. (From postcard in the McNeil family.)

On the following day, August 15:

> The "Cape Fear" came up just a minute ago and Dr. Boykin, Hugh and Tom have gone to see if there are any provisions on board for us. They have just returned and say there are none. We are nearly out of bread and don't know where to get any. This morning the pilot of one of the ships lying in the river died of yellow fever. Ships that came in the last few days, say that yellow fever is raging in Bermuda, so the "Ad-Vance" will not touch there but will proceed to Halifax. [The pilot who died was probably John Anderson of the *Mary Celestia*. If so, his death came somewhat later than indicated in the account of James Sprunt.][10]

August 16:

> Yesterday we had to borrow some bread for our supper from Mr. Morse, the pilot of the "Ad-Vance," but as Tom was going for it, he found a shop where biscuit could be bought, three for a dollar, so he got enough for supper and breakfast this morning . . . It is so monotonous here, every day passes alike. This evening Bro. Andrew took Kate, Sue and myself for a walk but we did not walk very far, it was so

sandy. We went on the margin of the river and counted ten vessels in quarantine near here, besides an old ironclad which they say is worthless from the number of barnacles fastened to the bottom.

August 18:

This morning by boat, we got plenty of fresh bread, old bacon, beef and vegetables . . . Capt. Wylie left this morning for the "Ad-Vance." He took tea with us and made a great deal of fun at our table.

On the night of August 18 the families enjoyed an impromptu concert given by Confederate signal officers. They played the violin, the flute, and the guitar and sang "Ben Bolt," "Bonny Jean," and other songs. (The flutist was Sidney Lanier; the guitarist was his brother. Both young men were signal officers.)
On August 20, Mary wrote:

This morning between ten and eleven o'clock we saw the "Ad-Vance" coming beautifully down from Wilmington, but she stuck on the bar and had to remain there until the next high tide, which was a little after seven, when she got afloat and came opposite this place and anchored.

August 21:

Today, though Sunday, is about like every other day down here. Capt. Wylie came ashore but was restless and didn't stay but a moment, scarcely. Last night, the serenaders, who are signal officers, were on duty just a little in front of this house, so they could not come here but played where they were and three or four ladies came and had a dance on our front porch, although they were perfect strangers to us.

August 22:

This A. M. Tom had a sore hand and on that account and others, it was thought best that we come aboard, so about 10:00 A.M. we came. Another attempt will be made tonight to run the blockade. About 13 steamers are in now. Eight large Yankee ships are so near that we can distinctly see them with the naked eye, but we will not encounter them as we go in the opposite direction, but there are five where we will have to go. [Captain Wylie and Kit Morse were planning to take the *Advance* out through New Inlet.]

The Third Attempt

Mary wrote on August 23:

Last night about 8:30 we started off to make the attempt. We went very well until we got to the inner bar and there, as usual, we got aground and while we were vainly attempting to get off, the moon rose and shown very brightly and then of course we were effectively prevented from trying any more. . . . A blockader was lying on the outer bar, just ahead of us last night and, if we had gone that far, would have had to come back, so it seems fortunate that we didn't go. But really it is trying to make three attempts to run out and get fast aground, to say nothing of the wearisomeness of staying nine days in Smithville. The "Lillian" came down today to run out tonight.

August 24:

The "Lillian" started out last night and it was thought she got out safely, but it is not certainly known. We stayed on the cotton bales to see it go out, saw the Yankees throw several rockets, the saw the flashes and heard the reports of fifteen guns. [The *Lilian* was captured outside of the harbor that night by the blockaders *Keystone State* and *Gettysburg*.][11]

August 26:

Last night we heard a quantity of guns firing and the occasion was not known until this morning, when it was found that the "Hope" was aground at Fort Fisher and a couple of sails were raised on board to get her off. The Yankees saw her then for the first time and began firing into her rapidly. The crew thought all was over and deserted the ship.

The next day sailors from the *Advance* helped unload the vessel, returning with eighteen barrels of sugar for their efforts. Mary observed that the *Hope* was 'a tremendous vessel, carrying 2,000 bails of cotton, double the cargo of the "Ad-Vance" carries, and does not draw as much water as the "Ad-Vance."' Mary also reported:

This model of the *Hope* shows a turtleback forward deck designed to slice throught the water in heavy seas. (Courtesy Mariners' Museum, Newport News, Virginia.)

Capt. Wylie says the officers did not do their duty on the "Hope" and the crew became unmanageable and they could do nothing until Capt. Wylie came and brought the men to order, and soon got the ship off. The Capt. [William C. Hammer, former commander of the *Annie Childs*] was so mortified that he could not manage his men, and so grateful to Capt. Wylie that he threw his arms around his neck and wept like a child.

August 30:

An attack on Wilmington is daily expected. There are nineteen blockaders in sight of here and a turreted monitor.

August 31:

This is father's 50th birthday . . . I wrote a letter to Sister today, in which I stated that we would once more run the blockade tonight, but the pilot has just sent a communication saying it would not be safe to attempt such a thing as it would be high tide on the bar before dark, so we are all down in the mouth again.

The Fourth Attempt

On September 2, Mary wrote:

Last night we got up steam about twilight and started out. We went splendidly, got over the rip as nicely as possible without touching and thought we would certainly go through, when the 1st officer discovered something on the bar, and when the glasses were turned on, a large blockader was distinctly seen lying directly in our path. She saw us and flashed her light, so of course we had to put back to Smithville. It was supposed to be a monitor, as no masts were seen, and if it was, we would have passed so near the we would have been blown to atoms.

September 3:

Last evening we got up steam, heaved the anchor and were just on the point of starting, when Capt. Wylie had a telegram sent him by a physician on shore, saying the he might not be well enough to navigate today if we got to sea and consequently just had all the steam turned off and the vessel anchored again. This was the greatest disappointment of all.

September 4:

Last night we started out, as Capt. Wylie is still unwell, with another navigator to steer in case our Capt. should have a relapse. We got beyond the bar and the range lights were [not] set, so we had to turn back, intending to try again, but the ship was so hard to turn that she had to be anchored and let the tide swing her around. We started out again, but by the time she got to the rips the tide had gone down so much that we could not cross them, so we are back again for the night.

Encounter with the *Old Dominion*

Mary wrote on September 5:

Last night for the 7th time an attempt was made to run out. We got to the rip, got aground and had just started off and were going at half speed, when the "Old Dominion," which had started a little after us, actually ran into us. Mother and the small children were down between the cotton bales, while Mrs. Boykin and I were on top of them. One of the stewards, who was on the cotton bales with us, saw the "Old Dominion" coming along at full speed, said, "Look at the Old Dominion, she's coming into us. Get a hold, get a hold." And with that he tumbled off. Mrs. Boykin

The *Old Dominion* in Bristol, England. (Photo courtesy of Chicago Historical Society)

and I were much nearer the shock, and we thought he was in fun and stayed up there. We saw the boat coming but thought, of course, that they would take care and not run into us, but the first thing we knew there was a most fearful crash. I tumbled over between the cotton but not before I had seen the bulwarks going away. All was in the greatest confusion and no one knew what was the damage . . . The bow of the "Old Dominion" was very strong, but our ship was so strong that it did not run in until it had scraped the length of three feet and a half, and the hole, which was quite large enough for a man to get in, was made just at our door, so that we could not open it on account of the pieces of timber knocked against it. The strong timbers were twisted into the smallest splinters, but the hole was 18 inches above the water. We came immediately back to Smithville and are going to Wilmington this morning.

On September 7 Mary wrote:

This morning we came down to Smithville and anchored in our old place. The "Will-o-the-Wisp," the "Helen," the "Owl" and the "Lynx" and other vessels are lying here in quarantine, having just come in.

The New Pilot Was as Drunk as a Fish

Mary wrote on September 8:

Last night as our pilot, Mr. Morse, had been ordered on another shift [ship], another pilot was detailed to carry us out. He got on a spree and was not notified he was to go out on the "Ad-Vance" until about an hour before time for him to come on board. When he did come, the guard had to wake him up and bring him on board as drunk as a fish. Of course, we could not risk ourselves with him and have to wait until tonight. [No information on the identity of the pilot could be found.]

But the evening for those aboard the *Advance* was not to be entirely wasted, as Mary recorded in her diary:

Last night after we had found out that we could not go and were in no pleasant humor, suddenly distant music struck on our ears. The same gentlemen who serenaded us so sweetly in Smithville, came out in a small boat and went round and round the ship very slowly, playing most beautifully. The tune next to the last was "Home, Sweet Home," and they went off playing "Dixie."

Back Home

For Mary, it was indeed to be "home, sweet home." A few days later, John White decided that traveling on a blockade runner was too dangerous for his family and sent them ashore and back to Warrenton. Mary wrote on September 15, from Warrenton:

> On the 8th we made our 9th attempt and failed. We got to sea that night and the pilot had just given the ship over to the Capt., when it was discovered that we were about to be surrounded. Three Yankee ships in front of us threw up rockets and one was on our side not more than 500 yards off, so our ship immediately put back and went with the speed of the wind until out of their reach. We anchored at Smithville the remainder of the night. It was remarkable calm, there was scarcely a ripple on the water and our paddles could be heard a mile and a half off.
>
> The next day, the 10th, the "Ad-Vance" left Smithville about 11:00 o'clock for New Inlet. The Capt. said that was the last night of the moon and they had either to go out or be blown up. She was anchored in sight of the Yankees all day, and everyone thought it would be so perfectly desperate that Father and Dr. Boykin took their families off. The "Ad-Vance" got out that night, on the 10th. 35 shots fired at her were heard in Smithville.
>
> We went to Mrs. Stewart's in Smithville, who keeps a public house. She took us in and we got dinner there. In the afternoon we went to the wharf to try to prevail on Gen. Whiting to let us go to Wilmington on the "Cape Fear," a river boat, as there were no passengers except himself, his staff, and Gen. Beauregard. But he promptly refused us. We journeyed back to Mrs. Stewart's again, weary and disheartened. She very kindly let us have lodging for the night.

Mary and her family made their way back to Warrenton. Captain Wylie got the *Advance* out to sea. But after clearing the blockaders she encountered the USS *Santiago de Cuba.*

The Capture of the *Advance*

The lookout on the swift Union warship sighted black smoke at 10:40 on the morning of September 10. She took up the chase. By one o'clock that afternoon, Captain Glisson of the *Santiago de Cuba* could see that he had a blockade runner on his hands. By sunset, he had closed to within four miles. At 7:40 P.M. the blockader fired a shot across the stem of the *Advance* and the chase ended.[12]

The chief engineer of the *Advance*, James Maglenn, blamed it on the coal. This was his description of the last voyage:

> Although the night was not altogether favorable, we started out as soon as the tide would permit. Of course, smoke, sparks and flames from the stack had to be kept down. This was very difficult to do, as our last shovelful of good coal was used shortly after crossing the bar and in plain sight of some of the fleet. Those that could see us would throw rockets, indicating the direction we were going. Then the dodging on our part and the frequent change of the ship's course to keep from running into them. The excitement at this time was very great. Yet all was quiet as the grave

on board and every man was at his post and doing his duty faithfully. The rocket firing and shooting were very heavy, and nothing but good management on the part of our officers could have pulled us safely through the fleet that night.

At sunrise there was nothing in sight, yet our black smoke was giving us away. Some of the fleet were following it, and about 8 o'clock a vessel was discovered chasing us and appeared to be gaining. Everything possible was done to increase the speed of the *Ad-Vance,* but the steaming qualities of the coal were against us. We were using Chatham, or Egypt coal, which was very inferior; in fact nothing but slate or the croppings of the mine. Our good coal at Wilmington was given to the Confederate cruisers, which accounts for our capture. [The *Tallahassee* got the good coal for her destructive run up the coast.][13]

Advance Chief Engineer James Maglenn. (Photo courtesy of Charleston County Library)

All but four of her crew were released by the captain of the *Santiago de Cuba* after claiming to be British subjects. According to Mary, the ones taken captive were Mr. Neal, Willie Muse, Mr. Field, and Mr. Byron. Three of these men were subsequently released, she said, leaving only Mr. Neal who ended up in prison.[14]

Mr. Neal was C. L. Neil, the signal officer. William T. (Willie) Muse was twelve years old at the time. In an 1893 letter to the *Southport Leader* he recalled that he spent three weeks in the Ludlow Street Jail in New York before he was released.[15]

So ended the blockade-running career of the *Advance,* which helped make the North Carolina troops the best-dressed and best-equipped in the Confederacy. She was eventually sold in a prize court to the U. S. Navy, and renamed the USS *Frolic.*[16]

Soon afterward, the blockade-running career of Kit Morse ended also. He was captured on another blockade runner and spent the rest of the war in Federal prisons, aboard the USS *Sabine* and then at Point Lookout in Maryland, according to his friend and fellow pilot, Jim Billy Craig.[17]

After the war Morse returned to his family in Smithville and resumed his career as a Cape Fear pilot. In April of 1877, he was at sea in his pilot boat *Uriah Timmons* when a terrible storm, which lasted for three days, struck Cape Fear. The pilot boat *Mary K. Sprunt* was lost in this same storm. The story of the *Timmons* and the *Sprunt* appears in the epilogue.[18]

Kit Morse died in 1903. His gravestone can be seen today in the Old Smithville Burying Ground, where so many of the Cape Fear pilots were laid to rest.

Mary kept her diary until June 7, 1865, when she wrote:

I don't go to school now. President Johnson has issued a proclamation, confiscating nearly every Southerner's property, and after their property is confiscated, they will not even be allowed to vote. Father is included in one of the classes. I don't expect to have a home long.

In 1930 Mary White made one final entry in her diary. She was living then in Petersburg, Virginia, as Mrs. E. R. Beckwith. She wrote:

> I seemed to have stopped the diary very suddenly. . . I really had no thought when I wrote it, of ever keeping any of it, but somehow it just seems to have survived.
>
> Mrs. Stuart, who kept the boarding house in Smithville (mentioned a number of times in the original diary), had a daughter named Kate. [Kate was a few years older than Mary.] She showed us a beautiful little watch that had been given her by a gentleman whose child she had saved. Years later, I knew a Mr. Darst, the Bishop's brother, who had been staying in Southport (our old Smithville) and he told me that Miss Kate was still living, then a very old woman, and keeping the house in much the same primitive fashion that her mother did. The father of the little boy she saved, when he fell overboard, was a ship captain. From that day to this, every ship of that line [the Clyde line] that passes the place salutes in honor of Miss Kate's heroism.

Although the last entry in Mary's diary concerned not the war but fond remembrances of a childhood friend, her earlier entries manage to convey from a unique viewpoint—literally perched on cotton bales stacked on the deck of an outbound steamer—a sense of the sometimes frustrating business of blockade running.

Mary White Beckwith
(Photo courtesy of Louise Holland)

Thomas Mann Thompson Jr. The Smithville pilot was known for his coolness under fire. Captain Mike Usina of the blockade runner *Atalanta* said that Thompson "was an officer who knew no fear." (Photo courtesy of Southport Maritime Museum)

CHAPTER 12

Thomas Mann Thompson

"I am ready, Sir, whenever you are."

> —*Smithville pilot Thomas Mann Thompson reporting to his captain that he is prepared to bring the* Atalanta *into the harbor on a moonlit night, even though the odds of capture are overwhelming.*[1]

O ne of the most successful of the Cape Fear pilots who ran the blockade was Thomas Mann Thompson of Smithville. Thompson piloted nine different steamers through the blockade, more, according to available records, than any other Cape Fear pilot. Of the blockade runners that Thompson piloted, three were captured and another, the *Elizabeth,* ran aground off Cape Fear.[2]

Thomas, the son of Thomas Mann Thompson Sr. and Rebecca Jane Dudley Rogers Thompson, was born in Brunswick County, probably in Smithville or on Bald Head Island, in 1831. In 1854 he married Mary Elizabeth Mintz. Together they had thirteen children. His older brother Joseph T. Thompson was also a pilot who ran the blockade at Cape Fear, as was their brother-in-law, Ephraim Gause.[3]

A Letter to Lily

In 1896, Thomas Thompson recalled some of the high points of his blockade-running days in a letter to his daughter Lily Thompson Fisher:

> As well as I can remember, I began running the blockade about the last day of Feby. 1864. Left here on str. [steamer] *Emma* as passenger for Nassau. When we arrived there I was employed as a pilot on her - made three trips in and out making seven times I ran the blockade on the *Emma* including the time I was a passenger. I then joined the str *Flora* made two round trips on her. Joined str *Florie* came out from Bermuda sprang a leak - returned - joined str *Thistle* ran blockade one time on her. Then joined the str *Atlanta [Atalanta]* ran eight times on her - then joined the

Armstrong ran three times on her. Joined the *Let Her Be* ran six times on her. Joined str *Coquett* ran blockade one time on her - Joined str. *Index* ran three times on her. Went out on steamer *Elizabeth* and ran blockade one time on her. I Ran Blockade from Feby 24th 1864 until a few days before the fall of Fisher. [January 15, 1965]. Made thirty-four trips and was fortunate enough never to be captured.[4]

In this letter to his daughter, Thomas Thompson also wrote of some of his experiences while piloting the *Atlanta* [This streamer, usually known as the *Atalanta*, once served in the Confederate Navy as the CSS *Tallahassee*.][5]

I came in on the *Atlanta* once when there were thirteen of the Yankee Blockaders in sight all lying around the bar in about two hundred yards of each other. I picked out the widest space between them and came full speed between them. They fired at us but did no damage. Another time I came in by one of them that was anchored in the channel on the bar - so that I had to come within five feet of her and never a sound did I hear from her. I thought at first I would run into her and sink her but saw that I could pass within a few feet without running ashore so thought better to get by if I had room than to take the chance of disabling our ship and being captured by the enemy's launches. Once we were fired upon by a ship and the ball passed between the Commander and myself. We were standing upon the bridge about four feet apart. It staggered both of us - but it was a spent ball or it would have stunned us. It fell about fifty yards beyond the ship.[6]

In July of 1864, the *Atalanta*, loaded with meat for the Confederate Army, slipped across the Western Bar and safely into port, passing closely two blockaders in the darkness.[7]

Captain Mike Usina of the *Atalanta* remembered that night well:

We approached the entrance to Wilmington Harbor on a beautiful moonlight night in July, only one day before the full moon. Before approaching the blockaders the officers and men were notified that the attempt was about to be made, with the chances very much against us. (There were thirty-five blockaders anchored there the afternoon before, counted from Fort Caswell.) But, I said that we had four hundred tons of meat for starving soldiers and I intended to make a run for it, and if any of them were unwilling to take the risk, they were at liberty to take the small boats and try to reach the beach. To their credit, not one man availed himself of the privilege.

When I said to Mr. Thompson, our fearless pilot, "Tom, I am going to make the attempt, what do you think of it?" his answer was "I am ready, Sir, whenever you are."[8]

Captain Usina said that as they slowly approached the Union flagship, the engineer told him that he could not maintain steam at a low level, that he would have either to speed up or open the safety valves to vent off pressure, which would have alerted the blockaders to their presence. The captain told him to hold steady. As Thompson guided the steamers between the blockaders, she was spotted. The cap-

tain of the flagship ordered them to stop or he would blow them out of the water.[9]
Captain Usina continues:

> "Hold on," I said, "until I speak to the engineer," which I did through the
> speaking tube; but instead of stopping the engines, he threw her wide open and she
> almost flew under our feet. Our neighbors soon found that we were not doing very
> much stopping and attempted to do the stopping themselves; but, fortunately for
> us, they failed to do so.[10]

Thompson recalled:

> The chief officer was a Virginia man named Charles Nelson. I ordered him to
> find out the depth of the water, for the *Atalanta* was getting into shoal water fast.
> Nelson went to the leadsman, found out the soundings but reported so slowly that
> I reproached him for it. I said, "Can't even a shell make you move faster? (Two of
> them had exploded between us a moment before.) His answer was, "What's the use
> sir? I might go just fast enough to get in the way of one of those damned shells."[11]

Adventures on the *Armstrong*

In his letter to his daughter, Thompson described a trip from Bermuda to Cape
Fear on the *Armstrong*. While in Bermuda he came upon a young Smithville man,
George Price. Thompson knew Price, who had been trained as an engineer and was
looking for a job on a blockade runner. Thompson persuaded the *Armstrong*'s captain, Charles Nelson, the former first officer of the *Atalanta*, to take Price aboard as
an oiler. This would turn out to be a most fortunate decision.[12]

The *Armstrong* departed from St. George's harbor on November 23, 1864, carrying 10 bales of gunny cloth, 200 bundles of iron hoops, 5 crates of earthenware,
and 1,370 cases of preserved meats. Also aboard as passengers were seven Confederate
soldiers who had escaped from a Yankee prison and managed to reach Bermuda by
way of Halifax.[13]

As the *Armstrong* steamed for the coast, the ship labored through the heavy seas
of a strong northern gale. The engineers boosted the steam pressure to give the ship
more headway. Shortly afterward, a steampipe ruptured. Steam filled the engine
room. The engineers and the firemen ran up the gangway to the deck. Without
power, the steamer lost headway and rolled uncontrollably in the deep swells.[14]

Thompson had just gone to his cabin when he heard the squeal of the hissing
steam. As he ran up on deck, the leadsman told him that the captain wanted to see
him. When Thompson arrived in the pilot house, Captain Nelson, obviously shaken
and unsure about how to recover from the loss of power, said to him, "What is best
to do? She will roll herself all to pieces."[15]

"Hoist the jib and get the ship before the wind," Thompson directed. The captain gave the order. With "steam from stem to stern," the deckhands rushed to set the

The blockade runner *Armstrong*. She was an iron-hull sidewheeler built in Glasgow, Scotland, in 1864. After five successful runs through the blockade, she was captured on an outbound voyage from Cape Fear on December 4, 1864. Her captain, Mike Usina of Savannah, said that she was "very poorly built." (Photo courtesy of Maritime Museum of the Atlantic, Halifax, Nova Scotia.)

sail. As the violent motion of the ship began to subside, the engineers and firemen looked around to determine whether all of the engine room gang had made it safely to the deck. They knew that anyone remaining behind would have been scalded to death. All were accounted for save one oiler, George Price. When they entered the engine room, they found to their astonishment that the boy had stayed behind to repair the steam leak. Working with white lead and canvas, drenched with sweat, scarlet from the steam, he was nearly finished.[16]

Home Before Dark

As the winds died down, the engineers managed to get up steam and the blockade runner pushed for Cape Fear. The next morning Thompson and the captain found themselves far to the south, below Charleston. Captain Nelson brought the ship slowly up the coast. Near the North Carolina line, he decided to anchor off the beach for the engineers to make more-permanent repairs to the ruptured steamline.[17]

Just before the anchor hit the water, Thompson and the captain saw men signaling from the edge of the woods near the beach. They turned out to be seven Union soldiers who had escaped a Confederate prison and managed to make their way to the coast to try to reach a Union cruiser.[18]

Thompson recalled: "They were nearly starved. We showed them the Confederate flag—they came down to the beach and waved us to take them aboard.

I took a boat and crew and brought them to the ship where we both fed and clothed them for they were nearly all naked. We gave them all they wished to eat." After the engineers finished their work, the *Armstrong* continued her voyage up the coast. Before preparing for the run into the harbor, Captain Nelson sent the seven Union soldiers ashore along with the mail from Bermuda. Just before sundown that evening, Thompson took the ship in across the Western Bar and "The brave boy who faced the steam and repaired the broken pipe when it was the duty of others and I were home before dark."[19]

(Drawing by Captain Robert Potter.)

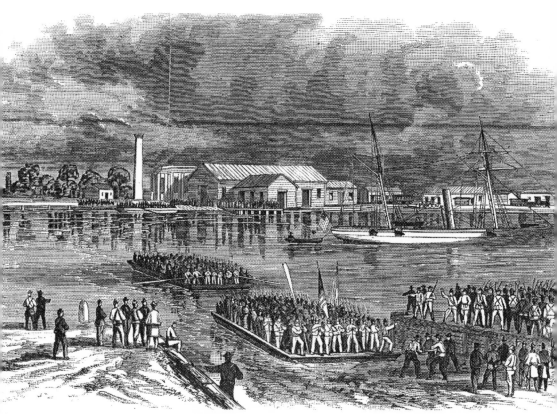

Union forces arrive in Smithville. The artist himself never came near the place, judging from his perspective on the river. (*Harper's Weekly*)

CHAPTER 13

The Legacy of the
Cape Fear Blockade Runners

Drucilla rode in her pony cart down to the water's edge at Federal Point, glared at the damned Yankees coming ashore and shook her little fists.

— *The defiant five-year-old daughter of pilot Thomas E. Burriss expressing her outrage at Federal troops.*[1]

For some families in Smithville and Federal Point, the melancholy days following the war's end were touched with joy, as men and boys who had served in the Confederate army came home to their families, along with the pilots who had been in prison. Some of the pilots took the long way home. A Halifax newspaper reported that on March 6, 1865, the schooner *Friend* arrived in port with seventeen passengers, most of whom were Confederate signal officers and pilots. The paper failed to mention the first names of the men, but among the group were pilots Sellers, Dosher, Burriss, and Thompson.[2]

Many residents of Smithville and Federal Point remained defiant, including families of the pilots. Seventeen-year-old Rebecca Gutherie, daughter of the pilot of the *Robert E. Lee*, helped make a Confederate flag and paraded in front of Yankee headquarters in Smithville with other girls, flaunting the flag and expressing her resentment for the occupying soldiers. The soldiers just laughed. Drucilla, the five-year-old daughter of Thomas E. Burriss of the *Banshee*, according to family tradition, rode down to the water's edge at Federal Point in her pony cart, glared at the damned Yankees coming ashore and shook her little fists.[3]

Despite the dangers in running the blockade, the pilots fared better than those who had served in the Confederate army. Seventy-seven men held licenses as pilots for Cape Fear during the Civil War. Most ran the blockade. Only five died in the service.[4]

Yellow fever claimed four of the Cape Fear pilots. John William Anderson died of yellow fever aboard the *Mary Celestia*, within sight of Smithville. Captain John W. Galloway brought the *Mary Celestia* across the bar on a run to Bermuda and died there of the disease. John B. Price died of yellow fever at Nassau.[5]

Price's son James, who was a boy of nine at the war's end, remembered his father telling him that he was going away on the ocean to get a ship at Nassau. Price died soon after going ashore. James later wrote, "The vessel on which he went (the steamer *Kent*) returned and was destroyed by the blockaders. For years the framework of her walking beam, sticking out of the water in front of our town, was a continual reminder of my great loss."[6]

George W. Burriss, the man who kept his whiskey in his coffin, died of yellow fever in Halifax in August of 1864. The fifth Smithville pilot who failed to survive the war was the unfortunate Thomas Dyer, who died at the hands of one of his shipmates aboard the *Georgiana McCaw*.[7]

The Cape Fear pilots of the Civil War, along with their fellow blockade runners, maintained what Dr. Wise called "the lifeline of the Confederacy." They helped sustain the Southern military forces and helped make life during the war years a little more bearable to those who remained home while others left to fight.[8]

Long after the war ended the Cape Fear pilots who ran the blockade remained heroes to their fellow townspeople. Their daring runs and narrow escapes, their tales of the British islands, of Confederate gold, and Yankee prisons, became the stuff of legends.[9]

But for most of them, the gold was quickly gone. Dr. Walter Curtis said that they "lent it to anybody they considered a friend without security and they spent very freely for everything they wanted and many things they did not want."[10]

Of the Smithville blockade runners, Thomas Thompson was not only one of the most successful, he also was one of the few to end up with anything to show for his efforts. After the war, he used some of the proceeds from his thirty-four trips through the blockade to build a fine home which stands today at the corner of Bay Street and Caswell Avenue in Southport. A Smithville lady once remarked that he was the only blockade runner she could think of off-hand that had anything to show for all the money he had made during the

The home of Thomas Mann Thompson.
(Photograph by the author.)

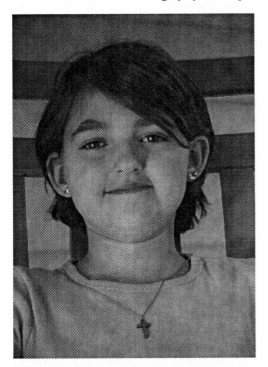

The gold cross brought home by Captain Ephraim Gause through the blockade, worn by his great-great-great-granddaughter.
(Photograph by the author.)

war. The others, she said, had spent their profits on "fast horses and fast women."[11]

But I know this is not entirely true, for my family still possesses a tortoise shell needle case, a pen, and a small gold cross that had been purchased in Nassau by my great-grandfather, Ephraim Gause, one of the Smithville pilots who ran the Union blockade at Cape Fear, on one of his voyages to the British island during the Civil War.[12]

Our mother always treasured these family heirlooms that recalled days long past—days of war when daring men skillfully guided sleek, steam-powered vessels through treacherous waters on nights of the unlit moon, slipping through the Union blockading fleet, carrying cotton to the British islands, and returning home with gold and scarce supplies for the Confederacy, and sometimes, with gifts for their loved ones.

(Drawing by Captain Robert Potter.)

PILOT TOWER

r. potter

Captain Robert Potter's drawing captures the essence of the Southport waterfront as it appeared during the latter part of the twentieth century. The pilot tower has since been torn down, although pilots still use the smaller structure to its right. The home on the left belonged to Captain Thomas Mann Thompson.

The Cape Fear Pilots after the Civil War

"A terrible storm of wind and rain raged all day long."

> —*The weather at Smithville on April 13, 1877, when the pilot boats* Uriah Timmons *and* Mary K. Sprunt *were found to be missing.*[1]

*I*n the decades following the Civil War, times of traumatic change for the defeated South, the pilotage at Cape Fear remained a vital profession. Although the money earned by the pilots was now a pittance compared to the handsome rewards of guiding a blockade runner, ship captains venturing into the harbor at Cape Fear remained beholden to the masters of the shoals.[2]

Ephraim Gause Tries to Collect His Pilot's Fees

Some pilots were never paid for their final voyages by owners of the blockade runners. Collecting these debts proved impossible, as in the case of Ephraim DeVaun Gause.[3]

Ephraim, who was born in Brunswick County, North Carolina, in 1825, was the pilot of the *Helen*. This iron-hull sidewheel steamer made seven voyages from Wilmington to Bermuda, Nassau, or Halifax, Nova Scotia in 1864. Two 1866 letters from British companies in London and Halifax tell of the futility of trying to collect such debts.[4] One, sent to G. P. Oxley & Company of Liverpool by J. H. Burney & Company of London reads:

> We called at Bigbee's respecting Mr. Gauzes claim for pilotage of the "Helen" which belongs to one of the trading companies of which Mr. B was manager, of course the claim was not admitted. They remarked that the voyage was not legal, but

they said if we would leave a copy of the acct with them they would write out to Bermuda if it was right. They then would see what could be done with it, but the company was insolvent and the prospects of a dividend very remote we shall accordingly leave a copy of your accounts with them which is all that can be done at present.[5]

In the years following the war, Ephraim was among the pilots who lived on Bald Head so they could "run competition," that is, race to become the first to reach an inbound ship. In 1887 he died on the island at age sixty-one. His family lived at 410 Brunswick Street on the old Southport yacht basin, in a house that still stands. Ephraim's son Charles Eyden was twelve when his father died. Charles eventually rose to prominence in Southport business and became one of the commissioners of the pilotage at Cape Fear.[6]

The steamer *Helen*, in a contemporary painting, probably by her captain, David Leslie. She made ten successful runs through the blockade. (From a private collection)

The Perils of the Open Sea

Wartime or not, pilots always face the perils endured by those who choose to brave the ocean in small boats. When a pilot boat fails to return as expected, especially with storm winds whipping the waters of Cape Fear, families wait anxiously. Sometimes, they wait in vain.[7]

On December 13, 1872, the families of five Cape Fear pilots awaited word of their men, who had been missing at sea for two days. Two of the pilots had been blockade runners: Joseph Bensel, of the *City of Petersburg*, and Thomas Brinkman of the *Condor*. The other three, too young to have run the blockade, were John D. Trott (24), James R. Sellers (21), and Robert St. George (22). Two days before, their boat had been caught in a storm. Searches of the area by the Revenue cutter *Seward* and the tug *Alpha* of the area where it had last been seen proved fruitless.[8]

Days passed with no trace of the missing men. Hopes faded, replaced by grim acceptance that the pilots had perished. Christmas came. A few days later word reached Smithville that the wreckage of a boat which could have been the sea dory of the Cape Fear pilots had washed ashore at Tub Inlet, near Little River. The following February, two months after the accident, the body of Thomas Brinkman was found near Battery Island. No one ever found the remains of the other men.[9]

In a single accident, five Cape Fear pilots had lost their lives. Over the following years the tragedy remained on the minds of many who lived at Cape Fear, a graphic reminder of the perils of a storm-swept sea. In August of 1875 residents of Bald Head Island told stories of ghosts who appeared at midday in the halls of houses, mysterious writing on floors, and unexplained moving of furniture. Some said the drowned pilots were responsible.[10]

The Travails of Charles Gause Dosher

On April 14, 1877, Smithville families were again anxiously awaiting word of pilots missing at sea. Two pilot boats carrying a total of ten pilots had failed to return to port after a fearful storm ravaged Cape Fear. Among the distressed parents who waited on shore were Charles Gause Dosher and his wife Susan. Their son Charles Jr. was among the missing, along with the husbands of two of their daughters.[11]

Charles Gause Dosher—farmer, Cape Fear pilot, and to his grandchildren, the beloved Papa Sol—was truly a man to whom tragedy was no stranger. Charles was born in 1821 on the family plantation west of Smithville at Frazier's Neck. His father, Colonel James Dosher, a prosperous farmer, had been an officer in the state militia. His mother, Sarah Brinson Dosher, was a granddaughter of Charles Gause, one of the founders of Smithville. Colonel Dosher and his wife maintained a residence in the town where the family spent the summers. Young Charles and his brothers and sisters—he had either nine or ten siblings—led a life of privilege on the plantation.

Servants took care of their every need. There was always a slave ready to "fetch and carry" and to take them in one of the family boats three miles up the Elizabeth River to Smithville.[12]

This privileged existence ended on Saturday, August 5, 1835, when Charles was fourteen. His family set out from Smithville in the colonel's sloop. They were going on a pleasure cruise down the Elizabeth River for a picnic at "the banks." It was to be an outing which included every member of the Dosher family except Charles's older brother John. Also aboard were Reverend William Hankins, his wife and their two children. Three young women completed the party: Clarissa Potter, Harriet Hankins, the sister of the Brunswick County sheriff, and a slave girl belonging to Colonel Dosher.[13]

The sloop left her mooring in Smithville and moved across the harbor. As it neared the mouth of the Elizabeth River the wind picked up. Rain pelted the passengers, many who sat on the bench which ran along the gunnels. In this "white squall," a small, intense thunderstorm of a type which sometimes bursts upon Cape Fear on clear days, the colonel attempted to swing the jib. The sloop capsized. The hours that followed were filled with horror. Colonel Dosher, his wife, and seven of his children drowned, along with the minister, Miss Potter, and the slave girl. The survivors owed their lives, according to a contemporary account in the Wilmington newspaper, to "a young Negro man, the property of Mr. John Dozier (brother of the deceased), named Fortune."[14]

Among the survivors was Charles and two of his younger brothers. All his life Charles would be haunted by the memories of that day. He would tell his grandchildren how Fortune helped him and his brothers cling to the side of the capsized boat so long that their fingernails came off. He said that some of the victims had been attacked by alligators. He remembered seeing the baby, who was six months old, float off, momentarily buoyed by its long white dress.[15]

One of Charles's brothers who had survived the accident died shortly afterward. Charles and young Benjamin, his other surviving brother, went to live with their uncle John V. Dosher until the next year when he, too, died. Then they went to live with their brother John. Six years later Benjamin died.[16]

No one is certain what happened to Fortune. A Fortune Dosher who years later established a black Baptist Church in Brunswick County may have been the same man.[17]

In 1842 Charles bought from his older brother 1,300 acres of the Frazier's Neck plantation that John had inherited from their father. About this time Charles married a Smithville girl, Susan Dunbar Davis. They lived in a house on the Frazier's Neck plantation and had a summer home in Smithville which stood on Moore Street. During this period Charles became a Cape Fear pilot. The pilotage was to him a part-time occupation for he continued to farm the plantation on Frazier's Neck. During the Civil War, he and Susan moved to Smithville with their growing family.[18]

According to family tradition, Charles ran the blockade a single time. He operated a salt works near Smithville, probably on the plantation. Like nearly every Southern family, Charles and Susan Dosher lost a son during the war, Frederick, General Whiting's messenger boy, who was captured at Fort Fisher and died at age seventeen a few months later in Elmira Prison.[19]

Then on that bleak Saturday of April 14, 1877, they feared that they had lost another son.

The *Timmons* and the *Sprunt*

Two days before in clear weather, four Cape Fear pilot boats had put to sea—the *Henry Westerman*, the *J. H. Neff,* the *Uriah Timmons,* and the *Mary K. Sprunt.* The *Westerman* and the *Neff* returned that evening.[20]

The next day, Friday the thirteenth, "a terrible storm of wind and rain raged all day long." At six o'clock in the morning the winds picked up from the east. Before the day ended more than three inches of rain had drenched the sandy streets of Smithville. Winds gusting to seventy miles per hour knocked down telegraph lines. The Frying Pan lightship broke her anchor line. Vessels were driven ashore, along with two pilot boats. But the *Timmons* and the *Sprunt* were not among them.[21]

The *Timmons* sailed under the command of one of the most experienced of the Cape Fear blockade runners, Captain Kit Morse. With him were Joseph T. Thompson, another blockade runner, along with Julius Weeks, C. Grissom, and Joe Arnold. The five pilots were accompanied by two black sailors. The *Timmons* had been built in 1873 for Kit Morse and Julius Dosher at the Cassidey shipyard in Wilmington and was known as a fast sailer, having opposed Charleston pilot boats in Fourth of July races.[22]

The *Mary K. Sprunt,* named in honor of a daughter of Alexander Sprunt, had been launched in Smithville in February of 1876. Built by William R. Dosher, Charles's cousin, she measured fifty-five feet overall, forty-three feet at the waterline, with a sixteen-foot beam and seven-foot depth of hold. She belonged to Charles Dosher Jr. and his two brothers-in-law, Robert S. Walker and Christopher C. Pinner.[23]

Captain Dosher and his brothers-in-law had been accompanied by three other pilots. On Thursday afternoon, eighteen to twenty miles north of Frying Pan Shoals, the *Sprunt* had pulled alongside the British brigantine *Baltic* for Jim Williams to board her to bring her into the harbor. The most experienced of the five pilots remaining on the *Sprunt* was Thomas B. Grissom, age thirty-nine, who had brought the *Lilian* through the blockade. The youngest at twenty-three was Lawrence Gillespie. A steward completed the crew.[24]

When the storm struck Cape Fear, both pilot boats stood well offshore. Neither could return to port. In the days which followed, news of the missing vessels came slowly. On Saturday, townspeople standing on shore could see the pilot boat *Swift* lying on oyster rocks in the bay with her keel sprung and the pilot boat *Nellie Neff* lying in the marsh. But they heard nothing of the *Timmons* and the *Sprunt.*[25]

On Sunday the fifteenth, the steamer *Lucille* arrived from Baltimore. Her master, Captain Bennett, reported that he encountered the gale south of Hatteras and had to scud his steamer to within thirty miles of Frying Pan Shoals before he could haul her to a stop. At eleven o'clock on Saturday morning he passed the Frying Pan lightship twenty miles southeast of her station. At the same time he passed a pilot boat. Judging by her rigging and her color, he made her to be the *Timmons.* According to Captain Bennett, the boat seemed "to be lying very comfortably." As the words of the captain were repeated in the town, the families and friends of Kit Morse and the other pilots aboard the *Timmons* could afford to ease their vigil. But the fate of the *Sprunt* remained uncertain.[26]

On Monday the sixteenth, the Revenue cutter *Colfax* left to look for the missing pilot boats and other vessels that might need assistance. That same day Captain Hall of the schooner *Nellie F. Sawyer* came into port and reported that he had seen the two

top masts of a vessel protruding from the surface at a point north by northeast of the lightship. The captain thought that the vessel had sunk during the storm. The next day the *Timmons* arrived in port. At 11:30 that morning she sailed across the harbor bringing cheers from the townspeople lining the shore at Smithville. As they looked at the vessel they could see remarkably little damage. One hatch was missing. Both of her skiffs were still aboard, to the surprise of everyone, although the larger one had its bow stove in.[27]

As the exhilarated townspeople talked to Kit Morse and the other pilots about their ordeal and the fate of the *Mary K. Sprunt,* the story began to unfold. Morse said that as the storm worsened he had to take in all sails except the foresail. The waves "rolled mountain high, the winds blowing so fiercely as to sometimes flatten the sea."[28]

One account by Colonel A. M.

The granddaughter of Charles Gause Dosher, Esther Dosher Eriksen, clipped this picture from a newspaper and kept it always because she said it looked just like the *Sprunt.* The *Timmons* also probably resembled this vessel.

Waddell told of a gray mist shrouding the sea and sky, the wind shrieking as the *Timmons* rode the heaving waves. Lashed to the cockpit was Julius Weeks. Late in the morning, Weeks, dead tired after thirteen hours at the helm, saw the jib halyard part. As the rope broke, the jib fell to hang, bag-like, below the bowsprit. Water filled the sail.[29]

The *Timmons* struggled on. But the pilots knew that she could not survive long. According to Colonel Waddell's account, one exclaimed, "We are lost. Unless we can cut that jib stay we are certainly gone. A man can't live there but it is our only hope."[30]

Volunteering for this task was the only unmarried man aboard, young Joe Arnold who had relieved Julius Weeks at the wheel. He shouted: "Hold on men. You are all married and have families; I am a single man; let me try it and if I go overboard it will be all right." Joe Arnold drew his sheath knife. With the boat pitching in the driving rain, Arnold slowly crawled forward along the deck, knife clinched tightly in his teeth. He managed to reach the foremast as the *Timmons* nearly capsized. Arnold clung to the mast as the little schooner slowly righted herself. Then he resumed his efforts to reach the bowsprit.[31]

Arnold finally grasped the bowsprit, just as the *Timmons* buried her bow into the sea. Arnold disappeared beneath the seething water. Moments later, the bow rose. The crew could see Arnold straighten himself into a sitting position, the knife still clinched in his teeth. He inched forward along the pole. Again and again the *Timmons* plunged her head beneath the waves. Still Joe Arnold clung on. At last, he reached the bow stay. He took the knife, and with a powerful stroke, severed the rope. As Arnold inched back down the bowsprit, the winds continued to howl and the waves crashed over the little vessel. But the men aboard the *Timmons* knew the worst was over.[32]

As the storm raged and darkness approached, they had lost sight of the *Sprunt.* Morse said the last time he saw her was Thursday evening, when she stood considerably to leeward of his vessel. After the *Timmons* rode out the gale, Morse found that they were far south of Cape Fear and put into Georgetown. The next day they ran up the coast to Cape Fear and saw a vessel lying off the bar awaiting a pilot. After putting one of the pilots aboard, Kit brought the *Timmons* home.[33]

As people listened to the story, hopes mounted for the *Sprunt.* But then word reached Smithville that the coroner had examined the body of a black sailor that had been discovered washed up on the beach at Federal Point the day before; it turned out to be the steward from the *Sprunt*. Captain Barr of the *Colfax* turned his cutter over to two seasoned pilots, Julius Potter and Julius Dosher, who searched up and down the coast, scanning the horizons with their glasses for signs of the missing boat. They saw two wrecks, but nothing of the *Sprunt*.[34]

In the days that followed, hopes for the missing pilots faded. On April 24, a Wilmington newspaper carried a letter from the mayor of Smithville, Dr. Walter Curtis. He began by putting into words what had become evident to those who awaited news of the *Sprunt*: "There seems little doubt the pilot boat *Mary K. Sprunt* is lost with all aboard." Dr. Curtis suggested that the paper help raise money for the families. The same day that people were reading the words of Dr. Curtis, they learned that Kit Morse had discovered the wreck. Kit had been cruising in the *Timmons* about seventeen miles southwest of Bald Head light when he saw the figure head of a vessel sticking above the water. He knew it was the *Sprunt*. Morse moved the *Timmons* in for a closer look. He could see the stump of the foremast and the bowsprit. He took some of the hoops from the foremast back to Smithville and passed along the dreaded news.[35]

On April 29, sixteen days after the storm, crewmen on the *Henry Westerman* found floating nine miles at sea the body of Thomas Grissom. They lowered the skiff, took the body onboard and brought it back to Smithville. From bruises on the chest they concluded that Grissom had been at the *Sprunt's* helm, lashed to the cockpit. The remains of the other pilots on the *Mary K. Sprunt* were never found. One of the Cape Fear pilots who visited the wreck said that she lay in water so clear that he could look down and "see her white sails shining and torn into ribbons, the shreds floating gently with the motion of the sea."[36]

In May of 1879, a monument to the pilots on the *Sprunt* and those who died in the 1872 storm was erected in the Smithville Burying Ground and a moving ceremony held in their honor. The names of the ten men who lost their lives are chiseled in stone, along with the following inscription:[37]

> The Winds and the Sea Sing
> Their Requiem
> And shall
> For ever more.

(Photo by the author)

Times of Change

For the Cape Fear pilots the last two decades of the nineteenth century were times of transition. New Inlet was gone. Most of the old blockade runners retired or died while still in the service, passing on to their sons their love of the sea and, in many cases, the fine art of the pilotage. Kit Morse's son Thomas became a pilot at Cape Fear and enjoyed a long career in the profession. Joseph Thompson's son Joseph Jr. became a pilot like his father as did John Savage's son, John Jr. And the pilot roles continued to be dominated with names such as Adkins, Burriss, Newton, and St. George. The numbers of pilots, which had swelled during the Civil War as many pilots were imprisoned, remained substantial; in 1891 forty-two pilots lived in Southport.[38]

In 1881 a hurricane caused havoc with Cape Fear shipping. The pilot boats *J. A. Lavensaler* and *Mystery* went aground near Smithville. The *Uriah Timmons*, the pilot boat of C. C. Morse, collided with a ship and sank in the channel, an embarrassing episode in the career of the former blockade runner, who later was able to salvage the boat. Two years later another hurricane at Cape Fear sent more ships upon the shore. In this storm the *Timmons* was sunk again. Captain Morse and his crew made it safely home.

The families of the drowned pilots gathered at the dedication of the pilot's monument. Sarah Ann Dosher Pinner (fourth from the left) was known as "Aunt Sal" in our family; Elitesto Dosher Walker (second from the left) was known as "Aunt Ess."
(Photo courtesy of Captain Roy Daniel.)

In 1884 Archibald Gutherie, the nephew of the man who ran the blockade as the Cape Fear pilot of the *Robert E. Lee*, bought a new pilot boat in New Bedford, Massachusetts, with fellow pilot Jim Williams. On the way home it developed an irreparable leak off the Virginia coast and foundered. The two pilots and their three-man crew had to be rescued.[39]

In these transitory times even the pilots' town had changed its name. In 1887 the town of Smithville, nearly a century after it was chartered in 1792, was renamed Southport.[40]

As young men took over the traditions of the pilotage at Cape Fear, many new pilot boats entered service. Some were new versions of the traditional fast sailing vessels, schooner-rigged clippers such as the *Mary K. Sprunt.*[41]

In 1884 Captains J. J. Adkins, J. L. Pinner, L. J. Pepper, and J. N. Burriss had built in Wilmington a new vessel named for the late wife of Captain Adkins, the *Addie*. At eighty-two feet in length with a nineteen-foot beam, she was one of the biggest of the new Cape Fear pilot boats. In 1887 Kit Morse sold the *Timmons* and bought a new, smaller and faster boat, the *Excelsior*. That same year Captain William St. George took the *Louise F. Harper*, his new boat built in Beaufort, North Carolina, on the run from Southport to Wilmington in two and one-half hours, the swiftest time on record. In 1890 Captains Kit Morse, Thomas Gray Burriss, Joe Arnold, Cornelius Piver, and Warren Mintz bought for use as a pilot boat a sixty-three-ton yacht with a reputation as a fast sailer, the *John D. Long* of Gloucester, Massachusetts.[42]

But the days of the little schooners that had graced the river for decades were numbered. Captain J. J. Adkins became the first defector to the powerboat ranks. In

This house on Lord Street in Southport was built by Captain Richard Dosher, pilot of the *Old Dominion*. (Photo by the author.)

1890 he bought to use as a pilot boat a twenty-five-foot launch powered by a four horsepower naphtha-fueled engine. Four years later the pilots' association converted from sails to steam. For $26,000 they purchased the steam tugs *Jones* and *Blanche*. Captain Adkins, president of the pilots association, took command of the *Jones* and Captain Dunn Burriss commanded the *Blanche*. Wilmington became the third port on the east and gulf coasts to convert its pilot boats to steam.[43]

But even as the pilots were moving toward the twentieth century with an eye to the future, the age-old value of the pilotage at Cape Fear remained undiminished. In October of 1894, the master of the Norwegian bark *Orig*, bound for Wilmington from Barbados, attempted to come into the harbor without a pilot. His vessel struck the Middle Ground. Despite efforts of the crew to free her from the shoal, she became a total loss.[44]

Despite the grounding of the Norwegian vessel, the conditions at the Western Bar had improved since the closing of New Inlet. In 1895 W. T. Sellers, J. R. Newton, and J. J. Thompson made a series of careful soundings at the bar and found the average depth to be sixteen feet at mean low water. The three pilots reported that the bar was in the best condition in years, the course being direct, favoring vessels of deep draft.[45]

In 1902 the writer of an article in a magazine about pilots attempted to capture the romance of the nineteenth-century pilotage. He wrote:

> The pilots were the dandies of the river towns. They wore fine ruffled shirts, tight fitting boots, long black coats and plug hats. Every river boy hoped some day to become a pilot. Even the young planters and merchants emulated their costumes and the belles of the river cities set their caps for them. The pilots were the great matrimonial catches of the territory. When the inhabitants of the country for miles round a landing place would travel to the rivers on Sunday to see the steamboat, the pilot, conscious of the important position according him in society by the backwoods people, would swagger up and down the hurricane deck, a glorious figure, hat tilted, smoking a great cigar and fitting his fingers into his magenta kid gloves.[46]

The Pilots of Today

The pilots of today are members of the Wilmington-Cape Fear Pilot's Association. Chartered in 1921, this organization is still governed by the Board of Commissioners of Navigation of the Cape Fear River, its five members appointed by the governor.[47]

About the time the pilot association was being established, Southport leaders were working to have the town established as the state port for North Carolina. They envisioned new state-owned shipping terminals springing up on the waterfront along with a host of new jobs. This effort finally failed, but not before the local weekly newspaper was named *The State Port Pilot*, a name which remains to this day.[48]

BOARD OF COMMISSIONERS
— OF —
NAVIGATION AND PILOTAGE

For the Cape Fear River and Bars

L. BROWN McKOY, Clerk.

COMMISSIONERS: { JAMES SPRUNT, Chairman
J. W. HARPER Vice-Chairman
H. G. SMALLBONES,
RICHARD DOSHER,
WILLIAM ST. GEORGE.

Wilmington, North Carolina 30 December 1920

Messrs. C.C.Chadbourn & Thomas F.Wood,

Committee on Information and Grievances of the Board of Commissioners

     of Navigation and Pilotage

Wilmington, North Carolina

Dear Sirs:-

     In reply to your inquiry asking if the Board of Commissioners
of Navigation and Pilotage have established a regulation requiring all
Cape Fear pilots to speak and board vessels approaching the Port of
Wilmington from a regularly licensed and numbered pilot boat, and not
from any other means or craft, I reply that such is the case and has been So
for a number of years past.

     I have not a copy of the regulation nor do I remember the date
of its adoption but it has been in force for a number of years past.

               Yours very truly,

              James Sprunt Chairman of the

              Board of Commissioners of

              Navigation and Pilotage.

Certified to and subscribed before me this
30th day of December 1920.

              Notary Public.

James Sprunt served as a commissioner of the pilotage well into the twentieth century. (Courtesy of Duke University Special Collections Library.)

When I was growing up in Southport in the 1950s, there were seven licensed pilots at Cape Fear. Six lived in Southport. I used to pump gas in their cars at my father's Esso station. I especially remember from those days Bertrum (Piggy) Burriss. He was always a pleasant and friendly man. But he had this idea that the best gas for his car was a mixture of regular and Esso Extra. So whenever he came to the station, we had to add five gallons of one type, then five gallons of the other to his tank. At my father's station customers always got prompt service with a smile: "fill the tank, check the oil and water and get the windshield, thank you sir, come back and see us." In Piggy's case, however, there was usually a little hesitation before one of us would arrive to pump his gas.

The president of the pilot's association then was Fred Willing. Harold St. George kept the records. The other Southport pilots were Robert (Toby) Thompson, John G. (Nuntie) Swan and William Styron. The seventh pilot, Jim Loughlin, lived at Harbor Island near Wrightsville Beach.[49]

Captain Thompson, who played first base on the town baseball team, was a fine athlete. His athletic abilities also served him well at sea. Thompson once had an accident boarding a ship which nearly cost him his life. One freezing cold morning he went to meet an inbound tanker and reached for the Jacob's ladder to climb aboard:

> A sea hit that ladder and knocked it away from me. It just went back toward the stern of the ship and left me hanging in space. I hooked my right arm, and by that time I was turned around facing the stern of the ship. The pilot boat was just a short distance away and saw I was in trouble, and they came back in to give me a hand. And I managed to throw my left leg aboard, but I couldn't get the right one out and she came in and caught me. [Doctors told Robert that he may never walk again. But a few months later he was back playing first base on the town team.][50]

A Battle Over a Battleship

During this period the pilots got involved with an issue that caused some dissension in the group. It concerned the battleship USS *North Carolina*, which the state had acquired as a war memorial. This ship, which is 728 feet long with a beam of 105 feet, drew nearly 29 feet of water. Because of her immense size, some of the pilots believed that she could not be taken safely up the river to her new mooring across from Wilmington. Some of the men argued bitterly. Piggy Burriss appeared on a Wilmington television station to explain his views.[51]

When the day finally arrived, Piggy took the battleship slowly to Wilmington. She did make it without running aground. But not before claiming her last victim, a floating restaurant named Fergus' Ark moored on the Wilmington side of the river, which her stern struck as tugs were moving her into her new berth. (The owner had refused to follow the pilot's advice to move his restaurant to provide room for the battleship to be maneuvered.)[52]

Most of the Cape Fear pilots of my youth were descendants of the pilots who ran the blockade during the Civil War. Both of Robert Thompson's grandfathers ran the blockade, as did his great-uncle Thomas Mann Thompson, who piloted nine different blockade runners into and out of the harbor. Piggy Burriss's grandfather and

The Southport waterfront in 1998. (Photo by the author.)

great-uncles ran the blockade. John Swan's grandfather Henry Swan, who came from Norway, ran the blockade as master of several blockade runners, including the little *Spunkie*. John's father was Captain Charlie Swan, long-time keeper of the new lighthouse at Bald Head.[53]

During most of its history the pilotage at Cape Fear has been a family affair. During the nineteenth century its roles were filled with fathers and sons, with brothers and uncles. During the Civil War era numerous members of the Burriss, Craig, Grissom, and Newton families were pilots, along with three or more men of the St. George, Davis, Dosher, and Thompson families. But eventually, two families so dominated the association that policies were established to prevent nepotism. Today, the son of a pilot rarely becomes one.[54]

The pilots of my youth displayed a quiet assurance born of well-honed skills and a mastery of the local waters, as do the local pilots of today. In 1998, the pilots of Cape Fear, the men who carry forth the legacy of the blockade runners of the Civil War, numbered ten:[55]

Captain Scott D. Aldridge
Captain Thomas L. Brendle
Captain Roy C. Daniel
Captain Davis C. Heering
Captain Carl W. Kirby

Captain Wayne W. "Rabbit" Ludlum
Captain Stephen M. Phillips
Captain Jackie W. Potter
Captain Robert E. "Buck" Smith
Captain Basil R. Watts

Captain Robert B. Thompson with his great grandson, Robert Downs, age two. Captain Thompson's grandfather ran the blockade, as did his great uncle, Thomas Mann Thompson. Robert became a Cape Fear pilot in 1932 and served in the pilotage for forty-one years. He built this skiff for his great grandson—lovingly crafting it from juniper and fitting it with stainless steel hardware so it would last a century—so the boy would have his own boat at an early age; Robert himself got his first skiff at age six. The Cape Fear pilots of today rarely pass directly to their sons and grandsons the art and mystery of the pilotage, as they did during the nineteenth century. But they still pass along a most enduring legacy, the love of the coastal waters of Cape Fear. (Photo courtesy of Captain Robert Thompson)

Appendix

The Cape Fear Pilots, 1861–1865

THE FOLLOWING LIST shows licensed Cape Fear pilots during the Civil War years. The second column indicates whether they were licensed as bar pilots (B) or river pilots (R). The third column shows where they lived: S = Smithville; FP = Federal Point; M = Masonboro Sound north of Fort Fisher; and B = Bald Head Island. Where records indicate that the pilots ran the blockade, their names appear in boldface and the steamers they piloted are listed, along with the number of attempts each vessel made and the number of its successes, and also the fate of the vessel. In some cases a vessel had other pilots besides those listed.

Notes at the end of the list identify sources on which the information is based. The principal sources are (1) pilot license records and (2) the writings of James Sprunt. The numbers of attempts and successes by the various vessels in running the blockade and their ultimate fates are taken from Stephen Wise's *Lifeline of the Confederacy* (3).

Pilot	B/R	Res.	Steamer	Attempts	Successes	Fate of Steamer [3]	Notes
Adkins, James N.	R	FP	*Ella and Annie (William G. Hewes)*	12	9	Captured near Cape Fear, 11/9/63.	1, 2
Anderson, John William	B, R	FP, S	*Mary Celestia*	8	8	Sank near Bermuda after striking rock 9/26/64.	1, 2
Bell, James			*Talisman*	6	5	Sunk in gale, 12/29/64.	2, 4
Bensel, Joseph W	R	S	*City of Petersburg*	16	16	Survived the war.	1, 2
Bowen, George F.	B	FP	USS *Keystone State*	-	-		1, 5
Brinkman, Thomas Washington	B	S	*Condor*	1	0	Ran aground near Fort Fisher, 10/1/64.	1, 2
			Blenheim	5	4	Captured in New Inlet, 1/25/65.	6
Burns, C. T.	B, R	FP					1
Burriss, Christopher William	B, R	FP, S					1
Burriss, Edward T. (Ned)	R	FP	*Wando (Let Her Rip)*	4	3	Captured off Cape Romain, 10/21/64.	1, 2

Pilot	B/R	Res.	Steamer	Attempts	Successes	Fate of Steamer[3]	Notes
Burriss, Edward T. (Ned)	R	FP	CSS *Tallahassee*	-	-	-	7
Burriss, George Washington	B	FP	*Hebe*	3	2	Destroyed trying to enter New Inlet, 8/18/63.	1, 2
Burriss, James Thomas Jr.	B, R	FP, M	vessel unknown				1, 8
Burriss, John Henry	R	FP					1
Burriss, John W.	B	FP					1
Burriss, Joseph Newton			*Hansa*	21	20	Survived the war.	2, 4
Burriss, Sylvester, Jr.[19]			*Beatrice*	3	2	Destroyed at Charleston, 11/29/64.	4, 6
Burriss, Thomas Edward	B	FP	*Let Her Be (Chicora)*	14	14	Survived the war.	1, 2
			Banshee I	15	14	Captured 11/21/63 near Cape Fear.	2, 9
Burriss, Thomas Edward	B	FP	*Owl*	7	4	Survived the war.	6, 20
Burriss, Thomas Gray	R	FP	Unknown				1, 10, 20
Clemmons, J. W.	R	FP					1
Craig, Charles W.	B, R	FP, M	*Margaret and Jessie*	20	18	Captured trying to enter New Inlet, 11/5/63.	1, 2
Craig, James N.	R	FP					1
Craig, James William (Jim Billy)	R	FP	*Annie*	14	13	Captured at New Inlet, 11/1/64.	1, 2

Pilot	B/R	Res.	Steamer	Attempts	Successes	Fate of Steamer[3]	Notes
Craig, James William (Jim Billy)	R	FP	*Don*	12	10	Captured off Beaufort, NC, 3/4/64.	2
			Gibraltar	2	2	Survived the war.	2
			Lilian	6	5	Captured off Wilmington, 8/24/64.	2
			Lynx	10	9	Destroyed at New Inlet, 9/25/64.	2
			Orion (Fannie)	20	20	Survived the war.	2
Craig, Jessie Sr.	R	FP					1
Craig, Jessie Jr.	B	FP					1
Craig, Joseph	B	FP					1
Craig, Thomas W·	B	FP	*Pet*	17	16	Captured 2/16/64 off Lockwood's Folly Inlet.	1, 2
Craig, W. T.	R	FP					1
Daniel, Edward F.	B	FP					1
Daniels, E. T.			*Coquette*	14	13	Survived the war.	2, 4
Davis, John	B	S					1
Davis, Joseph	B	S					1
Davis, Samuel B.	B	S					1
Dosher, Charles Gause	B	S	vessel unknown				1, 10
Dosher, Julius	B	S	*North Heath*	5	5	Damaged entering Wilmington 10/64, sunk as obstruction 1/65.	1, 2

Pilot	B/R	Res.	Steamer	Attempts	Successes	Fate of Steamer[3]	Notes
Dosher, Richard	B	S	*Old Dominion*	6	6	Survived the war.	1, 2
			Susan Bierne	1	0	Survived the war.	2
Dyer, Thomas K.	B	FP	*Giraffe (R. E. Lee)*	15	14	Captured 11/9/63 while heading to Wilmington.	1, 2, 11
Dyer, Thomas K.	B	FP	*Antonica (Herald)*	25	24	Destroyed at Old inlet, 12/19/63.	12
			Georgiana McCaw	1	0	Destroyed off Western Bar, 6/2/64.	2, 11
			Agnes E. Fry	6	4	Ran aground off Caswell Beach, 12/27/64.	19
Furpless, William S.	B	S					1
Galloway, J. W.		S					1
Ganor, E. D.	R						1
Garrason, Thomas B.	R	S	*Owl*	7	4	Survived the war.	1, 2
Gause, Ephraim DeVaun	R	S, B	*Helen*	10	10	Survived the war.	1, 2, 13
Grissom, Edgar A.	R	S					1
Grissom, Robert S.	R	S	*Little Hattie*	12	10	Survived the war.	1, 2
Grissom, Simon S.	R	S					1
Grissom, Thomas B.	B, R	FP, S	*Lilian*	6	5	Captured leaving Cape Fear, 8/24/64.	1, 2
Grissom, William J.	R	FP, S	*Vulture*	2	2	Survived the war.	1, 6
Gutherie, Archibald M.	R	B	*Robert E. Lee*	15	14	Captured 11/9/63.	1, 2

Pilot	B/R	Res.	Steamer	Attempts	Successes	Fate of Steamer[3]	Notes
Gutherie, James	R	S					1
Hill, John	R	FP, B	*Siren*	2	0	Captured off Beaufort, NC 6/5/64.	1, 2
			Banshee I	15	14	Captured 11/21/63 entering Cape Fear. (I)	2
			Banshee II	8	8	Survived the war. (II)	6
Howard, Henry	B	FP	*Orion (Fannie)*	20	20	Survived the war.	1, 2
Johnson, William	R	FP, B					1
Kent, Thomas			*Antonica (Herald)*	25	24	Ran aground and destroyed at Old Inlet, 12/19/63.	4, 19
Lockwood, Thomas			unknown				4, 19
Marshall, John			unknown				4,19
McKeithan, George			*Rothesay Castle*	5	4	Survived the war.	4, 19
McKensey, John			unknown				4, 19
Morse, Christopher Columbus (Kit)	B	S	*Advance (Lord Clyde)*	18	17	Captured leaving Cape Fear, 9/10/64.	1, 2,
			Cornubia (Lady Davis)	19	18	Captured 11/8/63 while entering Cape Fear.	2, 14
			Kate	20	20	Sunk at Cape Fear 11/18/62 after hitting obstruction.	2
Morse, Francis	R	S					1
Neill, John W.	R						1
Newton, James L.	B	FP					1
Newton, John L.	B	FP					1

Pilot	B/R	Res.	Steamer	Attempts	Successes	Fate of Steamer[3]	Notes
Newton, Joseph Henry	B	FP	vessel unknown				1, 10
Newton, Sterling F.	B	FP					1
Newton, Thomas W.	B	FP	*Eugenia, II*	10	10	Damaged coming into Cape Fear, 9/7/63.	1, 2
			Wild Rover	9	8	Survived the war.	6
Newton, William S.	B	FP					1
Pepper, Lewis	B	FP, M					1
Piver, Elijah	B	FP					1
Platt, Samuel							4, 20
Potter, William Julius	B, R	S	*Arabian*	4	3	Ran aground leaving New Inlet, 9/15/63.	1, 12, 15
			General Beauregard (Havelock)	17	16	Destroyed north of Fort Fisher, 12/11/63.	2
			Edith	19	19	Destroyed 2/25/65 at Indian Wells, NC.	12
Price, Jacob Aker Smith	R	S	*Virginia I*	7	6	Survived the war.	1, 6
Price, John	B	S					1
Savage, John R.	B, R	S	*Ella II*	6	4	Destroyed 12/1/64 while trying to enter Old Inlet.	1, 2
Sellers, Robert Augustus			*Venus*	7	6	Destroyed near New Inlet, 10/21/63.	2, 4
Sellers, William Raymond	R	S	*Advance*	18	17		1, 16

Pilot	B/R	Res.	Steamer	Attempts	Successes	Fate of Steamer[3]	Notes
Sellers, William Thomas	B	S					1, 18
Smith, C. G.			*Calypso*	7	6	Captured 6/11/63 while trying to enter Old Inlet.	2, 4
			Margaret and Jessie	20	18	Captured while trying to enter New Inlet, 11/5/63.	2
Springs, Joseph	R	FP	*Alice* (*Sirius*)	24	24	Survived the war.	1, 2
St. George, William	B	FP	*Don*	12	10	Captured off Beaufort, NC, 3/4/64.	1, 2
Swan, Henry G.		S	vessel unknown				4, 10
Thompson, Joseph T.	B	S	*Index* or *Thistle II*				1, 2
Thompson, J. W.	R						1
Thompson, Thomas Mann Jr.	B	S	*Armstrong*	6	5	Captured leaving Cape Fear, 12/4/64.	1, 2, 17
			Atalanta	10	8	Survived the war.	17
			Coquette	14	13	Survived the war.	17
			Elizabeth (*Atlantic*)	8	7	Ran aground off Cape Fear, 9/26/63.	17
			Emma II	8	7	Captured leaving Cape Fear, 7/26/63.	17
			Flora II	10	9	Lost at sea on 1/1/64 on way to Halifax, Nova Scotia' for repairs.	17
			Index	8	8	Survived the war.	17
			Let Her Be (*Chicora*)	14	14	Survived the war.	17
			Thistle II	3	2	Captured heading for Cape Fear, 6/4/64.	17

Pilot	B/R	Res.	Steamer	Attempts	Successes	Fate of Steamer[3]	Notes
Walker, George B.	B	FP					1
Wescott, John L.	R	S					1

Notes for Appendix

1. License records of the North Carolina Board of Commissioners of Navigation & Pilotage for Cape Fear River and Bar.
2. James Sprunt, *Chronicles of the Cape Fear River* and other books.
3. Stephen Wise, *Lifeline of the Confederacy.*
4. Not on licensed pilot list.
5. Report of Rear Admiral S. P. Lee.
6. Official diary of Colonel William Lamb.
7. Tallahassee officer list, August 6, 1864.
8. Bill Reaves, *Southport (Smithville): A Chronology,* Vol. I.
9. Thomas Taylor, *Running the Blockade.*
10. List of Smithville pilots who ran the blockade, compiled by Esther Dosher Eriksen based on those she personally remembered or had heard of.
11. John Wilkinson, *The Narrative of a Blockade Runner.*
12. William J. Potter, unpublished account of his experiences as a Cape Fear pilot.
13. J. H. Burney & Company, 1866 letter; G. P. Oxley & Company ,1866 letter.
14. Pay receipt for pilotage of the *Cornubia.*
15. James Sprunt lists pilot as J. W. Potter, when other sources indicate W. J. Potter.
16. Pay receipt for river pilotage of the *Advance.*
17. Letter from Thomas Mann Thompson to his daughter Lily, dated November 24, 1896.
18. Obituary of W. T. Sellers, 1905.
19. Marcus W. Price, "Masters and Pilots Who Tested The Blockade of Confederate Ports, 1861 - 1865."
20. Register of prisoners captured on blockade runners. The list of those captured on the *Deer* included three Wilmington pilots: Samuel Platt, E. Grissom, and Thomas Burress. Samuel Platt does not appear on the list of licensed pilots. E. Grissom was probably Egar A, Grissom. Whether the Thomas Burress was Thomas Edward Burriss or Thomas Gray Burriss is uncertain.

Notes

Prologue

1. James Ryder Randall, letter to his fiancee (and later wife) Kate, dated June 3, 1864.
2. United States census, Brunswick County, NC, 1860; Susan S. Carson, *Joshua's Dream: A Town With Two Names*, (Southport, NC, 1992), pp. 41-51, hereinafter cited as Carson, *Joshua's Dream*; Walter Gilmer Curtis, *Reminiscences of Wilmington and Smithville-Southport 1848-1900* (Southport, NC, 1900), hereinafter cited as Curtis, *Reminiscences*. Dr. Curtis was a physician who served as quarantine medical officer and as mayor of Smithville in the late 1870s. His *Reminiscences* serves as the best firsthand account of life in Smithville (Southport) during the latter half of the nineteenth century.
3. Curtis, *Reminiscences*, p. 6; Bill Reaves, *Southport (Smithville) A Chronology, Vol. I (1520-1887)* (Wilmington, 1978), hereinafter cited as Reaves, *Southport Chronology*. Bill Reaves, a local historian from Wilmington, compiled his chronologies of Southport (three volumes) based mainly on accounts in North Carolina newspapers. Also cited as Reaves, *Southport Chronology* is Mr. Reaves's *Southport (Smithville) A Chronology, Vol. II (1887-1920)*, Southport, NC: The Southport Historical Society, 1990.
4. Curtis, *Reminiscences*, p. 4.
5. Carson, *Joshua's Dream*, p. 39; Curtis, *Reminiscences*, p. 8; Emma Martin Maffitt, *The Life and Services of John Newland Maffitt* (New York,1906), pp. 85-95, hereinafter cited as Maffitt, *Life and Services*; Hamilton Corchran, *Blockade Runners of the Confederacy* (New York, 1958), p. 239, hereinafter cited as Corchran, *Blockade Runners*.
6. Carson, *Joshua's Dream*, p. 47; Curtis, *Reminiscences*, pp. 30-31.
7. United States census, New Hanover County, NC, 1850, 1860; James Henry Burriss III, *Burrows-Burriss-Newton and Allied families in VA and NC, Federal Point* (Wilmington,1980), hereinafter cited as Burriss, James, *Genealogy*.
8. M. P. Usina, *Blockade Running in Confederate Times* (Savannah, 1895) hereinafter cited as Usina, *Blockade Running in Confederate Times*, p. 29.
9. James Sprunt, *Chronicles of the Cape Fear River, 1660-1916* (Raleigh, 1916), pp. 395-396, hereinafter cited as Sprunt, *Chronicles*.

Chapter 1: The Art and Mystery of the Pilotage

1. "A Relation of a Voyage on the Coast of the Province of Carolina, 1666, by Robert Sandford," in Alexander Salley Jr., *Narratives of Early Carolina* (New York: Barnes & Noble, Inc., 1953), p. 83, hereinafter cited as Salley, *Narratives of Early Carolina*.
2. Carson, *Joshua's Dream*, p. 26; Burriss, James, *Genealogy*; Reaves, *Southport Chronology*, vol. I, p. 8.
3. Sprunt, *Chronicles*. Various charts of Cape Fear, such as the Preliminary Chart of Lower

Part of Cape Fear River, by Jenkins and Maffitt (1855), pp. 395-396, show the bars.

4. "A Brief Description of the Providence of Carolina on the Coasts of Floreda, and more perticularly of a New Plantation begun by the English at Cape Feare on the river now by them called Charles-River, the 29th of May, 1664 ," in Salley, *Narratives of Early Carolina*, pp. 67-68.

5. Claude V. Jackson III, *The Cape Fear - Northeast Cape Fear Rivers Comprehensive Study, A Maritime History and Survey of the Cape Fear and Northeast Cape Fear Rivers, Wilmington Harbor, North Carolina* (Kure Beach, NC, 1966), hereinafter cited as Jackson, *Cape Fear River*, offers perhaps the best technical description of the Cape Fear River and its harbor. This two-volume work contains numerous drawings, including those showing locations of all known shipwrecks at Cape Fear.

6. Reaves, *Southport Chronology*, vol. I, pp. 1-2; Salley, *Narratives of Early Carolina*, p. 78; Johnson, Charles, *A General History of the Robberies and Murders of the Most Notorious Pirates From Their First Rise and Settlement in the Island of Providence to the Present Year (1724)* (New York, 1927). [Daniel Defoe, *A General History of the Pyrates*, edited by Manuel Schonhorn, University of South Carolina Press (Columbia, 1972), pp. 101-102.]

7. Lawrence Lee, *The History of Brunswick County, North Carolina* (Charlotte, 1980), pp. 33, 45-46, hereinafter cited as Lee, *History of Brunswick County*.

8. Janet Schaw, *Journal of a Lady of Quality: Being the Narrative of a Journey from Scotland to the West Indies, North Carolina and Portugal, in the Years 1774 to 1776* (New Haven, 1923), pp. 144-215, hereinafter cited as Schaw, *Journal*.

9. Lee, *History of Brunswick County*, pp. 41-42, 55.

10. Schaw, *Journal*, p. 141.

11. Ibid., p. 141.

12. Ibid., p. 141.

13. Walter Clark, ed., *The State Records of North Carolina* (Goldsboro, 1905), pp. 586-592, hereinafter cited as Clark, *State Records*, which includes the 1784 law entitled "An Act for Regulating the Pilotage and facilitating the Navigation of Cape Fear River." Bill McDonald's February 12, 1974 article in The [Wilmington, NC] *Bulletin*, based primarily on interviews with Southport pilot Buck Smith, describes taking a ship up the river.

14. Author's 1997 interview with Captain Robert B. Thompson of Southport, who served as a Cape Fear pilot from 1932 to 1973.

15. Howard I. Chapelle, *American Sailing Craft* (Camden, Maine, 1975), pp. 187-232. The Cape Fear pilot boat lost with all hands in 1872, as described in the Epilogue, was a sea dory. The best descriptions of pilot schooners appear in the books of Howard Chapelle, especially *American Sailing Craft*.

16. Clark, *State Records*, pp. 586-592; North Carolina Board of Commissioners of Navigation & Pilotage for Cape Fear River and Bar, Pilot licensing records, 1861-1865, (located in the Manuscript Department, William R. Perkins Library, Duke University), hereinafter cited as N. C. pilot licensing records.

17. William L. Saunders, ed., *The Colonial Records of North Carolina* (Raleigh, 1890); Clark, *State Records*, pp. 586-592.

18. Clark, *State Records*, pp. 586-592.

19. Ibid., pp. 851-852.

20. Reaves, *Southport Chronology,* vol. I, p. 10.
21. Ibid., p. 15.
22. Ibid., p. 16.
23. N. C. pilot licensing records; J. Thomas Scharf, *History of the Confederate States Navy,* (New York, 1887), p. 481, hereinafter cited as Scharf, *History of the Confederate States Navy.* Colonel Scharf said pilots earned up to $3000; Marcus W. Price, "Ships That Tested the Blockade of the Carolina Ports, 1861-1865," *The American Neptune,* Vol. VIII. No. 3, July 1948, p. 213, hereinafter cited as Price, *Ships That Tested the Blockade.* Price quoted pilot rates up to 750 £; James Sprunt, *American Historical Society Papers,* Vol. XXIV (Richmond,1896), p. 160. James Sprunt said pilots earned as much as $5000. A CSA pay receipt made out to C. C. Morse on May 15, 1863 (in possession of the author) indicated $3000 for his pilotage of the *Cornubia.* Julius Potter said that he was paid $5000 for one voyage as pilot of the *General Beauregard.* (William Julius Potter, unpublished account of his experiences in piloting the *General Beauregard,* Sprunt papers, William R. Perkins Library, Duke University, Durham, NC, hereinafter referred to as Potter, *General Beauregard.*) The Potter account consists of a 30-page typescript. Due to its rambling nature, citing page numbers would not be meaningful.
24. N. C. pilot licensing records; Sprunt, *Chronicles,* pp. 404-405.
25. Confederate muster roll of the CSS *Caswell* (National Archives, Confederate Muster Rolls of Ships and Stations). The pilot of the vessel was Jacob A. S. Price. The other pilots in the crew were James N. Adkins, John W. Anderson, James Bell, Thomas K. Dyer, Thomas Garrason, and John L. Wescott. The *Caswell* was a wooden side-wheel steamer used by the Confederates as a tender in 1861 and 1862. (Jackson, *Cape Fear River,* vol. I, p. 277.)
26. Sprunt, *Chronicles,* pp. 395-396; Scharf, *History of the Confederate States Navy,* p. 465.
27. The [Wilmington, N. C.] *Daily Journal,* September 16, 1864.
28. Fort Fisher Logbook (1864) in North Carolina State Archives.
29. *ORN,* ser. I., vol. VIII, pp 402-403.
30. Ibid., ser. I., vol. VIII, p. 403.
31. Ibid., ser. I, vol. VII, p. 403-404.
32. *ORN,* Official Diary of Colonel William Lamb, ser. I, vol. XI, pp. 741-744.
33. Augustus C. Hobart-Hampden, (Captain Roberts), *Never Caught* (London, 1867), hereinafter cited as Hobart-Hampden, *Never Caught;* J. Wilkinson, *Narrative of a Blockade Runner* (New York, 1877), hereinafter cited as Wilkinson, *Narrative;* Sprunt, *Chronicles.*
34. Sprunt, *Chronicles,* p. 395; James Sprunt, *Derelicts* (Wilmington, 1920), hereinafter cited as Sprunt, *Derelicts;* James Sprunt, *Tales and Traditions of the Lower Cape Fear, 1661-1898* (Wilmington, 1898), hereinafter cited as Sprunt, *Tales and Traditions;* James Sprunt, "What Ship is That? Tales of the Cape Fear Blockade," articles in the *Southport Leader* (Southport,1894), hereinafter cited as Sprunt, *Southport Leader.* Sprunt also wrote the section on blockade running in Clark, *Regimental History.* A list of pilots of blockade runners also appears in Marcus W. Price, "Masters and Pilots Who Tested the Blockade of the Confederate Ports, 1861-1865," *The American Neptune* Vol. XV (April 1961), pp 81-106, hereinafter cited as Price, "Masters and Pilots." But Price's pilots list originated from Sprunt's writings, with a few exceptions.
35. Sprunt, *Chronicles,* p. 395.

Chapter 2: The Blockade at Cape Fear

1. James Russel Soley, *The Blockade and the Cruisers*, the Blue and Gray Press (No date given; first published in 1883 by Scribner), p. 27.
2. James M. McPherson, *The American Heritage New History of the Civil War* (New York, 1996), pp. 47-53, 581-584, hereinafter cited as McPherson, *New History of the Civil War;* Bruce Catton, *Reflections on the Civil War* (New York, 1994), p. 3, hereinafter cited as Catton, *Reflections.*
3. McPherson, *New History of the Civil War*, pp. 1-42; Catton, *Reflections*, p. 4.
4. Catton, *Reflections*, pp. 3, xvi.
5. Stephen R. Wise, *Lifeline of the Confederacy, Blockade Running During the Civil War* (Columbia, SC, 1988), pp. 24-25, hereinafter cited as Wise, *Lifeline*. Dr. Wise's exhaustively researched book, based on his Ph.D. thesis at the University of South Carolina, is the definitive work on blockade running during the American Civil War.
6. Howard P. Nash, *A Naval History of the Civil War* (New York, 1972), p. 82.
7. Wise, *Lifeline*, p. 25; Robert M. Browning Jr., *From Cape Charles to Cape Fear, the North Atlantic Blockading Squadron During the Civil War* (Tuscaloosa, 1993), pp. 1-5, hereinafter cited as Browning, *North Atlantic Blockading Squadron;* Chris E. Fonvielle Jr., *The Wilmington Campaign: Last Rays of Departing Hope* (Campbell, CA, 1997), pp. 5-7, hereinafter cited as Fonvielle, *Wilmington Campaign*. Dr. Fonvielle's exhaustively researched study is the definitive work on the Union efforts to capture the port of Wilmington.
8. Wise, *Lifeline*, pp. 12-13, 25-26; Browning, *North Atlantic Blockading Squadron*, pp. 1-7; Fonvielle, *Wilmington Campaign*, pp. 5-9.
9. Quoted in Kenneth A. Whittle, "Blockade of the Coast of the Carolinas," *The American Philatelist* (July 1982).
10. Wise, *Lifeline*, p. 11.
11. A broadside with the queen's proclamation can be found in the Peery Southern Maritime Collection of the South Carolina Historical Society.
12. Wise, *Lifeline*, pp. 12-13, 24-25; Browning, *North Atlantic Blockading Squadron*, p.4.
13. Wise, *Lifeline*, p. 25.
14. Wise, *Lifeline*, p. 25; Browning, *North Atlantic Blockading Squadron*, p.22; Fonvielle, *Wilmington Campaign*, p. 17. Dr. Fonvielle notes the the USS *Roanoke* took up station on July 12, 1861, and that the USS *Daylight* relieved her the following day. Stephen Wise (*Lifeline*, p. 25) said the *Daylight* became the first blockader at Cape Fear on July 21, 1861. The *Daylight's* log (*ORN* ser. I, vol. V, pp. 691-692) indicates that she was on station by July 17, 1861, when she fired a howitzer at a steamer heading in Old Inlet past Fort Caswell (and missed). Four days later, an officer and crewman from the *Daylight* took the ship's whaleboat with a flag of truce and delivered documents about the blockade to Confederates on shore. The *Daylight's* initial duty at Cape Fear turned out to be short-lived. On July 24, 1861, she developed mechanical problems, abandoned the blockade and limped to Hampton Roads. The USS *Penguin* replaced her in the blockade at Cape Fear. (*ORN*, ser. I, vol. V, p. 43.)
15. Wise, *Lifeline*, pp. 25, 128-132; Browning, *North Atlantic Blockading Squadron*, pp. 225, 232-236.
16. Clark, *Regimental History*, vol. V, p. 351.

17. Browning, *North Atlantic Blockading Squadron*, pp. 194-198; Fonvielle, *Wilmington Campaign*, pp. 93-94.

18. Wise, *Lifeline*, pp. 139-140; Browning, *North Atlantic Blockading Squadron*, pp. 235, 245; Navy, *Ship Dictionary*, vol. VII, p. 562.

19. Browning, *North Atlantic Blockading Squadron*, p. 209.

20. Scharf, *History of the Confederate States Navy*, p. 476.

21. Browning, *North Atlantic Blockading Squadron*, pp. 205, 216.

22. *ORN,* ser. I, vol. X, p. 443, ser. I, vol. X, p. 443. In the fall of 1861, several Cape Fear pilots were lured aboard blockaders, according to the Wilmington *Daily Journal.* The newspaper reported on September 25, 1861, that pilots had been lured out and held on board "Licolnite craft." Two days later the paper reported that the pilots captured were George Bowen and J. J. Puckett. The November 16, 1861, issue of the *Daily Journal* quoted a *New York Herald* report which listed four men from Wilmington among Confederate prisoners being moved from Fort Lafayette to Fort Warren: Robert S. Grissom, John L. Newton, Sterling F. Newton, and William St. George, all Cape Fear pilots. In regard to the pilots lured on board the blockaders, the *Journal* writer allowed that ". . . although not educated men, they are generally intelligent, more so than their avocation would lead those unacquainted with them to suppose. Without claiming for the Cape Fear pilots any extra patriotism, we may claim that they are about as good as their neighbors, and as patriotic as most men."

23. *ORN,* ser. I, vol. V, p. 85. A dispatch to the North Carolina governor, dated August 8, 1861, said that four Negroes escaped from Smithville and were believed to have gone to the blockading steamer, and that one or more were good pilots. (*ORN,* ser. I, vol. V, Part II, p. 218.)

24. Wise, *Lifeline,* p. 227; Fonvielle, *Wilmington Campaign,* pp. 13-17.

25. Wise, *Lifeline,* p. 16; Fonvielle, *Wilmington Campaign,* pp. 15-17.

26. Sprunt, *Chronicles,* p. 413.

27. Francis A. Litz, *Father Tabb: A Study of His Life and Works* (Baltimore,1923), pp. 9-10, hereinafter cited as Litz, *Father Tabb.*

28. Nash K. Burger, *Confederate Spy: Rose O'Neale Greenhow* (New York, 1967); *Confederate Veteran Magazine,* Vol. XL, 1932, p. 187.

29. John D. Bellamy, *Memoirs of an Octogenarian* (Charlotte, NC, 1942), p. 26.

30. Hobart-Hampden, *Never Caught,* p. 13.

31. Wise, *Lifeline,* p. 16; Browning, *North Atlantic Blockading Squadron,* p. 220; Fonvielle, *Wilmington Campaign,* p. 21; *ORN,* ser. I, vol. V, p. 86.

32. Reaves, *Southport Chronology,* vol. I, pp. 3, 74. The Wilmington *Daily Journal* of October 3, 1864, noted that Confederate spy Rose Greenhow drowned when her boat (a lifeboat from the steamer *Condor*) swamped upon "the rip."

33. Reaves, *Southport Chronology,* vol. I, p. 74.

34. Wise, *Lifeline,* pp. 16-17, 205-206; Browning, *North Atlantic Blockading Squadron,* p. 220.

35. *ORN,* ser. I, vol. 9, pp. 355-358.

36. *ORN,* ser. I, vol. 9, pp. 355-358; Browning, *North Atlantic Blockading Squadron,* pp. 225-248; "L." Letter to his brother Eddie dated November 18, 1862, recounting the grounding of the blockade runner *Kate* (East Carolina University Manuscript Collection).

Chapter 3: The Trade

1. F. N. Bonneau, article in *The Daily Journal,* Wilmington, NC, January 1864.
2. Hobart-Hampden, *Never Caught;* Wilkinson, *Narrative;* Sprunt, *Chronicles.*
3. Wise, *Lifeline,* p. 221.
4. Ibid., p. 13.
5. Ibid., p. 17.
6. Ibid., pp. 16-17, 227.
7. Ibid., pp. 15, 227.
8. Ibid., p. 15.
9. Wise, *Lifeline,* p. 16; Sprunt, *Chronicles,* pp. 393-396.
10. Wise, *Lifeline,* p. 17.
11. Ibid., pp. 15, 63, 121-143.
12. Ibid., p. 28.
13. Ibid., p. 107.
14. Wise, *Lifeline,* pp. 50-52; Ethel S. Nepveux, *George Alfred Trenholm and the Company That Went to War* (Charleston, 1973), pp. 33-34, hereinafter cited as Nepveux, *Trenholm.*
15. Wise, *Lifeline,* p. 58.
16. Leslie S. Bright, *The Blockade Runner Modern Greece and Her Cargo* (Raleigh, 1977), p.1, hereinafter cited as Bright, *Modern Greece.*
17. Ibid., pp. 4-6, 19-23.
18. Bright, *Modern Greece,* pp. 12-15; Clark, *Regimental History,* p. 351.
19. Bright, *Modern Greece,* pp. 49-58, 76, 96, 107-108, 112-127, 144-145.
20. Wise, *Lifeline,* pp. 58, 64, 95-96.
21. Wise, *Lifeline,* pp. 95-96; *Bermuda Historical Quarterly,* Winter, 1968, pp. 104-108.
22. *Bermuda Historical Quarterly,* Winter, 1968, p. 103.
23. Wise, *Lifeline,* pp. 57-58, 63-64.
24. Wise, *Lifeline,* p. 126; Fonvielle, *Wilmington Campaign,* pp. 19-20.
25. Wise, *Lifeline,* pp. 75-78.
26. Ibid., pp. 191-192.
27. Wise, *Lifeline,* pp. 240-241; Wilmington *Daily Journal,* September 20, 1864; Marquis, *In Armageddon's Shadow,* p. 248. Greg Marquis's book provides a detailed study of blockade runners at Halifax. Many ships made the voyage to take advantage of the excellent marine railways in the port, which allowed the steamers to be pulled out of the water for maintenance of their underwater hulls.
28. Wise, *Lifeline,* pp. 107-120, 134; Clark, *Regimental History,* vol. V, 335.
29. Wise, *Lifeline,* p. 49; Nepveux, *Trenholm,* p. 26.
30. Nepveux, *Trenholm,* pp. 21-84. The New York branch of the firm, Trenholm Brothers, did not flourish during the war for obvious reasons. But Dr. Charles Peery points out that Yankee goods often made their way to the South. Among evidence he cites is a brass padlock that he recovered from the wreck of the *Ella* off Bald Head Island. The *Ella* was chased ashore and destroyed on December 1, 1864, while trying to run into Old Inlet. (Charles Peery, "Clandestine Commerce: Yankee Blockade Running," *Journal of Confederate History, Special Commemorative Naval Issue CSS Alabama 1864-1989,* Brentwood, TN, 1989, p. 107).

31. Nepveux, *Trenholm*, p. 1.
32. Wise, *Lifeline*, pp. 101-102, 192-195. Officers of blockade runners also often purchased a few bales of cotton themselves to make more money on the voyages. (Clark, *Regimental History*, vol. V, p. 338.)
33. Ibid., p. 93.
34. Ibid., pp. 53-56.
35. Scharf, *Confederate States Navy*, pp. 483-487.
36. Sprunt, *Chronicles*, pp. 453-456; Clark, *Regimental History*, vol. V, p. 359. North Carolina also owned part interest in the *Don*, the *Hansa*, and the *Annie*.
37. Wise, *Lifeline*, p. 134; Frank E. Vandiver, ed., *Confederate Blockade Running Through Bermuda, 1861-1851* (Austin, 1947), pp. 6-103, hereinafter cited as Vandiver, *Confederate Blockade Running*.
38. Vandiver, *Confederate Blockade Running*, p. 96.
39. Wise, *Lifeline*, pp. 109, following p. 116.
40. Francis B. C. Bradlee, *Blockade Running During the Civil War* (The Essex Institute, 1925), pp. 101-102, hereinafter cited as Bradlee, *Blockade Running;* F. N. Bonneau, article in *The Daily Journal* (Wilmington, January 1864).
41. F. N. Bonneau, article in *The Daily Journal* (Wilmington, January 1864).
42. F. N. Bonneau, article in *The Daily Journal* (Wilmington, January 1864); Clark, *Regimental History*, vol. V, p. 445.
43. Wise, *Lifeline*, pp.59-60, 99-100; Maffitt, *Life and Services.*
44. Shingleton, Royce, *High Seas Confederate: The Life and Times of John Newland Maffitt* (Columbia, SC, 1994), p. 2, hereinafter cited as Shingleton, *High Seas Confederate;* Clark, *Regimental History*, vol. V, p. 385; Corchran, *Blockade Runners*, p. 239.
45. Shingleton, *High Seas Confederate*, pp. 9-10, 22.
46. Usina, *Blockade Running in Confederate Times*, pp. 37, 39.
47. Shingleton, *High Seas Confederate*, pp. 26-27, 35; Clark, *Regimental History*, vol. V, pp. 385-386.
48. Shingleton, *High Seas Confederate*, pp. 37, 39-46, 87, 93-94; Clark, *Regimental History*, vol. V, p. 387.
49. Wilkinson, *Narrative*, pp. 104-107; Sprunt, *Chronicles*, p. 410.
50. Wise, *Lifeline*, p. 109; Clark, *Regimental History*, vol. V, pp. 413, 425.
51. Hobart-Hampden, *Never Caught.*
52. Hobart-Hampden, *Never Caught*, p. 2; Wise, *Lifeline*, p. 296.
53. Hobart-Hampden, *Never Caught*, p. 12-13.
54. Thomas E. Taylor, *Running the Blockade* (London, 1896), p. 59, hereinafter cited as Taylor, *Running the Blockade.*
55. Wise, *Lifeline*, p. 196-198.
56. Wise, *Lifeline*, p. 109; Clark, *Regimental History*, vol. V, p. 413. Advance crew list in the possession of Dr. Charles Peery.
57. Advance crew list.
58. Kevin J. Foster, *The Search For Speed under Steam: The Design of Blockade Running Steamships, 1861-1865,* East Carolina University, (Masters thesis), hereinafter cited as Foster, *Speed Under Steam;* Kevin J. Foster, "Builders vs. Blockaders: The Evolution of the Blockade-Running Steamship," article in *Global Crossroads and the American Sea*, Clark G. Reynolds, ed. (Missoula, Montana, 1988), pp. 86-89.

59. Foster, *Speed Under Steam,* pp. 30-88; Richard Woodman, *The History of the Ship* (London, 1997), hereinafter cited as Woodward, *History of the Ship,* pp. 147-161.

60. Foster, *Speed Under Steam,* pp. 88-89; Woodward, *History of the Ship,* p. 138. Woodward notes that the *Savannah* arrived in England with her coal bunkers empty and completed the transatlantic voyage mostly under sail.

61. Clark, *Regimental History,* vol. V, p. 338; Foster, *Speed Under Steam,* p. 25.

62. Wilkinson, *Narrative,* pp. 165-166; Potter, *General Beauregard;* Foster, *Speed Under Steam,* p. 87-88.

63. Howard I. Chapelle, "Ships and Shipbuilding," Microsoft Encarta® 97, Microsoft Corporation, 1997.

64. Wise, *Lifeline,* pp. 107-108.

65. Wise, *Lifeline,* p. 108.

66. Wise, *Lifeline,* pp. 145, 148-149.

67. Foster, *Speed Under Steam,* pp. 100, 110, 135.

68. Foster, "Builders vs. Blockaders; The Evolution of the Blockade-Running Steamship," article in *Global Crossroads and the American Sea,* Clark G. Reynolds, ed. (Missoula, Montana, 1988), pp. 87-89.

69. McPhersons, *Lamson of the Gettysburg,* p. 194.

70. James Sprunt, Wilmington *Morning Star,* March 2, 1894; George Morrison, Wilmington *Morning Star,* March 2, 1894.

71. Clark, *Regimental History,* vol. V. p. 363. Sprunt quoted a letter by Colonel James G. Burr of Wilmington who cited Morrison's remarks.

72. George C. McDougal, letter to *Southport Leader,* dated March 2, 1894. McDougal said in this letter that the officers of the *Margaret and Jessie* boasted that this steamer once sprinted from Fort Anderson to Wilmington, a distance of some fifteen miles in forty-five minutes. Lamson's remarks appear in a letter contained in McPhersons, *Lamson of the "Gettysburg,"* p. 198.

73. McPhersons, *Lamson of the "Gettysburg,"* p. 210; *ORN,* ser. I, vol. X, pp. 534-535.

74. Foster, *Speed Under Steam,* pp. 87-88; Potter, *General Beauregard.*

75. Foster, *Speed Under Steam,* pp. 90-111; Hobart-Hampden, *Never Caught,* pp. 2-3.

76. Foster, *Speed Under Steam,* pp. 105, 110-111; Hobart-Hampden, *Never Caught,* p. 3.

77. Wise, *Lifeline,* pp. 106, 148-149, 286-287, 289-290, 293, 299, 301-303, 305, 310-311, 314, 319-322, 326.

78. *ORN,* ser. I, vol. VIII, p. 356; Wilkinson, *Narrative,* pp. 154-155.

79. *ORN,* ser. I, vol. IX, p. 355-358.

80. Fonvielle, *Wilmington Campaign,* pp. 135, 496. Dr. Fonvielle notes that while Colonel Lamb said the Mound Battery stood 60-foot high, its actual height may have been lower.

81. Clark, *Regimental History,* vol. V, p. 412.

82. Wilkinson, *Narrative,* p. 152.

83. Sprunt, *Chronicles,* p. 467.

84. *Bermuda Advocate,* May 18, 1864.

Chapter 4: The Pilots of the *Mary Celestia*

1. Usina, *Blockade Running in Confederate Times,* p. 33.

2. Wise, *Lifeline,* p. 312. The pilots were John William Anderson, John Wesley Galloway Sr. of Smithville, and John Virgin of Bermuda.

3. Sprunt, *Chronicles,* p. 408; Vandiver, *Blockade Running Through Bermuda,* pp. 131, 134, 136, 138; Confederate muster roll of CSS *Caswell.*

4. Usina, *Blockade Running in Confederate Times,* p. 33.

5. Vandiver, *Blockade Running Through Bermuda,* p. 138; Sprunt, *Chronicles,* pp. 408, 409; Usina, *Blockade Running in Confederate Times,* p. 32.

6. Sprunt, *Chronicles,* pp. 408-410.

7. Usina, *Blockade Running in Confederate Times,* p. 33.

8. Vandiver, *Blockade Running Through Bermuda,* p. 138; postscript added by Major General W. H. C. Whiting to an October 13, 1864, letter from Colonel C. H. Simonton to General Cooper concerning the death of Captain Galloway.

9. Galloway genealogy furnished by Doreen Holtz of the Southport Historical Society. Her sources include the Brunswick County tax roles and the Council Journals of Brunswick.

10. United States census, Brunswick County, NC, 1850; *Wilmington Messenger,* January 19, 1898.

11. Wilmington *Journal,* October 15, 1864; Compiled Confederate Service Records, NC State Archives, Raleigh, NC.

12. Compiled Confederate Service Records, NC State Archives, Raleigh, NC; N. C. pilot licensing records.

13. Wise, *Lifeline,* p. 247; postscript added by Major General W. H. C. Whiting to an October 13, 1864, letter from Colonel C. H. Simonton to General Cooper concerning the death of Captain Galloway; death notice in Wilmington *Journal,* October 15, 1864.

14. Vandiver, *Blockade Running Through Bermuda,* p. 138; David L. Horner, *The Blockade-Runners, True Tales of Running the Yankee Blockade off the Confederate Coast* (New York, 1968), pp. 109-110, hereinafter cited as Horner, *The Blockade-Runners; Bermuda Historical Quarterly,* Winter, 1968, p. 108.

15. Horner, *The Blockade-Runners,* p. 111; *Bermuda Historical Quarterly,* Winter 1968, p. 108, and Spring, 1962.

Chapter 5: Thomas Brinkman and the *Condor*

1. C. K. Graham, *Under Both Flags* (Richmond, 1896), hereinafter cited as Graham, *Under Both Flags,* p. 340. Graham's book includes the chapter "What a North Carolina Boy Saw of the Civil War," by James Eastus Price of Southport.

2. Brinkman family genealogy, compiled by Joseph S. Loughlin of Piqua, Ohio; United States census, Brunswick County, NC, 1860.

3. Brinkman family genealogy; N. C. pilot licensing records. Since the *Condor* stopped at Halifax on her way to Wilmington (Wise, *Lifeline,* p. 196), it should be a good assumption that Brinkman boarded her there rather than in England or at some other point.

4. Wise, *Lifeline,* p. 150.

5. Ibid., p. 197. Some writers have identified the *Condor*'s captain as Hobart-Hampden. Dr. Wise indicates that it was indeed Hewett, which is confirmed by the writings of James

Sprunt and by an entry in Colonel William Lamb's diary (*ORN*, ser. I, vol. XI, p. 743).

6. Burger, *Confederate Spy*, pp. 51-52.

7. Burger, *Confederate Spy*, pp. 62-81, 189-199. One bleak winter day, I sat in the Special Collections Library at Duke University and read her diary. Or tried to. I found the writing almost indecipherable. Perhaps it reflected the pitching and rolling of the *Condor* as she crossed the Atlantic.

8. Ibid., pp. 219-220. Some sources indicated that the bag of coins was sewn into her dress.

9. Wise, *Lifeline*, pp. 196-198; *ORN*, ser. I, vol. X, p. 531.

10. Wise, *Lifeline*, p. 197; *ORN*, ser. I, vol. X, p.531

11. Robert Carse, *Blockade, The Civil War at Sea* (New York, 1958), pp. 160-161.

12. Burger, *Confederate Spy*, p. 220.

13. Taylor, *Running the Blockade*, p. 112; Wise, *Lifeline*, p. 197.

14. *ORN*, ser. I, vol. XI, p. 745.

15. Graham, *Under Both Flags*, p. 340.

16. Ibid., p. 340.

17. *ORN*, ser. I, vol. XI, p.741.

18. Reaves, *Southport Chronology*, vol. I, p. 60.

Chapter 6: The Burriss Boys of Federal Point

1. Taylor, *Running the Blockade*, p. 51.

2. James Burriss, *Genealogy*; United States census, New Hanover County, 1850, 1860 1870; Sprunt, *Chronicles* and other writings.

3. James Burriss, *Genealogy*.

4. Ibid.

5. James Burriss, *Genealogy;* N. C. pilot licensing records; Sprunt, *Chronicles,* p. 395; Wise, *Lifeline* p. 303.

6. Sprunt, *Chronicles* p. 395; Wise, *Lifeline* p. 293.

7. Sprunt, *Chronicles* p. 395; Betty Cappo, recollections of Burriss family traditions, as told to Jim McNeil; Royce Shingleton, *John Taylor Wood: Sea Ghost of the Confederacy* (Athens, 1979), pp. 133-134, hereinafter cited as Shingleton, *Sea Ghost.*

8. Wise, *Lifeline*, pp. 101-102, 234, 243; *ORN; The Hebe Skirmish Centennial and the Fort Fisher Visitor Center-Museum Groundbreaking Program* (Wilmington,1963), hereinafter cited as *The Hebe Centennial Program.*

9. *ORN*, ser. I, vol. IX, p. 166-167; *The Hebe Centennial Program.*

10. *ORN*, ser. I, vol. IX, p. 165-166; *The Hebe Centennial Program;* Clark, *Regimental History,* vol. V, p. 352; Wilmington *Daily Journal,* August 1863.

11. Shingleton, *Sea Ghost*, pp. 124-132; *New York Times*, August 1863.

12. Shingleton, *Sea Ghost*, pp. 128-129.

13. Ibid., pp. 133-141.

14. Halifax *Acadian Recorder*, August 27, 1864.

15. Sprunt, *Chronicles*, p. 395; Taylor, *Running the Blockade*, pp. 51-54.

16. Taylor, *Running the Blockade*, pp. 50-54. As supercargo, Taylor managed the commercial interests of the blockade running voyages of his company.

17. Wise, *Lifeline*, pp. 112-113; Taylor, *Running the Blockade*, p. 47.

18. Taylor, *Running the Blockade*, pp. 51-54; Sprunt, *Chronicles*, p. 395.

19. Taylor, *Running the Blockade*, pp. 49, 51.
20. Ibid., pp. 51, 52, 53, 54.
21. James Burriss, *Genealogy;* Betty Cappo, *Burriss Genealogy.*
22. James Burriss, *Genealogy;* Sarah Ann McNeil, recollections of conversations with her great-aunt Esther Dosher Eriksen; N. C. pilot licensing records; Sprunt, *Chronicles*, p. 408.
23. Sarah Ann McNeil, recollections from conversations with her grandfather, Charles Eyden Gause.

Chapter 7: The Misfortunes of Thomas Dyer

1. Wilkinson, *Narrative*, p. 129.
2. U. S. census Brunswick County, NC 1860; military records of Thomas Dyer in National Archives; N. C. Pilot licensing records.
3. Military records of Thomas Dyer; Confederate muster rolls of CSS *Beaufort* and CSS *Caswell;* Navy, *Ship Dictionary*, vol. II, p. 503, 506.
4. Sprunt, *Chronicles*, p. 395; Wilkinson, *Narrative*, p. 129.
5. Wise, *Lifeline*, pp. 99-100.
6. Dumbarton (Scotland) *Herald*, November 20, 1862.
7. Wilkinson, *Narrative*, pp. 126-127.
8. Wilkinson, *Narrative*, pp. 128-129; Litz, *Father Tabb*, pp. 15-16.
9. Wilkinson, *Narrative*, pp. 126-127.
10. Ibid., pp. 136-137.
11. Sprunt, *Chronicles*, p. 395.
12. Wise, *Lifeline*, p. 115; Potter, *General Beauregard.*
13. Bradlee, *Blockade Running During the Civil War*, p. 105.
14. *ORN*, ser. I, vol. IX, pp. 362-366.
15. *ORN*, ser. I, vol. IX, pp. 363-365.
16. *ORN*, ser. I, vol. IX, p. 365.
17. *ORN*, ser. I, vol. IX, pp. 363-364.
18. *ORN*, ser. I, vol. IX, pp. 363-364.
19. *ORN*, ser. I, vol. IX, p. 364.
20. *ORN*, ser. I, vol. IX, p. 365. It is not certain that Thomas Dyer piloted the *Antonica* on her last voyage. Julius Potter said that he piloted the steamer at Cape Fear. Marcus Price listed Thomas Kent as her Cape Fear pilot, but Kent's name does not appear in the pilot licensing records. Thomas Kent's name does appear as pilot on the list of those captured on the *Antonica* in a letter listing prisoners from that steamer (National Archives, Records Group 45, Letters received related to Confederate Prisoners of War). But since in most cases Cape Fear pilots upon capture claimed to be foreign nationals and were released accordingly, Dyer may have been the steamer's pilot.
21. Sprunt, *Chronicles*, p. 395.
22. Wise, *Lifeline*, p. 302; *ORN*, ser. I, vol. X, p. 114.
23. *ORN*, ser. I, vol. X, pp. 114-115.
24. Sprunt, *Chronicles*, p. 461.
25. Wilkinson, *Narrative*, pp. 137-138.
26. Reaves, *Southport Chronology*, vol. I, p. 78.

Chapter 8: The Pilot Who Became a Preacher

1. Sprunt, *Chronicles*, p. 405.
2. Burriss, James, *Genealogy;* U. S. census, New Hanover County, NC, 1850, 1860; Sprunt, *Chronicles*, p. 395.
3. Reaves, *Southport Chronology*, vol. I, p. 10; U. S. Census, New Hanover County, 1850.
4. James Burriss, *Genealogy;* Sprunt, *Chronicles*, pp. 397-398.
5. Sprunt, *Chronicles*, pp. 396-406.
6. Ibid., pp. 397-398.
7. Ibid., pp. 393-395.
8. Wise, *Lifeline*, pp. 119-200.
9. Ibid., p. 120; Sprunt, *Chronicles*, p. 398.
10. Sprunt, *Chronicles*, p. 398.
11. Ibid., p. 399.
12. Ibid., p. 399.
13. Ibid., p. 399.
14. Ibid., p. 399.
15. Sprunt, *Chronicles*, p. 400; Wise, *Lifeline*, p. 296.
16. Sprunt, *Chronicles*, p. 400; Wise, *Lifeline*, p. 288.
17. Sprunt, *Chronicles*, pp. 400-401. The ironclad CSS *Raleigh* was built in Wilmington for defense of the harbor. She ran aground and broke her keel on New Inlet's inner bar in May 1864 (Fonvielle, *Wilmington Campaign*, p. 81).
18. Ibid., p. 401.
19. Sprunt, *Chronicles*, p. 401; Vandiver, *Blockade Running Through Bermuda*, p. 136.
20. Sprunt, *Chronicles*, pp. 401-403.
21. James Morris Morgan, *Recollections of a Rebel Reefer* (Boston: Houghton Mifflin Company, 1917), p. 193.
22. Sprunt, *Chronicles*, p. 403.
23. *ORN*, ser. I, vol. IX, p. 390.
24. Edwin W. Beitzell, *Point Lookout Prison Camp for Confederates* (private publishing, 1972), pp. 1, 120-121, hereinafter cited as Beitzell, *Point Lookout*. Mr. Beitzell's book contains a list of all recorded deaths of Confederate prisoners at Point Lookout.
25. Beitzell, *Point Lookout*, pp. 2-3, 21-23, 122; Sprunt, *Chronicles*, p. 404.
26. Aubrey H. Stark, *Sidney Lanier, A Biographical and Critical Study* (New York, 1964), p. 59.
27. Sprunt, *Chronicles*, pp. 404-405.
28. Ibid., p. 405.
29. Ibid., p. 403.
30. Wise, *Lifeline*, p. 290; Sprunt, *Chronicles*, p. 403.
31. Sprunt, *Chronicles*, p. 403; *ORN*, ser. I, vol. IX, p. 547.
32. *ORN*, ser. I, vol. IX, p. 547.
33. Ibid., ser. I, vol. IX, p. 548.
34. Sprunt, *Chronicles*, p. 404.
35. Sprunt, *Chronicles*, p. 404.
36. Sprunt, *Chronicles*, p. 405; Bradlee Reaves, *Blockade Running During the Civil War*, p. 108.

37. *Wilmington Star*, December 4, 1870; September 25, 1880; October 3, 1880; October 15, 1880; October 29, 1880.
38. Sprunt, *Chronicles*, p. 406.

Chapter 9: The Tale of Julius Potter

1. Potter, *General Beauregard.*
2. Potter, *General Beauregard.* This typescript does not identify its author. According to James Sprunt (Sprunt, *Chronicles*, p. 395) Julius Potter was the Cape Fear pilot of the *General Beauregard.* Mr. Sprunt actually transposed Julius's initials, using throughout his writings J. W. Potter instead of W. J. Potter. According to other sources such as pilot licensing records and the U. S. census, W. J. (for William Julius) is correct.
3. Potter family genealogy, provided by Robert Potter of St. Marys, Georgia.
4. N. C. pilot licensing records; Potter, *General Beauregard.*
5. Wise, *Lifeline*, p. 304; Potter, *General Beauregard.*
6. Wise, *Lifeline*, pp. 235, 256, 304; Potter, *General Beauregard.*
7. Potter, *General Beauregard.*
8. Ibid.
9. Ibid.
10. Ibid.
11. Ibid.
12. Ibid.
13. Ibid.
14. Ibid.
15. Ibid.
16. Potter, *General Beauregard;* Navy, *Ship Dictionary*, vol. II, p. 433.
17. Potter, *General Beauregard.*
18. Ibid.
19. Ibid.
20. Ibid.
21. Ibid.
22. Potter, *General Beauregard;* Navy, *Ship Dictionary*, vol. II, p. 433.
23. Potter, *General Beauregard.*
24. Ibid.
25. Ibid.
26. Potter, *General Beauregard;* Sprunt, *Chronicles*, p. 395.
27. Potter, *General Beauregard.*
28. Potter, *General Beauregard;* author's interview with Leslie Bright of the Fort Fisher Underwater Archaeology Unit. Another reference to the "blue pigeon" can be found in Bradlee, *Blockade Running During the Civil War*, p. 105.
29. Potter, *General Beauregard.*
30. Ibid.
31. Potter, *General Beauregard;* Wise, *Lifeline*, p. 115.
32. Potter, *General Beauregard.*
33. Ibid.
34. Ibid.

35. Ibid.
36. Ibid.
37. Ibid.
38. Ibid.
39. Ibid.
40. Ibid.
41. Ibid.
42. Ibid.
43. Ibid.
44. Ibid.
45. Potter, *General Beauregard;* Horner, *The Blockade-Runners,* pp. 161-172.
46. Potter, *General Beauregard.*
47. Potter, *General Beauregard; ORN,* ser. I, vol. VIII, p. 354.
48. Potter, *General Beauregard.*
49. Potter, *General Beauregard; ORN,* ser. I, vol. VIII, p. 354.
50. Potter, *General Beauregard.*
51. Ibid.
52. Ibid.
53. *ORN,* ser. I, vol. IX, p. 354.
54. E. Lee Spence, *Treasurers of the Confederate Coast* (Charleston, 1995), p. 270.
55. Reaves, *Southport Chronology,* vol. I, p. 77.

Chapter 10: Christopher Columbus Morse

1. Sprunt, *Chronicles.*
2. Sprunt, *Chronicles,* p. 395; Wise, *Lifeline,* pp. 286, 294, 307.
3. Morse family genealogy, complied by Sarah Ann McNeil of Southport, NC.
4. Morse family genealogy; Price, "Masters and Pilots Who Tested the Blockade," p. 97.
5. Morse family genealogy; U.S. Census, Brunswick Cty, NC; N. C. pilot licensing records.
6. Wise, *Lifeline,* pp. 233, 242, 307.
7. Ibid., pp. 59, 307.
8. Wise, *Lifeline,* p. 68; Clark, *Regimental History,* vol. V, p. 403.
9. Wise, *Lifeline,* p. 126; Fonvielle, *Wilmington Campaign,* pp. 19-20.
10. Wise, *Lifeline,* pp. 126-127; Fonvielle, *Wilmington Campaign,* pp. 19-20.
11. Wise, *Lifeline,* p. 127; Wilmington *Daily News,* November 11, 1862.
12. "L," letter to his brother Eddie dated November 18, 1862, recounting the grounding of the blockade runner *Kate,* East Carolina University Manuscript Collection.
13. "L," letter to his brother Eddie dated November 18, 1862; Wise, *Lifeline,* p. 127.
14. Jackson, *Cape Fear River,* vol. I, pp. 268-269; author's 1998 interview with Leslie Bright of Carolina Beach, who has dived on the wreck. James Randall, who visited Smithville during the Civil War, wrote that the wreck of the *Kate* became "a famous fishing ground" where he lashed his boat to one of the sunken paddle wheels. (Jackson, *Cape Fear River,* vol. I, p. 269.)
15. Sprunt, *Chronicles,* pp. 395, 299; Wise, *Lifeline,* pp. 194-295.
16. CSA pay receipt made out to C. C. Morse for piloting the *Cornubia,* dated May 15, 1863.

17. Sprunt, *Chronicles.*
18. Clark, *Regimental History,* vol. V, pp. 406-407.
19. Ibid., vol. V, p. 407.
20. Wise, *Lifeline,* p. 139; Vandiver, *Blockade Running Through Bermuda,* p. 121.
21. Vandiver, *Blockade Running Through Bermuda,* p. 121.
22. *ORN,* ser. I, vol. IX, pp. 273-274.
23. *ORN,* ser. I, vol. IX, pp. 275, 277-286; Navy, *Ship Dictionary,* vol. II, p. 511.
24. Clark, *Regimental History,* vol. V, p. 363; George Morrison letter to the *Wilmington Star,* dated March 2, 1894.
25. Clark, *Regimental History,* vol. V, p. 359; Wise, *Lifeline,* pp. 106, 286.
26. Clark, *Regimental History,* vol. V, p. 361; Wise, *Lifeline,* p. 286.
27. Clark, *Regimental History,* vol. V, pp. 343-344. The passenger was Reverend Moses D. Hoge; the date was October 12, 1863.
28. Hamilton Corcoran, *Blockade Runners of the Confederacy* (New York, 1958), p. 175.

Chapter 11: Through the Eyes of a Girl

1. Mary J. White, *Diary, August 2, 1864–June 7, 1865,* hereinafter cited as Mary White's diary. (Courtesy United Daughters of the Confederacy, Richmond, VA). The original of Mary's diary was acquired by the Roanoke Rapids, NC, chapter of the UDC and later moved to the UDC's Raleigh headquarters. Her entries date from August 2, 1864, to June 7, 1865, with a final postscript that she wrote in 1930. The copy I obtained consists of a 30-page typewritten transcription produced by the UDC. (Its pages are not numbered.) All of the excerpts in this chapter are taken from this diary.
2. Ibid.
3. Mary White's diary; Clark, *Regimental History,* vol. V, p. 341. The description of Captain Wylie came from Reverend Moses Hoge.
4. Ibid.
5. Ibid.
6. Mary White's diary; Sprunt, *Chronicles,* pp. 408-410.
7. Mary White's diary; Sprunt, *Chronicles,* p. 395.
8. Mary White's diary.
9. Mary White's diary. James Sprunt said that Captain Gutherie of Smithville was captain of the *Cape Fear.* This was probably Cape Fear pilot Archibald Gutherie.
10. Ibid. Frank Vandiver in *Blockade Running Through Bermuda,* p. 138, shows the *Mary Celestia* departing St. George's for the coast under Arthur Sinclair, master, on August 2, 1864. Port records in Stephen Wise's *Lifeline of the Confederacy* show her arriving in Wilmington on or about August 6. (This date would have been the arrival in the harbor, not at Wilmington, given the quarantine then in effect.) Mary's reference to the death of a pilot on August 15, 1864, doesn't match up with other accounts if the pilot was indeed John Anderson. I could find no record of the death of another pilot near Smithville during that period.
11. *ORN,* ser. I, vol. IX, pp. 388-389.
12. Mary White's diary; *ORN,* ser. I, vol. IX, p. 453.
13. Clark, *Regimental History,* vol. V, pp. 337-338.
14. *ORN,* ser. I., vol. XI, pp. 453-454; Mary White's diary. The Register of Prisoners

Captured on Blockade Runners lists the four persons taken prisoner as Cyrus F. Neill, William E. Mayo, William Muse, and J. G. Byron. William Muse was listed as third steward in a letter listing prisoners of war captured on the *Advance* (National Archives, Records Group 45)

15. Crew list of the *Advance;* Muse, William T., 1893 letter to the *Southport Leader.*
16. Navy, *Ship Dictionary*, vol. I, p. 78. Proceeds from the sale of the *Advance* amounted to $288,286.49, according to Admiral David Porter's book *The Naval History of the Civil War* (reprint, Sacaucus, NJ, 1984).
17. Sprunt, *Chronicles*, p. 404.
18. Reaves, *Southport Chronology*, vol. I, p. 70.

Chapter 12: Thomas Mann Thompson

1. Sprunt, *Chronicles*, p. 424.
2. Sprunt, *Chronicles*, p. 395; Thomas Mann Thompson, letter to his daughter Lily, November 24, 1896 (in N. C. State Archives), hereinafter cited as Thompson letter; Wise, *Lifeline*, p. 289.
3. Thompson family genealogy, compiled by Sarah Ann McNeil of Southport, NC.
4. Thompson letter.
5. Wise, *Lifeline*, p. 289; Wood, *Sea Ghost*, pp. 118-122.
6. Thompson letter.
7. She left St. George's on July 11, 1864 (Vandiver, *Blockade Running Through Bermuda*, p. 136).
8. Usina, *Blockade Running*, p. 29.
9. Ibid., p. 30.
10. Ibid., p. 30.
11. Thompson letter.
12. Ibid.
13. Vandiver, *Blockade Running Through Bermuda*, p. 141; Thompson letter; Usina, *Blockade Running*, p. 32.
14. Thompson letter.
15. Ibid.
16. Ibid.
17. Thompson letter; Usina, *Blockade Running*, p. 32.
18. Thompson letter; Usina, *Blockade Running*, p. 32.
19. Thompson letter.

Chapter 13: The Legacy of the Cape Fear Blockade Runners

1. Betty Cappo, recollections of Burriss family traditions, as told to Jim McNeil.
2. Curtis, *Reminiscences*, p. 37; *Halifax Express*, March 1865 (courtesy of Greg Marquis, Saint Mary's University, Halifax).
3. Sarah Ann McNeil, recollections of conversations with her grandparents Charles Gause and Gertrude Dosher Gause; Betty Cappo, recollections of Burriss family traditions.
4. N. C. pilot licensing records; Curtis, *Reminiscences*, p. 30.

5. Curtis, *Reminiscences*, p. 30; Captain Galloway's death notice in *Wilmington Journal*, October 15, 1864; Graham, *Under Both Flags*, p. 339.

6. Graham, *Under Both Flags*, p. 339. No references to the steamer *Kent* appear in Wise, *Lifeline* or Price, *Ships That Tested the Blockade*. James Price may have meant the *Kate*, which sunk in the river just off Smithville on November 18, 1862.

7. *Acadian Recorder* [Halifax], August 27, 1864; Wilkinson, *Narrative*, pp. 137-138.

8. Wise, *Lifeline*.

9. Sprunt, *Chronicles*, pp. 395-410.

10. Curtis, *Reminiscences*, p. 27.

11. Carson, *Joshua's Dream*, p. 45. Recollections of Sarah Ann McNeil of Dosher family traditions.

12. These objects remain in the possession of the McNeil family.

Epilogue: The Cape Fear Pilots after the Civil War

1. Louis T. Moore, unpublished article on the lost pilots of Smithville, 1872 and 1877, hereinafter cited as Moore, *Lost Pilots*. Mr. Moore's account, found in the New Hanover County Public Library in Wilmington, consists chiefly of direct quotes from three Wilmington newspapers: the *Daily Journal*, the *Sun*, and the *Star*.

2. Reaves, *Southport Chronology*, vol. I, p. 66, others following.

3. Burney, J. H. & Company letter to G. P. Oxley & Company of Liverpool concerning the *Helen*, London, July 6, 1866, hereinafter cited as Burney letter; Oxley, G. P. & Company, letter to E. D. Gauze [Gause] concerning fee for piloting the *Helen*, Halifax, October, 21, 1866. Copies of both letters are in the possession of the author.

4. Gause family genealogy, prepared by Sarah Ann McNeil of Southport.

5. Burney letter.

6. Gause family genealogy.

7. Moore, *Lost Pilots*.

8. Moore, *Lost Pilots;* Reaves, *Southport Chronology*, vol. I, p. 59.

9. Reaves, *Southport Chronology*, vol. I, p. 60.

10. Moore, *Lost Pilots;* Reaves, *Southport Chronology*, vol. I, p. 66.

11. N. C. pilot licensing records; Dosher family genealogy, compiled by Sarah Ann McNeil, hereinafter cited as Dosher genealogy.

12. Dosher genealogy.

13. *The Peoples Press*, Wilmington, NC, August 14, 1835, hereinafter cited as *Peoples Press* article.

14. *Peoples Press* article; Dosher family tradition related by Esther Dosher Eriksen (granddaughter of Charles Gause Dosher) to Sarah Ann McNeil.

15. Dosher family tradition.

16. Dosher genealogy.

17. Dosher family tradition.

18. Dosher family tradition; Dosher genealogy.

19. Dosher family tradition; Dosher genealogy.

20. Moore, *Lost Pilots*

21. Moore, *Lost Pilots;* Reaves, *Southport Chronology*, vol. I, p. 70.

22. Moore, *Lost Pilots;* Reaves, *Southport Chronology*, vol. I, p. 60.

23. Moore, *Lost Pilots;* Reaves, *Southport Chronology,* vol. I, p. 67.

24. Moore, *Lost Pilots;* Sprunt, *Chronicles,* p. 395.

25. Moore, *Lost Pilots.*

26. Ibid.

27. Ibid.

28. Col. A. M. Waddell, "Heroes of the Deep: Incidents in the Lives of Two Cape Fear Pilots," correspondence of the *New York World,* hereinafter cited as Waddell, *Heroes.* An undated copy of this article, which does not show the newspaper in which it appeared, is available in the local history room at the New County Public Library in Wilmington. It was likely published around 1880. Colonel Waddell attended the dedication of the monument to lost pilots in the Southport cemetery in 1879 (Reaves, *Southport Chronology,* vol. I, p. 74).

29. Waddell, *Heroes.*

30. Moore, *Lost Pilots;* Waddell, *Heroes.*

31. Moore, *Lost Pilots;* Waddell, *Heroes.*

32. Waddell, *Heroes;* Moore, *Lost Pilots.*

33. Moore, *Lost Pilots.*

34. Ibid.

35. Ibid.

36. Ibid.

37. Reaves, *Southport Chronology.* Vol. I, p. 74.

38. Ibid., vol. II, p. 37.

39. Ibid., vol. I.

40. Ibid., vol. II, p. 1.

41. Ibid., vol. I, 66.

42. Ibid., vol. I, p. 87, Vol. II, pp. 2, 32.

43. Ibid., vol. II, pp. 32, 62.

44. Ibid., vol. II, p. 62.

45. Ibid., vol. II, p. 65.

46. Ibid., vol. II, p. 146. This article likely described pilots on rivers such as the Mississippi, but the Cape Fear pilots were probably much like this.

47. Keaton, Gary, "Gentleman Pilots of Cape Fear," *Wilmington Magazine,* Oct-Nov 1995, p. 35.

48. Briefing booklet advocating Southport as the state port, in the possession of the McNeil family.

49. Author's recollections; J. W. Long, "Quarterbacks of the River," article in *The State* magazine, May 19, 1956.

50. Jim Harper, "Down to the Sea," article in Southport, NC *State Port Pilot,* Apr. 1, 1998.

51. Author's recollections; author's 1997 interview with retired Cape Fear pilot Robert Thompson; Navy, *Ship Dictionary,* V, p. 108.

52. Author's recollections; author's 1997 interview with retired Cape Fear pilot Robert Thompson.

53. Thompson genealogy compiled by Sarah Ann McNeil; Swan genealogy compiled by Helen Thomas Pearce.

54. Sprunt, *Chronicles,* pp. 395-396; author's 1998 interview with Cape Fear pilot Roy Daniel.

55. List of pilots provided by Captain Roy Daniel of Southport.

Photo Notes

Page 6: Wise,, *Lifeline*, p. 311. National Archives Record Group 45, "Register of Prisoners Captured on Blockade Runners, September 1862 - July 1865," hereinafter cited as Register of Prisoners Captured on Blockade Runners. Captain Craig was one of the few Cape Fear pilots identified by name and occupation on the lists of prisoners. To avoid capture, most of the Cape Fear pilots on captured blockade runners did not give their true name nor admit to being a pilot, and were released after signing a parole of honor like most of the crew and passengers. Otherwise, they would have languished in Union prisons until the end of the war. Taped to the inside cover of the Register of Prisoners Captured on Blockade Runners is a copy of a letter from the Union Secretary of Navy, Gideon Wells, to Rear Admiral S. P. Lee, dated May 9, 1864, which includes the following statement of Union policy, "Pilots and seafaring men, excepting bona fide foreign subjects, captured on neutral vessels are always to be detained." The Union recognized early in the war the great importance of the Cape Fear pilots to the Confederate cause.

Page 7, bottom: Markings on the back of the photo show that it was taken in a studio across from the Halifax Club. Halifax during the Civil War is vividly described in Greg Marquiss's *In Armageddon's Shadow: the Civil War and Canada's Maritime Provinces* (Montreal, 1998), hereinafter cited as Marquis, *In Armageddon's Shadow*. I initially believed the man on the left to be Lt. John Wilkinson. He was in Halifax with the *Robert E. Lee*, along with his Cape Fear pilot Archibald Gutherie. It stands to reason that the two of them would be photographed together. Although the man on the left bears some resemblance to Lt. Wilkinson as he is shown in other pictures, I could not definitely establish that he is Lt. Wilkinson.

Page 7, top: *ORN*, ser. I, vol. XI, p. 744; Curtis, *Reminiscences*, p. 6; Confederate muster rolls of the CSS *Caswell*.

Page 17: Navy, *Ship Dictionary*, vol. I, p. 288-429.

Page 18: Navy, *Ship Dictionary*, vol. II, p. 247; Wise, *Lifeline*, p. 25.

Page 20: Navy, *Ship Dictionary*, V, p. 95-96.

Page 25: Browning,, *North Atlantic Blockading Squadron*, p. 263.

Page 26: Jackson,, *Cape Fear River*, vol. I, p. 268. Mr. Jackson notes that Lightship "D" mounted two lights, both standing 40 feet above the water level.

Page 34, top: Bright, *Modern Greece*, pp. 6-12.

Page 40: Wilmington, NC *Daily Journal*, January 1864.

Page 43, bottom: Wise, *Lifeline*, pp. 8-9, 57-60, 117, 165.

Page 43, top: Shingleton, *High Seas Confederate*, following p. 81; Sprunt, *Chronicles*, p. 395.

Page 47, top: Price, *Ships That Tested the Blockade*, pp. 202-203; Wilkinson, *Narrative*, p. 166.

Page 47, bottom: *ORN*, ser. I, vol. IX, pp. 287-288; Navy, *Ship Dictionary*, Vol. VII, p. 562.

Page 51: Bradlee, *Blockade Running During the Civil War*, pp. 42, 117.

Page 70: Wise, *Lifeline*, p. 310; *ORN*, ser. I, vol. X, p. 504.

Bibliography

Acadian Recorder, Halifax, Nova Scotia, August 27, 1864.

American Neptune, The. "Pictorial Supplement III, Blockade Runners," Salem, MA, 1961.

Anderson, Bern. *The Naval History of the Civil War, By River and By Sea.* New York: Alfred A. Knopf, 1962.

Beitzell, Edwin W. *Point Lookout Prison Camp for Confederates.* Private publishing, 1972.

Bellamy, John D. *Memoirs of an Octogenarian.* Charlotte, NC: Observer Printing House, 1942.

Bermuda Advocate, May 18, 1864.

Bermuda Historical Quarterly, Spring, 1962

Bermuda Historical Quarterly, Winter, 1968.

Blockade-Runners and Raiders, The. Alexandria, VA:Time-Life Books, 1983.

Bonneau, F. N. Article in *The Daily Journal,* Wilmington, NC, January 1864.

Bradlee, Francis B. C. *Blockade Running During the Civil War.* The Essex Institute, 1925.

Bright, Leslie S. *The Blockade Runner Modern Greece.* Raleigh: Division of Archives and History, June 1977.

Brinkman family genealogy provided by Joe Loughlin of Piqua, Ohio.

Browning, Robert M. Jr. *From Cape Charles to Cape Fear, the North Atlantic Blockading Squadron During the Civil War.* Tuscaloosa: The University of Alabama Press, 1993.

Burger, Nash K. *Confederate Spy: Rose O'Neale Greenhow.* New York: Franklin Watts, Inc., 1967.

Burney, J. H. & Company. Letter to G. P. Oxley & Company of Liverpool concerning the *Helen,* London, July 6, 1866.

Burriss, George Washington, genealogy, compiled by Betty T. Cappo of Wilmington, NC.

Burriss, James Henry III. *Burrows-Burriss-Newton and Allied families in VA and NC, Federal Point,* private printing, 1980.

Campbell, R. Thomas. *Fire and Thunder, Exploits of the Confederate States Navy.* Shippensburg, PA: The Burd Street Press, 1997.

Cappo, Betty. Recollections of Burriss family traditions, as told to Jim McNeil.

Carse, Robert. *Blockade, The Civil War at Sea.* New York/Toronto: Rinehart and Company, Inc., 1958.

Carson, Susan S. *Joshua's Dream: A Town With Two Names.* Southport, NC: Carolina Power and Light, 1992.

Catton, Bruce. *Reflections on the Civil War.* New York: Berkley Books, 1994.

Chapelle, Howard I. *American Sailing Craft.* Camden, ME: International Marine Publishing Company, 1975.

Chapelle, Howard I. "Ships and Shipbuilding," article in Microsoft Encarta® 97 encyclopedia, Microsoft Corporation, 1997.

Chartin, Peter M. *The Civil War: The Coastal War, Chesapeake Bay to the Rio Grande.* Alexandria, VA: Time-Life Books, 1984.

Clark, Walter, ed. *Histories of the Several Regiments and Battalions from North Carolina in the Great War 1861-65, Written by Members of the Respective Commands.* Vol. V, State of North Carolina, 1901.

Clark, Walter, ed. *The State Records of North Carolina.* Goldsboro: Nash Brothers Publishing Company, 1900.

Confederate Naval Records, vessel muster rolls, National Archives.

Confederate Service Records, National Archives.

Confederate Service Records, N. C. State Archives.

Confederate Veteran Magazine, Vol. VI, 1898.

Confederate Veteran Magazine, Vol. XXIV, 1916.

Confederate Veteran Magazine, Vol. XL, 1932.

Corcoran, Hamilton. *Blockade Runners of the Confederacy.* New York: The Bobbs-Merrill Company, Inc., 1958.

Craig family genealogy, compiled from information developed by Bill Reaves.

Curtis, Walter Gilmer. *Reminiscences of Wilmington and Smithville-Southport 1848-1900.* Southport, NC: Herald Job Office, 1900.

Denny, Robert E. *Civil War Prisoners and Escapes, A Day-by-Day Chronicle.* New York: Sterling Publishing Company, Inc., 1993.

Dosher family genealogy, compiled by Sarah Ann McNeil of Southport, NC.

Drury, Ian and Tony Gibbons. *The Civil War Military Machine, Weapons and Tactics of the Union and Confederate Armed Forces.* New York: Smithmark Publishers, Inc., 1993.

Drysdale, Richard. "Blockade-Running from Nassau," article in *History Today,* May 1997.

Dumbarton [Scotland] *Herald,* November 20, 1862.

Earnhart, Hugh G., ed. "Aboard a Blockade Runner: Some Civil Experiences of Jerome DuShane," *The North Carolina Historical Review,* Vol. XLIV, Number 4, October 1967.

Eriksen, Esther Dosher. Conversations recalling Smithville blockade runners she had known or heard of, with Sarah Ann McNeil.

Farley, M. Forster. "Ships of Wood, Nerves of Steel," *South Carolina Heritage,* May 1975.

Fonvielle, Chris E. Jr. *The Wilmington Campaign: Last Rays of Departing Hope.* Campbell, CA: Savas Publishing Company, 1997.

Fort Fisher logbook [1864] in N. C. State Archives.

Foster, Kevin J. "Builders vs. Blockaders; The Evolution of the Blockade-Running Steamship," article in *Global Crossroads and the American Sea,* Clark G. Reynolds, ed. Missoula, Montana: Pictorial History Publishing Company, 1988.

Foster, Kevin J. *The Search For Speed under Steam: The Design of Blockade Running Steamships, 1861-1865,* East Carolina University (Masters thesis).

Frank Leslie's Illustrated Newspaper, 1864.

Galloway family genealogy provided by Doreen Holtz of Boiling Springs Lakes, NC.

Gause family genealogy, compiled by Sarah Ann McNeil of Southport, NC.

Gragg, Rod. *The Illustrated Confederate Reader.* New York: Harper and Row, Publishers, 1989.

Graham, C. K. *Under Both Flags.* Richmond, 1896.

Gutherie, Archibald Menzies, family genealogy, compiled by Sarah Ann McNeil, Southport, NC.

Halifax *Evening Express.*

Harper, Jim. "Down to the Sea," article in Southport, NC *State Port Pilot,* April 1, 1998.

Harper's Weekly, November and December, 1864.

Hebe Skirmish Centennial and the Fort Fisher Visitor Center-Museum Groundbreaking

Program. North Carolina Department of Archives and History, Wilmington: Commercial Printing & Mailing Service, August 24, 1963.

Hobart-Hampden, Augustus C. (Captain Roberts). *Never Caught.* London: John Camden Holton, 1867. (Reprint: Wilmington: The Blockade Runner Museum, 1967.)

Horner, David L. *The Blockade-Runners, True Tales of Running the Yankee Blockade off the Confederate Coast.* New York: Dodd, Meade and Company, 1968.

Jackson, Claude V. III. *The Cape Fear–Northeast Cape Fear Rivers Comprehensive Study, A Maritime History and Survey of the Cape Fear and Northeast Cape Fear Rivers, Wilmington Harbor, North Carolina,* N. C. Division of Archives and History Underwater Archaeology Unit, Kure Beach, NC, April 1966.

Johns, John. "Wilmington During the Blockade," *Harper's New Monthly Magazine* XXXIII (January-December 1914), 497-503.

Johnson, Charles. *A General History of the Robberies and Murders of the Most Notorious Pirates From Their First Rise and Settlement in the Island of Providence to the Present Year (1724).* New York: Dodd, Meade & Company, 1927.

Johnson, George Jr. *Rose O'Neal Greenhow and the Blockade Runners,* private printing, 1995.

Keaton, Gary. "Gentleman Pilots of Cape Fear," *Wilmington Magazine,* Oct-Nov, 1995.

"L." Letter to his brother Eddie dated November 18, 1862, recounting the grounding of the blockade runner *Kate,* East Carolina University Manuscript Collection.

Lamb, William. *Colonel Lamb's Story of Fort Fisher.* Wilmington: Wilmington Printing Company, 1966.

Lee, Lawrence. *The History of Brunswick County, North Carolina.* Charlotte: Heritage Press, 1980.

Lee, Lawrence. *The Lower Cape Fear in Colonial Days.* Chapel Hill: UNC Press, 1965.

Levin, Alexandra Lee. "To Canada Via the Blockade," article in *The State* magazine, April 1978.

Litz, Francis A. *Father Tabb: A Study of His Life and Works.* Baltimore: Johns Hopkins Press, 1923.

Lobban, Malcolm. "The Clyde Built Blockade Runners," article in *The Highlander* magazine, Sept.-Oct., 1990.

Long, J. W. "Quarterbacks of the River," article in *The State* magazine, May 19, 1956.

Lounsbury, Carl. *The Architecture of Southport.* Southport, NC: The Southport Historical Society, 1979.

Maffitt, Emma Martin. *The Life and Services of John Newland Maffitt.* New York: The Neal Publishing Company, 1906.

Maffitt, John Newland. "Blockade Running," *United Service* VI (June 1882), 626-633, VII (July 1882), 14-22 new series, VII (February 1892), 147-173.

Marquis, Greg. *In Armageddon's Shadow.* Montreal: McGill-Queen's University Press, 1998.

McDonald, Bill. "River Pilots on the Cape Fear," article in *The Bulletin,* February 12, 1974.

McNeil, Sally. Recollections from conversations with her grandparents, Charles Eyden Gause and Gertrude Dosher Gause.

McPherson, James M. *The American Heritage New History of the Civil War.* New York: Penguin Books, 1996.

McPherson, James M. and Patricia McPherson. *Lamson of the Gettysburg.* New York: Oxford University Press, 1997.

Merkel, Andrew. *Tallahassee: A Ballad of Nova Scotia in the Sixties.* Halifax: The Imperial Publishing Company, 1945.

Morgan, James M. *Recollections of a Rebel Reefer.* New York: Houghton, Mifflin, 1917.

Morse family genealogy, complied by Sarah Ann McNeil of Southport, NC.

Moore, Louis T. Unpublished article on the lost pilots of Smithville, 1872 and 1877.

Nash, Howard P. *A Naval History of the Civil War.* New York: A. S. Barnes, 1972.

National Archives, Washington, DC. Records Group 45, Letters received related to Confederate Prisoners of War.

National Archives, Washington, DC. Records Group 45, Register of Prisoners Captured on Blockade Runners, September 1862-July 1865.

Navy Department. *Dictionary of American Naval Fighting Ships.* Washington: Government Printing Office, 1963-1981.

Navy Department. *Civil War Chronology, 1861-1865.* Washington: Government Printing Office, 1971.

Nepveux, Ethel S. *George Alfred Trenholm and the Company That Went to War.* Charleston: private printing, 1973.

North Carolina Board of Commissioners of Navigation & Pilotage for Cape Fear River and Bar. Pilot licensing records, 1861-1865. (Located in the Manuscript Department, William R. Perkins Library, Duke University.)

North Carolina State Archives, Fort Fisher Logbook, 1864.

Oxley, G. P. & Company. Letter to E. D. Gauze [Gause] concerning fee for piloting the *Helen*, Halifax, October, 21, 1866.

Peery, Charles. "Clandestine Commerce: Yankee Blockade Running," *Journal of Confederate History, Special Commemorative Naval Issue CSS Alabama 1864-1989.* Brentwood, TN: Southern Heritage Press, 1989.

Peoples Press, The [Wilmington, NC], August 8, 1835.

Porter, Admiral David D., USN. *The Naval History of the Civil War.* Sacaucus, NJ: Castle, 1984. (reprint)

Potter family genealogy, provided by Robert Potter of St. Marys, Georgia.

Potter, William Julius. Unpublished account of his experiences in piloting the *General Beauregard*, Sprunt papers, William R. Perkins Library, Duke University, Durham, NC.

Price, Marcus W. "Masters and Pilots Who Tested the Blockade of the Confederate Ports, 1861-1865," *The American Neptune*, Vol. XV, April 1961, 81-106.

Price, Marcus W. "Ships That Tested the Blockade of the Carolina Ports, 1861-1865," *The American Neptune*, Vol. VIII. No. 3, July 1948.

Randall, James Ryder, letter to his fiancee (and later wife) Kate, June 3, 1864. (Quoted by Bill Reaves in *The Whitters Bench*, Southport Historical Society, November, 1993.)

Reaves, Bill. *Southport (Smithville) A Chronology, Vol. I (1820-1887).* Wilmington, NC, 1978.

Reaves, Bill. *Southport (Smithville) A Chronology, Vol. II (1887-1920).* Southport, NC: The Southport Historical Society, 1990.

Rivenbark, Celia. "A star to steer her: pilots let river's ships flow," Wilmington *Morning Star,* October 4, 1996.

Robinson, Bob. "Adventures of blockade-runner come to life in girl's diary," Wilmington *Star News,* October 3, 1993.

Ross, Robert B. "Running the Blockade During the Civil War," article in *Wilmington Star,* March 29, 1914.

Salley, Alexander Jr., *Narratives of Early Carolina.* New York: Barnes & Noble, Inc., 1953.

Sanders, Mary F. Eyewitness account of run of the *Little Hattie* into New Inlet in Oct.1864.

Saunders, William L., ed. *The Colonial Records of North Carolina.* Raleigh: 1890.

Scharf, J. Thomas. *History of the Confederate States Navy.* New York: Rogers & Sherwood, 1887.

Schaw, Janet. *Journal of a Lady of Quality: Being the Narrative of a Journey from Scotland to the West Indies, North Carolina and Portugal, in the Years 1774 to 1776.* New Haven: Yale University Press, 1923.

Schmidt, Dorcas W., compiler, and Carson, Susan S., ed. *The Cemeteries of Southport (Smithville) and Surrounding Area.* Southport, NC: Southport Historical Society, 1983.

Sellers genealogy, Lucy Blocker of Bowie, MD, and Ellen Butters of Margate, FL.

Shingleton, Royce. *High Seas Confederate: The Life and Times of John Newland Maffitt.* Columbia, SC: USC Press, 1994.

Shingleton, Royce. *John Taylor Wood: Sea Ghost of the Confederacy.* Athens: University of Georgia Press, 1979.

Silverstone, Paul H. *Warships of the Civil War Navies.* Annapolis: U. S. Naval Institute Press, 1989.

Soley, James Russell. "The Blockade and the Cruisers," the *Blue and Gray Press* (undated). (The first edition was published by Scribner in 1883.)

Southport [NC] *Leader,* 1893 and 1894.

Spence, E. Lee. *Treasures of the Confederate Coast.* Miami-Charleston: Narwhal Press, Inc., 1995.

Speer, Lonnie R. *Portals to Hell: Military Prisons of the Civil War.* Mechanicsburg, PA: Stackpole Books, 1997.

Sprunt, James. *American Historical Society Papers,* Volume XXIV. Richmond: American Historical Society,1896.

Sprunt, James. *Chronicles of the Cape Fear River.* Raleigh: Edwards and Broughton Printing Co. 1916.

Sprunt, James. *Derelicts: An Account of Ships Lost at Sea in General Commercial Traffic and a Brief History of Blockade Runners Stranded along the North Carolina Coast, 1861-1865.* Wilmington, NC, 1920.

Sprunt, James. *Tales and Traditions of the Lower Cape Fear, 1661-1898.* Wilmington, LeGwin Brothers, 1898.

Sprunt, James. "What Ship is That? Tales of the Cape Fear Blockade," articles in the *Southport Leader,* Southport, NC, 1894.

Stancil, Bill. "Suited to Command," article in *The State,* September, 1974.

Stark, Aubrey H. *Sidney Lanier, A Biographical and Critical Study.* New York: Russel and Russel, Inc. 1964.

Steelman, Ben. "Marine's Diary Details Life in Confederacy," article in *Wilmington Sunday Star-News,* March 6, 1988.

Stick, David. *Bald Head: A History of Smith Island and Cape Fear.* Wendell, NC: Broadfoot Publishing Company, 1985.

Stick, David. *Graveyard of the Atlantic.* Chapel Hill: UNC Press, 1952.

Swan family genealogy, compiled by Helen Thomas Pearce.

Bibliography

Taylor, Thomas E. *Running the Blockade*. London: J. Murray, 1896.

Thompson family genealogy, compiled by Sarah Ann McNeil of Southport, NC.

Thompson, Robert. His recollections on career as a Cape Fear pilot, as told to Jim McNeil.

Thompson, Thomas Mann. Letter to his daughter Lily, November 24, 1896.

United States census, New Hanover County, NC, 1850, 1860, 1870

United States census, Brunswick County, NC, 1850, 1860, 1870.

United States War Department, Civil War military records in the National Archives.

Usina, M. P. *Blockade Running in Confederate Times*. Savannah: George N. Nichols Press, 1895.

Vandiver, Frank E., ed. *Confederate Blockade Running Through Bermuda, 1861-1851*. Austin: University of Texas Press, 1947.

Waddell, Col. A. M. "Heroes of the Deep: Incidents in the Lives of Two Cape Fear Pilots." Correspondence of the New York World. (This article is available at the New Hanover County Public Library in Wilmington, NC. It was probably published in a Wilmington newspaper around 1880.)

War of the Rebellion: The Official Records of the Union and Confederate Navies, Government Printing Office, 1896.

White, Mary J. *Diary, August 2, 1864 - June 7, 1865*. (Courtesy United Daughters of the Confederacy, Richmond, VA).

Whittle, Kenneth A. "Blockade of the Coast of the Carolinas," *The American Philatelist*, July, 1982.

Wilkinson, J. *The Narrative of a Blockade Runner*. New York, NY, 1877.

Williams, Capt. Edgar D. "Captain Williams Compiles Records of Blockade Ships," article in Wilmington, NC *Star*, September 23, 1924.

Wilmington, NC *Daily Journal*.

Wilmington, NC *Sun*.

Wilmington, NC *Star*.

Wilson, Ash. Paper entitled "River Pilots of the Lower Cape Fear River in the Years Prior to the to the War of Northern Aggression," November 22, 1992.

Wilson, Frank L. Letter to Captain J. J. Guthrie of the Steamer *Advance*, April 6, 1864.

Wise, Stephen R. *Lifeline of the Confederacy, Blockade Running During the Civil War*. Columbia, SC: USC Press, 1988.

Wise, Stephen R. *Lifeline of the Confederacy, Blockade Running During the American Civil War*, University of South Carolina, 1983. (Ph.D. thesis)

Woodman, Richard. *The History of the Ship*. London: Conway Maritime Press, 1997.

Index

Act for Regulating the Pilotage and Facilitating the Navigation of the Cape Fear River, 5

Adair, W. F., 73-*74*

Adkins, James N., 12, 41, 149

Advance (blockade runner), 12, 38, 45, 48, 49, 101, 105-107, *108*, 109-120, 153, 154

Agnes E. Fry (blockade runner), 37, 48, 152

Alexander Collie & Company, 37, 44, 59, 64, 80, 105-106

Alice (blockade runner), 12, 92, 155

Anaconda Plan, 15

Anderson, Edward, 37-38

Anderson, John William, 12, 53-55, 113, 130, 149

Anna Deans (blockade runner), 101

Annie, 37, 80, 105, 111, 150

Antonica (steamer), 73-75, 94, 152, 153

Arabian, 90, 154

Argyle (blockade runner), 101

Aries, USS (blockader), 74

Armstrong, 37, 124, 125-127, 155

Arnold, Joe, 137, 139

Astor, USS (blockader), 19

Atalanta (blockade runner), 12, *65*, 123, 124, 155

Atlanta (ironclad) (ex-*Fingal*), *38*

Atlantic, 155

Badger (blockade runner), 48

Bald Head Island, 1, 6, 23, 135

Banshee (blockade runner), 12, 45, 48, 66-68, 150, 153

Barnes, A. I., 107

Bat (blockade runner), 48, 85

Beatrice (blockade runner), 9, 150

Beaufort, CSS (gunboat), 71

Beaufort Harbor, 30

Beckwith, Mary White. *See* White, Mary

Bell, James, 12, 82, 149

Bensel, Joseph W., 12, *58*, 112, 135, 149

Bermuda, 7, 22, 33-34, 35, 36, 38, 39, 51, 53, 55, 56, 79, 81, 82, 103, 104, 111, 113, 125, 130

Bermuda (blockade runner), 32

Bijou (steamer), 53

Blenheim (blockade runner), 149

blockade, Union, setup of, 14-20, 24-26

Board of Commissioners of Navigation and Pilotage, 5, 6, 78

Bonneau, Frank, 29, 39-41

Bora. See *General Beauregard*

Bourne, John T., 38-39

Bowen, George F., 6, 8, 21, 149

Boykin, Thomas J., 107

Brinkman, Thomas W., 12, *58*, 59-62, 135, 149

Browning, Robert, 20

Brunswick Town, 3

Burns, C. T., 149

Burriss, Bertram "Piggy," 63, 144-145

Burriss, Christopher William, 63, 149

Burriss, Drucilla, 129

Burriss, Edward Thomas (Ned), 12, *63*, 64, 149-150

Burriss, George Washington, 12, 64, 65, 130, 150

Burriss, James Henry, 63

Burriss, James Henry III, 68

Burriss, James Thomas, 63, 150

Burriss, John Henry, 63, 150

Burriss, John Newton, 63, 64

Burriss, John W., 150

Burriss, Joseph Newton, 12, 150

Burriss, Sylvester Jr., 9, 150

Burriss, Thomas Edward, 12, 63, 66-68, 129, 150

Burriss, Thomas Gray, 12, 68-69, 150

Caird & Company, 48

Calypso (blockade runner), 12, 155

Cape Fear (steamboat), 112

Cappo, Betty, 64

Captain Galloway's Coast Guard Company, 55
Carolina (steamer), 102
Caswell Beach, 76
Caswell, CSS (steamer), 6, 71
Catton, Bruce, 14-15
Cecile (blockade runner), 41
Charleston, SC, 29-30
Chicora (blockade runner), 64, 150
Chicora Importing and Exporting Company, 37, 73, 90
City of Petersburg (blockade runner), 12, 36, 48, 49, 112, 149
Clemmons, J. W., 150
Clyde-built steamers, 47
Colfax (Revenue cutter), 138
Colonel Lamb (blockade runner), 48, *51*
Condor (blockade runner), 12, 37, 45, 59-62, 149
Confederate Ordnance Bureau, 44, 103
Confederate Point, xvii. *See also* Federal Point
Constance (blockade runner), 106
Coquette (blockade runner), 12, 124, 151, 155
Cornubia (blockade runner), 79, 101, 103-105, 153
Coxetter, Louis, 73
Craig, Charles William, *6,* 12, 82, 150
Craig, James N., 91, 150
Craig, James William (Jim Billy), 12, 77-87, 150-151
Craig, Jessie Jr., 151
Craig, Jessie Sr., 151
Craig, Joseph, 95, 151
Craig's Landing, xv, *78*
Craig, Thomas W., 12, 151
Craig, W. T., 151
Crenshaw & Company, 37
Crossan, Thomas M., 106
Crusader, USS, 41
Curtis, George, 107
Curtis, Walter, 130
Cushing, William B., 9

Daniel, Edward F., 151

Daniel, Roy, 89
Daniels, E. T., 12, 151
Davis, John, xiv, 55, 151
Davis, Joseph, 151
Davis, Samuel B., 151
Daylight, USS (blockader), 18
Dolphin, USS (brig), 41
Don (blockade runner), 12, 37, 44, 80, 105, 151, 155
Dosher, Charles Gause, xiii, 135-137, 151
Dosher, Charles Gause Jr., 135, 137
Dosher, Fortune, 136
Dosher, John, 136
Dosher, Julius, 12, *58,* 140, 151
Dosher, Richard, 12, 151
Dosher, Sarah Brinson, 135
Dyer, Thomas K., 12, 71-76, 130, 152

Edith (blockade runner), 106, 154
Elizabeth (blockade runner), 123, 124, 155
Elmira Prison, 137
Ella and Annie (blockade runner), 12, 29, 39-41, 149
Ella II, 12, 154
Emma, USS (blockader), 73
Emma II (blockade runner), 123, 155
Emma Henry (blockade runner), 9
Eugenia II (blockade runner), 12, 154

Falcon (blockade runner), 59
Fannie, 151, 153
Fanny and Jenny (blockade runner), 68
Federal Point, xv, xvii, 2, 6, 9, 23,63, 68, 77, 87, 129, 140, 149
Fingal (blockade runner), 37-38
Five Fathom Hole, 91, 95
Flamingo (blockade runner), 59
Flora Macdonald, CSS (transport), 86
Flora II (blockade runner), 123, 155
Florida (Confederate raider), 42
Florida, USS (blockader), 20
Florie, 123
Fort Anderson, 92
Fort Campbell, 95
Fort Caswell, 1, *26,* 27, 50, 76, 95, 102, 103

Fort Donnelson, USS (formerly *Robert E. Lee*), *47*

Fort Fisher, xv, 1, 9, 19, 23, 33, 45, 50, 54, 61, 64, 68, 72, 79, 80, 96, 149

Fort Jackson, USS (blockader), 81, *88,* 91, 92

Fort Johnston, 3, 5, 55, 62

Fort Macon, 84-85

Fort Sumter, 13

Foster, Kevin, 46

Fox (blockade runner), 48

Fraser, Trenholm and Company, 37, 73, 85

Friend (schooner), 129

Frolic, USS (ex-*Advance*), 120

Frying Pan Shoals, 1, 4, 23, 74, 94

Frying Pan Shoals lightship, 55, 95, 96, 137

Furpless, William S., 152

Galloway, John Wesley Sr., 55-56, 130, 152

Ganor, E. D., 152

Garrason, Thomas B., 12, 55, 152

Gause, Ephraim D., xiii, 12, 69, 111, 123, 131, 133-134, 152

Gayle, Richard N., 103, 105

Gemsbok, USS (blockader), 8

General Beauregard "Bora" (blockade runner), 12, 73, 89-98, 154

General Buckingham (blockader), 73, 74-75

Georgiana McCaw (blockade runner), 75-76, 152

Gettysburg, USS (blockader), 49, 82-83

Gibraltar (blockade runner), 78-79, 151

Gillespie, Lawrence, 137

Giraffe (steamer) (later *Robert E. Lee*), 12, 44, *47, 70,* 71-73, 152

Gorgas, Josiah, 36

Greenhow, Rose, 22, 59, 60-61

Gregory, Frederick, 104

Grissom, C., 137

Grissom, Edgar A., 152

Grissom, Robert S., 12, 111, 152

Grissom, Simon S., 152

Grissom, Thomas B., 43, 82, 83, 137, 140, 152

Grissom, William J., 152

Gutherie, Archibald Menzies, xiii, xiv, *7,* 12, 73, 152

Gutherie, James, 55, 153

Gutherie, J. J., 107

Gutherie, Rebecca, 129

Halifax, Nova Scotia, 36, 59, 61, 65, 85, 129

Hammer, William C., 116

Hankins, Harriet, 136

Hankins, William, 136

Hansa (blockade runner), 12, 37, 64, 105, 150

Harvey, Blind Isaac, 56

Havana (steamer), 79

Havelock (British steamer), 73, 89, 154. *See also General Beauregard*

Hebe (blockade runner), 12, 20, 37, 64, 150

Hebert, Louis, 7, 9

Helen (blockade runner), 12, 36, 111, 118, 133, 152

Henry Westerman (pilot boat), 137

Herald (English steamer), 153

Hewett, William N. W., 44, 45, 60, 61

Hill, John, 12, 153

Hobart-Hampden, Charles Augustus, 44-45, 80

Holgate, Harry, 90, 95, 96

Home (schooner), 9

Hope (blockade runner), 115-116

Horner, David, 56, 96

Howard, Henry, 12, 153

Howquah, USS (blockader), 98

Huse, Caleb, 36-37

Hutchins, Lou, 55

Index (blockade runner), 12, 37, 124, 155

James Adger, USS (blockader), *17,* 19, 64, 105

James Funk (pilot boat), 65

J. H. Neff (pilot boat), 137

John Fraser and Company, 37, 102

Johnson, William, 153

Jones & Quiggin, 48

Jones, William C., 107

Jones, William H., 107

Kate (blockade runner), 18, 35, 101, 102-103, 153
Kelly, James A., 9
Kent (blockade runner), 130
Kent, Thomas, 153
Keystone State, USS, (blockader) 8, 149
"King Cotton" doctrine, 16-17

Lady Davis. See *Cornubia*
Lamb, William, 19, 45, *46*, 64, 78, 95, 96, 104
Lamson, Roswell, 8
Lanier, Sidney, 84
Lee, Samuel Phillips, 24-26, 64
Let Her Be (blockade runner), 124, 150, 155
Lilian (blockade runner), 10, *11*, 42, *43*, 115, 151, 152
Little Hattie (blockade runner), 12, 111, 152
Lockwood, Robert, *43*
Lockwood, Thomas, *43*, 102, 153
Lord Clyde (British steamer), 153
Lucille (steamer), 138
Lucy (blockade runner), 48, 95
Lynx (blockade runner), 12, *24*, 48, 81-82, 118, 151
Lyon, Thomas, 90, 94, 95

Maffitt, John Newland, xv, *xvi*, 41-43, 83
Maglenn, James, 119-120
Maglenn, William, 107
Malvern, USS (blockader) (ex-*Ella and Annie*), 41
Margaret and Jessie (blockade runner), 12, 48, 49, 82, 150, 155
Marshall, John, 153
Martin, D. S., 83
Mary Celestia (blockade runner), 12, 37, *52*, 53-57, 111-112, 149
Mary K. Sprunt (pilot boat), 133, 137, 138, 139-140
McDougal, George, 49
McKeithan, George, 153

McKensey, John, 153
Merlin (steamer), 33
Minnesota, USS (blockader), 64
Modern Greece (blockade runner), 19, 32-33
Montgomery, USS (blockader), 85, 86
monument to pilots, 140
Moore, Joe, 90
Morrison, George, 49, 107
Morse, C. C. "Kit," 12, 79, 86, 100, 101-107, 110, 111, 112, 118, 120, 137, 138, 139, 140, 141, 142, 153
Morse, Francis, 153
Morse, James Madison, 101-102
Morse, John, 101
Morse, Thomas, 141
Mound Battery, *24*, *27*, 50, 92
Muse, William T. "Willie," 120

Nansemond USS (blockader), 8
Nassau, Bahamas, 7, 22, 33, 34-35, 90, 91-92, 102, 130
Neil, C. L., 107, 120
Neill, John W., 153
Nellie F. Sawyer (schooner), 138
Nelson, Charles, 125
New Inlet, xv, 23, 25, 30, 50, 79, 92
Newton, James L., 153
Newton, James Stokes, 95
Newton, John L., 153
Newton, Joseph, *58*, 154
Newton, Sterling F., 154
Newton, Thomas W., 12, 79, 154
Newton, William S., 154
Nighthawk (blockade runner), *24*, *61*, 66
Niphon, USS (blockader), 20, 40-41, 51, 64, 105
Norfolk, VA, 30
North Carolina, USS (battleship), 145
North Heath (blockade runner), 12, 151

Oak Island, 23
Old Dominion (blockade runner), 12, 36, 48, 117-118, 152
Old Inlet, 23, 25, 30, 50, 92
Old Smithville Burying Ground, 120, 149
Orion (blockade runner), 12, 80, 151, 153

Owl (blockade runner), 12, 42, 48, 118, 150, 152

Pepper, Lewis, 154
Pet (blockade runner), 12, 106, 151
Pilot boats, evolution of after war, 142-143
Pinner, Christopher C., 137
Piver, Elijah, 95, 154
Platt, Samuel, 154
Point Lookout, 20, 83-*84*, 86
Port Lafayette prison, 41
Potter, Clarissa, 136
Potter, Julius. *See* Potter, William Julius
Potter, Robert, 132
Potter, William Julius, 12, 89-99, 140, 154
Price, George, 125, 126, 127
Price, Jacob A. S., xiv, *7*, 154
Price, James, 59, 62, 130
Price, John B., xiv, 130, 154
Ptarmigan (blockade runner), 59

Raleigh, USS (ironclad ram), 80
Rebel Rose. *See* Greenhow, Rose
Reid, E. C., 79
Retribution (Confederate privateer), 86
Ridge, Samuel. *See* Hewett, William N. W.
Ridgely, Daniel, 98
Robert E. Lee (blockade runner), 7, 12, 19, 44, 46, *47*, 50, 152. See also *Giraffe*
Roberts, Captain. *See* Hobart-Hampden, Charles Augustus
Rothesay Castle (blockade runner), 153

Sabine, USS (prison ship), 86
Sages, Jimmie, 93
Saltonstall, W. G., 73, 74, 75
Sandford, John, 1
Santiago de Cuba, USS (blockader), 119-120
Savage, John R., 12, 21, 55, 86, 141, 154
Savage, John R. Jr., 141
Savannah (coastal packet), 41, 46
Savannah, GA, 30
Schaw, Janet, 3-4
Scott, Winfield, 15
Sellers, James R., 135

Sellers, Robert A., 154
Sellers, William R., 12, 154
Sellers, William T., 155
Semmes, Raphael, 79
Shenandoah, USS (blockader), 41
Shokokon, USS (blockader), 64
Sinclair, Arthur, 55
Siren (blockade runner), 12, 153
Sirius, 155
Smith, Cornelius G., *5,* 12, 55, 155
Smithville, xiv-xv, 2, 5, 6, 9, 76, 103, 111, 119, 129, 137, 140, 142, 149.
Southport, 1-2, 142. *See also* Smithville
Springs, Joseph, 12, 92, 155
Sprunt. See *Mary K. Sprunt*
Sprunt, James, xiii, 10, 43, 49, 54, 77, 84-85, 106
Spunkie (blockade runner), 146
Stansbury, Smith, 39
State of Georgia, USS (blockader), 73
Steele, Jonathon, 45, 66
St. George, Harold, 145
St. George, Robert, 135
St. George's, Bermuda, 22, 33, 53, 104
St. George, William, 12, 80, 155
St. Louis, USS, 41
Stokes, Jim, 91
Styron, William, 145
Sumter (Confederate cruiser), 79
Susan Bierne (blockade runner), 152
Swan, Charlie, 146
Swan, Henry, 146, 155
Swan, John G., 145, 146

Talisman (blockade runner), 12, 149
Tallahassee (Confederate raider), 64, 65, 120, 150
Taylor, B., 107
Taylor, Tom, 66
Theodora (blockade runner), 34
Thistle II (blockade runner), 12, 123, 155
Thompson, Joseph T., 12, 82, 123, 137, 141, 155
Thompson, Joseph T. Jr., 141
Thompson, J. W., 155
Thompson, Robert "Toby," 145, 147

Thompson, Thomas Mann Jr. 12, *122,* 123-127, 130, 155
Tioga, USS (Federal warship), 90
Timmons. See *Uriah Timmons*
Trenholm, George Alfred, 37, 42
Trott, John D., 135
Tuscarora, USS (blockader), 98

United States Coast Survey, xiv
Uriah Timmons (pilot boat), 133, 137, 138-139, 141, 142
Usina, Mike P., 53-55, 124-125

Vance, Zebulon, 38, *39,* 105
Venus (blockade runner), 12, 37, 154
Victoria, USS (blockader), 75-76
Violet, USS (steam tug), 75
Virgin, John, 56
Virginia (blockade runner), 154
Vulture (blockade runner), 152

Waddle, A. M., 139
Walke, Henry, 91
Walker, George B., 156
Walker, Norman, 39

Walker, Robert S., 137
Wando (blockade runner), 12, 149
Weeks, Julius, 137, 139
Wescott, John, 156
Western Bar, 23, 50, 75, 79, 82, 102, 124, 127, 143
White, John, 109-110, 112, 116, 118-119
White, Mary J., 109-120
Whittle, William Conway Jr., 103
Wild Darrell (blockade runner), 48
Wild Rover (blockade runner), 154
Wilkerson, John, 7, 22, 41, 44, 46, 50, 72, 76
Williamson, Obediah H., 9
Willing, Fred, 145
Will-o-the-Wisp (blockade runner), 118
Wilmington-Cape Fear Pilots Association, 143
Wilmington, NC, xiv, 3, 6, 7, 9, 10, 19, 20, 21-23, 27, 30, 33, 35, 45, 54, 61, 64-65, 102-103, 143
Wise, Stephen, 29
Wood, John Taylor, 65
Wylie, Joannes, 45, 107, 110, 111, 112, 116, 117

LaVergne, TN USA
23 February 2010
173901LV00003BA/100/A